GENERAL INSURANCE

by

B. BENJAMIN
Ph.D., F.I.A.

*Special edition for sale to members
of the Institute of Actuaries and members or
students of the Faculty of Actuaries*

Butterworth-Heinemann Ltd
Linacre House, Jordan Hill, Oxford OX2 8DP

PART OF REED INTERNATIONAL BOOKS

OXFORD LONDON BOSTON
MUNICH NEW DELHI SINGAPORE SYDNEY
TOKYO TORONTO WELLINGTON

First published 1977
Reprinted 1978, 1987, 1990, 1991

© The Institute of Actuaries and the Faculty of Actuaries in Scotland 1977

All rights reserved. No part of this publication may be reproduced in any material form (including photocopying or storing in any medium by electronic means and whether or not transiently or incidentally to some other use of this publication) without the written permission of the copyright holder except in accordance with the provisions of the Copyright, Designs and Patents Act 1988 or under the terms of a licence issued by the Copyright Licensing Agency Ltd, 90 Tottenham Court Road, London, England W1P 9HE. Applications for the copyright holder's written permission to reproduce any part of this publication should be addressed to the publishers.

ISBN 0 7506 0446 8

Printed and bound in Great Britain by
Redwood Press Limited, Melksham, Wiltshire

CONTENTS

Preface *page* vii

Chapter	1	The Nature of General Insurance	1
	2	British Legislation Governing Insurance Companies	34
	3	The Investment and Taxation of General Insurance Funds	54
	4	Documentation and Data Collection	62
	5	The Risk Premium	114
	6	Expenses in General Insurance	139
	7	The Office Premium	156
	8	Experience Rating	177
	9	Reinsurance	206
	10	Technical Reserves in General Insurance	234
	11	Solvency	271
	12	Analysis of Profit	302

Index 311

PREFACE

General Insurance is a highly technical field and it would be foolish for any actuarial student to imagine that this textbook, dealing as it does with statistical and other actuarial contributions to management, offers a complete guide to general insurance or indeed that any textbook could be more than a foundation to be built upon with hard experience. The purpose of this textbook is modest and I hope realistic. It is generally agreed that the profitability of general insurance requires to be safeguarded by the application of rational procedures for the classification and assessment of risks and the establishment of adequate premium bases and reserves. A beginning has been made and is being continually pursued to develop suitable techniques for this purpose. In this development actuaries and other statisticians, together with those currently engaged in the management of general insurance with a wealth of experience behind them, have collaborated to a point at which it is felt that the fruits of their work should be made a compulsory part of the actuarial discipline. This is what this textbook seeks to do. It seeks to bring together the existing state of knowledge and the existing state of practice in the general insurance field. These two states are different. In all fields of industry science tends to forge ahead of practice. New techniques have to be proven before they are adopted in general practice. So the book is a compromise between knowledge and practice. As practice catches up with knowledge the book will have to be revised. In a sense the very rapidity with which this book becomes outdated and inadequate will be a measure of its usefulness.

This volume is based upon the contributions of a large number of actuaries who have given their spare time and experience to the production of papers on different aspects of general insurance. The Institute owes a tremendous debt to them. Many of their names are unknown to me since they were members of working groups from which only one individual reported. Some of their names appear as authors of papers in the chapter bibliographies. I am personally grateful to them and to many other colleagues, actuarial and non-actuarial, who led me patiently by the hand through this venture. I am particularly grateful to my scrutineers, Len Coe and Brian Corby, for their forebearance and constructive advice and, not least, friendliness; they contrived to make the whole exercise a very pleasant one. Last, I must express my appreciation of the unfailing support of Jacqueline Millar of the Actuarial Tuition Service who deciphered my manuscripts however messy with corrections, typed the whole of the text, and saw it through the press with tremendous good humour.

CHAPTER I

THE NATURE OF GENERAL INSURANCE

1.1 The easiest way of describing general insurance is to say that it is the provision of an insurance contract other than for life assurance. A life assurance contract is one 'which secures the payment of an agreed sum of money on the happening of a contingency, or of a variety of contingencies, dependent on a human life' [Fisher & Young *Actuarial Practice of Life Assurance*. Cambridge University Press, 1971]. However this is not only uninformative but it is not entirely accurate because, in some kinds of general insurance, death although only the outcome of a contingency (injury) and therefore not itself the contingency which brings the contract to fruition may nevertheless determine the amount of the liability to be met. Indeed in some cases of death arising from employment it may be difficult to separate the contingency from the outcome.

1.2 While there are several fundamental differences between life and general insurance there are also important similarities which to a non-technical observer would be unexpected and which appear often to have been ignored.

1.3 First, the fundamental differences are as follows.

1 While life assurance contracts are usually made for a long period of several years, general insurance contracts are usually, though not invariably, made for a short period of one year or less and at the end of that period are renewable by mutual consent of the insurer and the insured.

2 For both types of contract the principle of *uberrima fides*, i.e. utmost good faith, must be observed by both parties but in life assurance once the contract has been made, the insured is generally under no obligation to report any changes of circumstances affecting the risk insured unless a change in the actual nature of the contract is requested by the insured, for example a change in the maturity date

of an endowment assurance. In general insurance however, there is at each renewal an onus on the insured to observe utmost good faith in informing the insurer of any changes in circumstances which may affect assessment of the cost of the risk borne by the insurer. This assessment is carried out by skilled underwriters who will, for example, take note of information that a factory insured against fire risk has begun to use more inflammable material or that, in the case of insurance against burglary, security measures have been improved.

3   In consequence the premium for a general insurance contract may vary at each renewal either because of these changes of individual circumstances or because the general level of premiums for a particular class of business needs to be reviewed in order to ensure, for example, that the insurer is not operating at a loss or making excessive profits or that premiums are at such a level that loss of business to a competitor may be likely. Such general changes become necessary in times of inflation (monetary depreciation) and also when overall risk conditions change, for example when a general worsening of traffic conditions increases the frequency of accidents. In contrast the premiums for a life assurance contract remain fixed.

4   In life assurance and in a limited number of general insurance classes of insurance, for example, personal accident, the size of the claim is predetermined at the outset (except in the case of bonus applicable to with-profit policies but these are fixed once declared and do not affect the principle). In general insurance the size of the claim (per unit of premium) may vary enormously even within a class of business which is fairly homogeneous in relation to the risk of a claim of any sort occurring. Not only does the distribution of size of claim (for any class) have a wide range but it is usually very skew (a lot of small claims, a few extremely large claims) so that averages do not give sufficient information to provide an adequate base for management. While a deterministic approach (the life table) may be adequate for the valuation of life assurance

NATURE OF GENERAL INSURANCE

liabilities, a stochastic approach (with statistical models more complicated than the life table) has to be considered for general insurance. Furthermore there is a principle of indemnity which places some constraint on the claim distribution. Most, but not all, insurance policies are contracts of indemnity. Under such a contract, the insured claimant will be placed by the insurer in the same financial position after settlement as before the occurrence of the event insured against.

5   In life assurance the risk of a claim normally increases progressively throughout the duration of the policy. This means that a level annual premium which over the whole period of the policy is adequate, is at the outset larger than necessary to cover the risk of the early years. The insurer is thus required to invest the excess to build up a reserve against later years when the premium is less than the cost of each year's coverage of risk. In general insurance the risk is not usually subject to a rising gradient; it may even be greater in the earlier than in the later days of the contract (the insured may install additional safety equipment, e.g. sprinklers).

6   In life assurance, payment of a claim completes and extinguishes the contract. In general insurance the policy continues to run to the end of its period despite the payment of a claim and a subsequent claim may be made within the period of the contract though once the total sum insured in respect of any part of the cover provided by a contract has been paid that part of the contract would terminate. The important point is that more than one claim can be made in each year of insurance.

1.4   Nevertheless there are some points of similarity between general and life insurance.

1   The statistical problems of measurement of risk are basically similar. The basis of insurance is that there is a degree of stability, at least over relatively short periods of time, in the probability of occurrence of an event leading to a claim and that this probability can be estimated from experience. In this process of estimation there is, as for life assurance, the problem of relating the insured events to

the exposures to risk from which they arise; and there is also, the problem of heterogeneity (historically referred to as 'class selection' in life assurance). A number of different factors affect the probability (of an event leading to a claim) which must therefore be calculated separately for different classes of risk representing differing combinations of these factors. For example in life assurance regard must be had to sex, age, initial selection, and types of contracts; in motor insurance regard may have to be paid to sex, age of driver, size and model of vehicle, use of vehicle (commercial or pleasure), area of country in which driven (busy or quiet), duration of driving experience.

2 While general insurance contracts are short-term, there is a delay between payment of the premium and the incurrence of a liability and between incurrence of liability and the reporting of that incurrence, and normally a further delay, sometimes long, before settlement so that problems of investment and inflation cannot be ignored.

3 Just as in life assurance there are problems of equity between different groups of general insurance policyholders. In with-profit life assurance an attempt is made to declare bonuses in such a way that regard is had to the different contributions to the distributable profits of different generations of policyholders. In making changes of tariff in motor insurance or instituting a gradient of no-claim discounts, an insurance company must try to be as fair as possible between different groups of insured.

1.5 So we must say what general insurance *is* and not what it is not. Current legislation is embodied in the Insurance Companies Act of 1974 (which consolidated the provisions of the Insurance Companies Acts of 1958 to 1973) and this requires a more detailed classification; this classification first separates long-term business viz. industrial assurance business and life assurance, annuity business and sickness and injury insurance effected for not less than five years and sinking fund business, and defines 'general business' as 'insurance business not being long-term business'. The classes of general business are:

NATURE OF GENERAL INSURANCE

1 Liability
2 Marine, aviation and transport
3 Motor vehicle
4 Pecuniary loss
5 Personal accident and sickness
6 Property

1.6 Table 1.1 (kindly provided by Professor R. L. Carter of Nottingham University) gives an indication of the relative volume of each class of business transacted in the U.K.

TABLE 1.1 World-wide net premiums of British insurers

	1945 (£m)	1955 (£m)	1965 (£m)	1974 (£m)
(1) *U.K. registered companies*				
Ordinary life and annuities	117·5	331·0	849·3	2818·0
Industrial life	79·4	127·4	204·0	382·0
Total life ... (a)	196·9	458·4	1053·3	3200·0
Motor	33·8	180·5	478·2	1277·0
Fire & Accident (non-motor)	128·7	477·8	704·3	2268·0
Marine, Aviation & Transit	22·6	65·4	104·4	410·0
Total non-life ... (b)	185·1	723·7	1286·9	3955·0
Total ... (a) & (b)	382·0	1182·1	2340·2	7155·0
(2) *Lloyd's*				
Life ... (c)	N.A.	0·04	0·4	1·0
Motor (U.K. only)	N.A.	8·2	27·2	85·0
Fire & Accident	N.A.	118·7	257·7	511·0
Marine & Aviation	N.A.	105·5	176·1	546·0
Total non-life ... (d)	N.A.	232·4	461·0	1142·0
Total ... (c) & (d)		232·4	461·4	1143·0

Note: Lloyd's figures are not directly comparable with the companies because of their different systems of accounting. Making certain assumptions regarding commission paid (which is excluded from the figures) and the extent to which Lloyd's figures include self—reinsurance for closed years, *Policy Holder* calculate that in 'company premium' terms Lloyd's 1974 premium income would have been about £975 million.
Sources: Annual Abstract of Statistics.
  Lloyds.
  Policy Holder Insurance Journal.

LIABILITY

1.7 Liability insurance is insurance against the risk that the person insured may incur liabilities to third parties. This kind of insurance is normally divided into two risk groups: employers' liability and general liability. [Liability arising from the use of motor vehicles, the use of vessels or aircraft or risk incidental to the construction, repair or docking of vessels and aircraft are excluded from this category.]

Employers' liability

1.8 The Employers' Liability (Compulsory Insurance) Act, 1969, which came into force on 1 January 1972, requires that every employer (except local authorities, police authorities, nationalised industries and any other employer specifically exempted) must maintain an approved policy of insurance with an authorised insurer against liability incurred as a result of bodily injury, disease or death sustained by their employees (excluding close relatives of the employer) in the course of employment in Great Britain, with a minimum limit of indemnity of £2,000,000. An authorised insurer is defined in the 1974 Act (referred to above) as one authorised by the Secretary of State for Trade.

General liability

1.9 There is a wide range of policies available but in addition to other liabilities they generally all cover the policyholder for:

(i) sums which the insured becomes legally liable to pay for compensation and claimants' costs and expenses in respect of (a) bodily injury to or illness of any person other than those covered by employers' liability or (b) loss of or damage to property not belonging to the insured and, occurring as a result of an accident happening in connection with the business of the insured; and

(ii) costs and expenses of litigation in respect of a claim against the insured.

1.10 Other liabilities which may be covered include the following.
(a) Product liability. This is a legal liability for injury to third parties or loss of or damage to their property, caused by products sold, supplied, installed, repaired, serviced or tested by the insured.
(b) Professional men, e.g. solicitors, accountants, surveyors etc. These policies indemnify against loss arising from claims in respect of breach of professional duty by reason of error, neglect or omission.
(c) Property owners' liability. These policies indemnify property owners against liability to others arising from defects in buildings.
(d) Liabilities attaching to private citizens and their families to cover accidents arising otherwise than out of their employment or use of cars.
(e) Golfers and other sportsmen, who are indemnified against liability to others caused by the insured whilst engaged in sport.

1.11 It is standard practice for general liability policies to carry monetary limits for individual claims and, often, for all claims arising in a single policy year.

1.12 In many of these types of liability insurance there is a risk of a claim for a very large sum of money and as we have already said (para 1.3) the distribution of claims is liable therefore to be very skew. Where there has been a criminal act the insurance company may seek to recover money from the culprit but this is only infrequently successful and even then the recovery is only partial. There is not therefore any serious abatement from such actions of the range of claims.

MARINE, AVIATION AND TRANSPORT

Marine insurance

1.13 The Marine Insurance Act of 1906 (which codifies case law relating to marine insurance) defines marine insurance as 'a contract whereby the insurer undertakes to indemnify the assured in manner and to the extent thereby agreed against marine losses, that is to say, the losses incident to marine adventure'. Marine insurance probably began in northern Italy about the end of the 12th century but it was not until towards the end of the 17th century that financiers and merchants were specialising in the underwriting of marine adventures. The negotiations were conducted in various coffee houses which were popular meeting places of the time. One such was opened around 1680 by Edward Lloyd in Tower Street, London, frequented as it grew by shipowners, merchants and sea captains. It soon became the centre of marine underwriting, encouraged by Lloyd who provided his patrons with pen, ink, paper and shipping information, and in 1696 he published a news sheet called *Lloyd's News*. Even though it was short lived due to legal difficulties, it can be said to be the forerunner of what we know today as the *Lloyd's List* which first appeared in 1734, London's oldest daily newspaper. Lloyd's grew in influence and strength and in 1772 a Committee of Lloyd's was founded and in 1774 Lloyd's moved into rooms in the Royal Exchange.

1.14 Today Lloyd's is a society incorporated by Act of Parliament in 1871 operating from Lloyd's Building in the City of London.

1.15 It is important to note that the Corporation does not underwrite insurance contracts but merely provides facilities for its members, which number approximately 8,000, formed into 135 marine, 123 non-marine, 35 aviation, 34 motor and 10 short-term life syndicates.

1.16 Each syndicate is represented by an underwriting agent. These agents, normally referred to as 'underwriters', occupy seats at 'boxes' in the Underwriting Room. Only members, associates and annual subscribers of Lloyd's are permitted to enter the 'Room' so that merchants and ship owners must approach an accredited Lloyd's broker if they wish to place their business at Lloyd's. These brokers are not restricted to Lloyd's but also place business with the other equally important section of the marine market, namely the insurance companies.

The company market

1.17 There is an extensive company market outside Lloyd's for underwriting marine risks in London. Most insurance companies writing marine business are joint stock companies with a liability limited to its assets unlike Lloyd's underwriters who have no such limit of liability. The majority of companies appoint an underwriter to accept business on behalf of the company. The underwriter is a salaried employee of the company and has no personal liability for the risks he writes; it is the company which is liable for the commitments undertaken by the underwriter.

1.18 The company and Lloyd's markets work very well together using similar systems and with little discrimination from brokers.

1.19 An insurance broker must be accredited to Lloyd's before he can place business there. Firms of Lloyd's brokers may be either one-man businesses, partnerships, or limited companies. At least one of the partners or directors must be either an underwriting member or an annual subscriber to Lloyd's. A substantial deposit must be made with Lloyd's as a security for the broker's obligations to underwriters. The broker whether at Lloyd's or in the company market is the agent of the proposer not of the underwriter. Pending the issue of the policy the broker sends the insured a cover note and a debit note for the premium. The broker at Lloyd's is responsible for the preparation of the policy which he deposits at Lloyd's Policy Signing Office with the 'slip' which is the basis of transactions between brokers and underwriters and on which is written particulars of the risks and the proportions accepted by the underwriters on behalf of their syndicates. At this office the policy is checked with the slip and the names of the underwriters are added. The policy is then sealed and sent through the broker to the insured.

1.20 Lloyd's serves as a nerve centre of shipping intelligence. Shipping intelligence is received from Lloyd's agents, coast radio stations and shipowners. This information is collated and made available to the public in *Lloyd's List and Shipping Gazette* referred to earlier. Lloyd's shipping index is published daily, and contains information regarding the movement of vessels.

The Salvage Association

1.21 The Salvage Association is operated by a committee composed of representatives of many marine insurers. The Association provides expert technical assistance regarding salvage and arranges surveys of damaged ships, cargoes and other maritime property. It is a non-profit making concern and was incorporated by Royal Charter in 1867. Lloyd's Recoveries Department acts for both Lloyd's underwriters and insurance companies in the collection of general average refunds (see para. 1.29) and deals with the distribution of such refunds and also of recoveries obtained in connection with cargo claims which have been paid by insurers in collision cases.

The overseas market

1.22 In most of the economically developed nations of the world there is a substantial marine market, although a proportion of the business accepted there ultimately finds its way back to London by way of reinsurance.

Lloyd's agents

1.23 In many world ports a Lloyd's agent is appointed. He does not underwrite any marine insurance business, his duty is to provide service. For example, when a ship is in trouble or a cargo has been discharged in a damaged condition, the agent will arrange surveys and will deal with claim settlements.

Marine insurance company agents

1.24 Most large companies appoint agents to represent the parent company provincially and in many of the major cities overseas. These agents may be appointed solely to represent the parent company, but the majority of such agents are business firms operating in the area who undertake the agency as part of their business. One firm may hold several agencies for different companies. The company agent, unlike the Lloyd's agent, underwrites business on behalf of the parent company.

His agency appointment stipulates limitations on the type of business and the maximum amounts to which he may commit the company. Any business outside these limits is submitted to the parent company for approval before acceptance. The agent is generally empowered to settle claims, although in some cases head office approval may be necessary. As remuneration, the agents collect commission from the premiums they collect and usually receive a profit commission based on the profit accruing from the business written by them.

Institute of London Underwriters

1.25 This is an organisation which represents the interests of its members in the London marine insurance company market. Its membership comprises more than one hundred and twenty companies.

1.26 A committe elected from the members runs the affairs of the Institute. The purpose of the Institute is to further the interests of insurance, by co-ordinating facilities regarding wording, clauses and conditions and to find grounds for common agreement on problems affecting the marine insurance market. The work of the Institute is conducted through a number of committees on some of which Lloyd's underwriters and other marine interests are represented. The committees exercise great influence over the day-to-day workings of the marine insurance market in the United Kingdom and abroad. The I.L.U. provides the secretariat for these committees. The Institute clauses, drafted by the Technical and Clauses Committee and published by the Institute are, in general, used throughout the world.

Marine risks

1.27 The risks to be covered in marine insurance include 'all perils of the sea' (wrecking, stranding, sinking, damage by bad weather or by sea water), fire, violent attack, wilful errors of the master or crew (scuttling, abandonment), war risks or seizure.

1.28 The insured is expected to take normal precautions to safeguard the insured property and the policy provides that the insurers will meet a share of the cost of these precautions.

1.29 Archaic language survives in customary use. The term 'average' is used to describe damage. Partial damage to a ship is 'particular average'. The term 'general average act' relates to an act where an 'extraordinary sacrifice or expenditure is voluntarily and reasonably made or incurred in time of peril for the purpose of preserving the property imperilled in the common adventure' [Marine Insurance Act, 1906; section 66(2)]. An example is the jettisoning of cargo to lighten the load and thus to prevent a damaged ship from sinking before reaching port. The loss is referred to as a 'general average loss' and by the law of most countries has to be spread over all those who benefitted from the action taken and does not fall solely on the owner of the jettisoned cargo. 'Freight' is the money paid to the shipowner for carrying goods. One commonly speaks of insuring an 'adventure' (i.e. a voyage).

1.30 Marine insurance may be undertaken on either a voyage or a time basis, i.e. either to cover a specific voyage or for the duration of a specific period (normally a year).

1.31 It is accepted by law that in any marine policy there is the implication that the voyage (or 'adventure') is lawful and will be conducted lawfully. In voyage policies only, it is further implied that at the commencement of the voyage the ship is seaworthy, i.e. in good condition, and properly manned but the onus of proof that a ship is not seaworthy rests with the insurer. In cargo insurances, since the cargo owner cannot be expected to give any warranty about the ship, it is customary for the insurers to endorse the policy to admit the seaworthiness of the vessel.

Insurance of a ship

1.32 A ship is insured against total loss or damage in part up to the value stated in the policy. A distinction is drawn between actual and constructive total loss. An actual total loss occurs when the ship is destroyed or so damaged that it is no longer recognisable as the object which was insured, or if the insured is permanently deprived of it. A constructive total loss occurs when the ship has been reasonably abandoned either in the face of inevitable total loss or because the cost of avoiding total loss would exceed the insured value.

1.33 A marine policy may commonly include a collision or running down clause providing that if the ship collides with another vessel, and in consequence the insured has to pay damages to a third party, the insurer will pay a specified proportion of the damages up to the value of the insured ship. Running down clauses do not include an indemnity for liability in respect of the death or physical injury to a third party, or for damage to harbour or dock structures.

Protection and indemnity

1.34 Certain risks such as, for example, indemnity for liability in respect of claims for loss of life or personal injury resulting from accidents, or liability for damage to harbours or for the cost of removing wrecks are commonly covered not by a marine insurance policy but by mutual insurance between shipowners who group themselves together for this purpose into protection and indemnity associations (or clubs as they are called).

Insurance of freight

1.35 Frequently the shipper of goods pays freight in advance and adds the cost to the value of the goods for insurance purposes. On the few occasions when the freight is not to be paid until after shipment, the shipowner has an insurable interest in the freight and can insure it. A claim may arise if the total freight is increased as a result of a reasonably justified diversion of the ship or transhipment of the cargo as a result of some hazard on the voyage.

Insurance of cargo

1.36 The cargo may be insured either under a 'valued' policy which specifies the goods to be insured and their value, or under an 'open' or 'floating' policy, i.e. the insurers agree to cover all transmissions up to a specified limit per shipment for particular classes of goods, the transmissions being notified as they occur. A floating policy is more appropriate for a related series of shipments; it is issued for a single total sum which is progressively reduced by the value of each shipment of the series successfully completed.

1.37 As in all forms of insurance, any one proposing to insure the cargo must have an insurable interest in it. Normally the shipper effects the insurance either as principal or agent. Cargo policies are assignable from one person to another (provided an insurable interest is transferred). The policy changes hands with the goods.

1.38 The cargo will usually be insured for its full value on arrival at destination, the original cost being increased by the cost of the insurance, the freight, and any duty becoming due (the latter being covered only after the date when the cargo becomes subject to duty). In the case of partial loss the difference between the original value and the value of the damaged goods must be assessed.

Average adjusters

1.39 As indicated in paragraph 1.29 a 'general average loss' has to be shared among all those with a financial interest in the marine adventure. Each person's share will be in proportion to his financial interest. It therefore becomes necessary to ascertain the financial interest of the shipowner and the owners of the cargo so as to make an 'adjustment' of the loss between them. This assessment is made by a firm of professionally skilled people called 'average adjusters', the choice of firm being made by the shipowner. The process necessarily takes time during which the shipowner has a lien on the cargo. In practice the cargo is usually released on payment of a 'general average deposit' estimated to be sufficient to cover the ultimate share of loss. Underwriters are not legally liable to make these deposits on behalf of the insured but again in practice they will reimburse the insured or alternatively provide the ship-owner with a certificate that they will meet the eventual share of the loss; the latter may be sufficient to secure release of cargo.

Aviation insurance market

1.40 The financial risks in aviation are large and most of the aviation insurance risks are widely distributed between many insurers by means of co-insurance or reinsurance. The main division of the London market is between the following.

(a) *Specialist aviation insurance companies* which are wholly owned by consortia of major British insurance companies and which specialise in aviation insurance. Most of their business is effected through London-based insurance brokers, through branch offices overseas and through reciprocal arrangements with overseas companies and pools.

(b) *General insurance companies* Many major British insurance companies maintain specialist aviation departments and transact aviation business both directly with the public and through London-based insurance brokers.

(c) *Lloyd's underwriters* Many Lloyd's underwriters transact aviation insurance through the intermediary of Lloyd's brokers. Lloyd's underwriters who engage in aviation insurance are members of Lloyd's Aviation Underwriters' Association and the insurance companies dealing in aviation insurance are members of the Aviation Insurance Offices' Association. The aim of these organisations is to represent members in their relations with many official bodies and to exchange information, draft standard policy and clause wordings. The Associations do not fix rates, there is a free competition between all members.

International conventions

1.41 A single operator may maintain air services over many different countries and because the claims resulting from a single accident may be extremely high, it is desirable to maintain international agreements as to the circumstances in which liability arises and as to the limits of liability. These agreements are embodied in a series of conventions, the most important of which was the Warsaw Convention of 1929. This agreed that the liability for injury to passengers and goods carried by aircraft should be absolute up to certain limits and that aircraft operators should not be allowed to contract out of these liabilities. The limits allowed have since been increased by later conventions.

Aviation insurance practice

1.42 Not unnaturally aviation insurance practice tends to resemble that of marine insurance. Details of the risk are entered on a slip which is shown round the market, each underwriter taking a share. There is also a leader underwriter who negotiates the insurance.

Comprehensive aviation cover

1.43 A comprehensive policy may be secured which provides cover, to the pilot as well as to the operator, for liability for:

(i) Accidental damage to the aircraft, including damage by fire.
(ii) Legal liability for injury or damage to persons or property on the ground.
(iii) Legal liability to passengers for personal injury or damage to their personal effects.

1.44 A partial return of premium is sometimes made if no claim arises during the period of the insurance and returns may also be made if the aircraft is grounded for a period.

1.45 There is frequently an excess clause in the policy providing that the insurers shall not be liable for the first part (a sum or fraction) of the claim. Large air operators may obtain excess-of-loss insurance which will exclude losses of value below a specified moderate amount and apply only to losses of very large dimensions as in an air disaster. It should be borne in mind that except for minor landing and taxiing mishaps, there is no such thing as a *small* aviation accident. Air accidents are remarkably infrequent but tend, when they come, to be disasters, especially in the age of jumbo-jets. It is therefore the rare disaster that the air companies (large enough to meet the cost of their small losses) are most concerned to cover.

Cargo insurance

1.46 Here again the practice is as for marine insurance. The carriage of goods by air can be insured either on the basis of individual flights or for all transmission during a period of

NATURE OF GENERAL INSURANCE

time. In the latter case the insurance may be by *declaration*, i.e. a specified sum is fixed at the outset which is progressively reduced by the value of each consignment declared to have been sent, (like the floating policy of marine insurance) or by *open cover*, i.e. the insurers agree to cover all transmissions up to a specified limit per aircraft for particular classes of goods, the transmissions being notified as they occur.

Personal accident insurance

1.47 Personal accident insurance (to which further reference is made in paragraph 1.62) provides for the payment of fixed amounts to air-crew and passengers who are accidentally injured, regardless of legal liability for the accident. Air operators normally have group policies for their crews while passengers make personal arrangements either by policies for individual flights or by policies for all flights during a period, usually 1 year. Twenty-four hour policies may be obtained by slot machine at most airports.

Other aviation insurance

1.48 The risk of an aircraft being out of service as result of an accident can be covered usually on the basis of a specified sum related to the period in which the aircraft is grounded. Airport operators may insure against their liability for accidental damage or injury. The manufacturers of aircraft or aircraft components may protect themselves against the liability arising from an accident attributable to defects in their products.

MOTOR VEHICLE

1.49 Motor vehicle insurance covers loss or damage to motor vehicles, and liabilities to third parties, arising out of the use of motor vehicles but it specifically excludes the transit risks covered under marine, aviation and transport insurance.

1.50 The trend has been for the number of vehicles on the roads to increase, and for more and more people to be driving although recently there has been some tendency for the frequency of accidents relative to total mileage to fall. Many of those who drive have limited resources and without the assistance of insurance would be unable to meet their liability to a third party in the event of an accident causing injury to such a third party. The law (specifically the Road Traffic Act, 1972) requires that anyone using a motor vehicle on the road must have, in force, an insurance in respect of this legal liability to third parties including passengers for bodily injury. The insurance must be evidenced by possession of a cover note or certificate of insurance containing certain prescribed particulars which is to be delivered to the insured by the insurer. Motor insurance is usually renewable annually (though insurance can be effected for shorter periods than 1 year) and in order to secure against any lapse of insurance due to delay in payment, a temporary Road Traffic Act cover certificate is usually issued with each annual renewal notice. (It usually extends to 15 days beyond expiry of the current insurance.)

Private cars

1.51 Full third party cover almost invariably extends to legal liability for damage to the property of third parties as well as to injury; it may be extended to include protection against the loss of the insured's own vehicle by fire or theft. Most owners are, however, not satisfied merely to have third party cover even with a fire and theft extension. It is usual to effect what is known as a comprehensive policy which provides indemnity for the loss of or damage to the insurer's own private car, liability for injury to third parties or damage to their property together with extra benefits such as personal accident cover for the insured, payment of medical expenses incurred by injured occupants of the insured's car and loss of or damage (subject to low monetary limits) to rugs, clothing or personal effects carried in the insured car. With regard to the passengers in the insured car, the Motor Vehicle (Passenger Insurance) Act 1971 specifically makes it compulsory to insure liabilities for injuries suffered by them.

1.52 Generally the higher mileage travelled within a specified period and the denser the traffic conditions, the higher the risk of accident, and insurers require higher premiums if a car is used for professional or commercial purposes rather

NATURE OF GENERAL INSURANCE 19

than if solely for social and domestic purposes or for pleasure. Other underwriting factors are (i) geographical district of normal use—usually identified by reference to the place where the car is garaged, (ii) youthfulness of the driver as an indication of comparative inexperience or carelessness, (iii) occupation of driver—if this is one encouraging higher risks or one attracting people more liable to take risks, and (iv) make of car especially if it is one which may be expensive to repair or is a heavier or faster car; not only because the risk of accident may be higher but because, other things being equal, a heavier or faster car will do more damage.

No-claim discount

1.53 An important and well-established feature of motor insurance is the provision of a cumulative no-claim discount. The rate of discount increases progressively with each further year free of claim, from perhaps 25% after one claim free year to 60% after 4 years without claim. A claim may break this progression; no-claim discount is treated in detail in Chapter 8. Other rebates are allowable e.g. for the restriction of driving the car to one named person or when the car is laid up for a time and prior notice has been given. An excess provision also commonly applies whereby a rebate is allowed if the insured bears the first £X of any claim.

Overseas travel

1.54 By agreement between the insurance industries of the principal European countries it is possible for cars to carry their insurance with them for short periods of foreign travel. A certificate issued on behalf of the British insurer (the so called 'green card') is recognised at frontiers as proof that the motor insurance requirements of the country visited outside the E.E.C. are satisfied. A certificate is no longer necessary within the E.E.C. but it continues to be issued in those cases where the insured wishes to obtain and pay for the full cover provided by his policy instead of the limited insurance required by the legislation of the E.E.C. country concerned.

Commercial vehicles

1.55 The insurance of commercial vehicles may be limited to the liability imposed by the Road Traffic Act ('Act liability only'), may be full third party protection, or may be comprehensive. In the latter case the degree of comprehensiveness may be less than for private car insurance, the extra benefits being rarely provided. A commercial vehicle may be any shape or size ranging from a hire car or small van to a motor coach or modern articulated juggernaut. In which group the vehicle comes (within this range) and its working conditions (e.g. long haul over motorways or local delivery in relatively easy traffic) will affect the premium rating. No-claim discounts are given.

1.56 A special 'fleet' rating may be offered where several vehicles are in single ownership. In this case no-claim discounts are not given but the premium is reviewed each year in the light of the claims experience of the fleet.

Motor cycles

1.57 The popular image of the average motor cycle rider as young, tough and wild is a product of experience though by no means true of all riders. Accidents are frequent amongst such riders and are often serious. A rider or a passenger on two wheels is much more exposed to serious injury than a driver or passenger inside the shell of a car and held by safety belts. Not all insurers seek such business; those that do have to charge higher premiums for young riders or require them to meet the first part of any claim. A comprehensive policy is relatively expensive and less comprehensive than for a private car.

Claim settling agreements

1.58 To avoid the waste of time and the cost of legal actions, many insurers have 'knock-for-knock' agreements with each other so that in the event of an accident between two vehicles insured by two different insurers, each insurer meets the cost of the repairs to the vehicle it has insured without any investigation as to which of the insured is legally liable, and without attempting therefore to recover the cost from the other insurer. Where a number of vehicles are involved it is likely that legal liabilities will be fairly evenly shared so that even if every legal liability were to be pursued in the courts, the overall distribution of costs would not be very different from that resulting from the 'knock-for-knock' agreement; and the overall financial result to the insurers would be less favourable because they would all have been involved in litigation expenses. These claim agreements also extend to the sharing of third party claims subject to monetary limits and legal costs are saved here too.

1.59 These agreements usually mean that the insured loses his no-claims discount unless it is clear that he was not to blame for the accident. In these cases the insurers will agree to preserve the no-claim discount, but in the absence of clear evidence they will usually stand firm since they have had to pay out money and blame is difficult to attribute in the absence of adequate information. Claim settling agreements do cheapen insurance but they can create aggrieved customers who are not especially convinced of the overall benefits; they are only conscious of their own grievances. There is a public relations problem here which insurers have to deal with.

Protection of injured third parties

1.60 An agreement effective from 1 July 1946 was reached between the Minister of Transport and the Motor Insurers' Bureau (a group comprising the majority of insurance companies and Lloyd's underwriters) which gives an effective right to a third party to recover if necessary from the Bureau in all cases of liability towards him covered by the Road Traffic Acts—that is for personal injury as a third party whether in or outside the vehicle concerned. The object of the agreement is to ensure that those who would have been able to recover by reason of the insurance of the negligent driver but who in fact cannot do so (e.g. because the driver is untraced or uninsured) can seek recovery from the M.I.B. The agreement between the Bureau and the Ministry requires payment 'if judgment ... is obtained against any person...' but it is common practice for the Bureau to take over the settlement of the majority of claims before judgment and even before legal proceedings are commenced. In fact even where the driver is untraced and therefore unknown (so that judgment can never be obtained) the Bureau accept and settle these claims on an ex gratia basis.

PECUNIARY LOSS

1.61 Pecuniary loss insurance covers risks arising from:
1. Insolvency of debtors.
2. Failure of debtors to pay their debts when due.
3. Having to carry out a contract of guarantee (e.g. to make good a debtor's failure to meet obligations to another creditor).
4. Interruption of or reduction in the scope of business carried on (e.g. by some accidental damage to the business premises).
5. The incurring of unforeseen expenses. This class of insurance covers fidelity insurance and consequential loss insurance. Fidelity guarantee insurance has replaced the old system of personal sureties which an employee in a position of trust used to have to provide as a protection against loss suffered by his employer as a consequence of the employee's misbehaviour. This system was never adequate or secure. In this type of insurance, the insurer, in consideration of a premium, undertakes to reimburse the employer for any loss caused by dishonesty of one or more employees up to a stated amount. Where the guarantee is for more than one employee it is known as collective. The amount of the guarantee may be stated with a separate limit for each 'named employee' or as a single sum for all employees within the guarantee (in the latter case, called a floating guarantee). The principle of good faith applies and an insurer will require the employer to provide a frank record of the past behaviour of the employees.

PERSONAL ACCIDENT AND SICKNESS

1.62 Personal accident insurance provides cash benefits payable in the event of disablement or death due to accident or disablement due to illness. The insurance is normally on an

NATURE OF GENERAL INSURANCE

annual contract basis and may vary in scope from (1) benefits only for injury by accident to (2) benefits arising from an accident or certain specified diseases (e.g. cancer) and (3) benefits arising from 'accident and all sickness'.

1.63 Benefits for accidental death or injury are commonly arranged in a scale of decreasing severity similar to that shown below (the figures are shown to indicate relativity since in a time of high inflation they are likely to be out of date before publication).

1	Death	£1,000
2	Loss of both hands or both feet or the sight of both eyes; or of one hand *and* one foot; or of one hand or one foot *and* the sight of one eye	£1,000
3	Loss of one hand or one foot or the sight of one eye	£500
4	Permanent total disablement (other than as in 2 or 3 above)	£100 p.a. (or £1,000 cash depending on company)
5	Temporary total disablement	£10 per week for 104* weeks
6	Temporary partial disablement	£10 per week for 104* weeks

1.64 Normally the policy will provide that payment in respect of any one accident will be limited to benefit under one of these headings except that benefit could be paid consecutively under both 5 and 6. Benefit for sickness disablement would not include capital sums. Medical or surgical expenses can be covered for an additional premium.

1.65 A medical examination is not required but the proposal form is searching in respect of the present occupation and of the previous accident, insurance and medical history as well as the present physical condition. The premium rating is related to occupation. Individuals in occupations with a heavy accident risk, e.g. building workers, attract a higher risk rating than those with only light risk, e.g. clerical workers. New pro-

---

* If there are periods of both total and partial disablement the total of 104 weeks applies to the combined benefits, i.e. no more than 104 weeks' disablement benefit can be drawn in total.

posers over a certain age, say 55 to 60, would not be accepted and renewals at older ages would be discouraged because the risk of accident or illness increases sharply as age 60 approaches as also does the duration of any temporary disablement.

1.66 Personal accident insurance benefits are payable regardless of the actual monetary loss suffered by the insured; such insurances are not contracts of indemnity. Naturally, the insurer would avoid an adverse option by making sure that the level of periodic payments was not substantially in excess of the normal earnings of the insured, and not therefore an inducement to delay a return to work. As part of this precaution the insurer would seek information as to all other policies held by the insured with other insurers; the insured would be required to notify the insurer of any other additional policies. Because the contracts are not of indemnity, all benefits have to be paid in full however many insurers there may be; furthermore there is no question of recovery of the benefits from a third party who might have caused the accident by negligence.

1.67 An insurer may refuse to offer renewal to an insured who has a series of accidents or illness and thus turns out to be an abnormally heavy risk. Some insurers will offer *permanent* sickness and accident insurance up to a specified age, binding themselves to renew the contract annually up to that age. Such permanent sickness and accident insurance is considerably more expensive than ordinary personal accident and sickness insurance but the duration of benefit for temporary disablement can be reduced to say 6 months, to make it less expensive. Also as in permanent sickness insurance as such this cost can be reduced by the imposition of a waiting period. Where such contracts are for a period of 5 years or more they are classified as ordinary long-term insurance business (see para. 1.5 above).

1.68 Short periods of extra risk, e.g. winter sports or touring holidays, can be covered by special policies. This category would include very short period risks such as air flights for which heavy cover can be obtained at low cost. Mention must be made here of coupon or ticket insurance. A ticket giving cover for railway accidents can be bought at a station booking office with the railway ticket and at most airports there are slot machines from which insurance coupons can be bought (and posted to a next of kin) before departure of flight. Some diaries include coupons which can be sent to a named company together with a small premium in order to obtain limited accident cover.

Hospital expenses

1.69 Many people would like to be able to afford private facilities when they need to enter hospital. Private medicine is however increasingly expensive and as the need for treatment may arise quite suddenly there has been a demand for insurance against the contingency. Initially, because most people were content to rely upon the National Health Service the demand was not large and was mainly met by specialist non-profit making societies which collected annual contributions graded according to age on entry into the scheme and paid hospital expenses up to a specified limit. More recently shortage of resources in the National Health Service has led to an increase in the demand for insurance and a number of insurance companies have entered the field which has become more competitive. As a result of the increased cost of private treatment, the cost of insurance has increased and it is likely that in future more attention will have to be paid to other factors than age in premium rating.

PROPERTY

1.70 Property insurance is insurance against loss of or damage to material property, but does not include property falling within the scope of marine, aviation and transport insurance and of motor vehicle insurance. The principal peril covered is that of fire but many policies cover additional perils such as engineering failures, or theft. A number of other perils may be covered. These include: explosion; riot and civil commotion; malicious damage; damage from aircraft or from articles dropped from aircraft; storm; tempest and flood; bursting or overflowing of water tanks, apparatus and pipes; impact damage, e.g. from vehicles.

The fire insurance market

1.71 A very high proportion of fire insurance business in the United Kingdom is transacted by insurance companies, the remainder by Lloyd's underwriters. A few companies transacting fire insurance specialise in particular classes of business. Some companies have been formed as subsidiaries of large industrial and commercial groups in order to insure the parent companies' property. A few mutual companies insure property in a particular trade or industry in which the members of the company are interested.

1.72 As already indicated underwriting members of Lloyd's operate as individuals for the purpose of accepting insurance. Each member of a syndicate will take a proportion of the total risk. Fire insurance is accepted mainly in the non-marine syndicates although there are subsidiary syndicates maintained by marine underwriters to accept a small amount of non-marine business incidental to their marine business.

1.73 All fire insurance at Lloyd's must be placed through a Lloyd's broker, but insurance with a company is either arranged direct or through an agent or broker. Agents act for particular insurance companies and introduce business on a commission basis. Many agencies are part-time and are held by solicitors, bank managers, accountants, estate agents, etc., who in the course of their main occupation are frequently in contact with people who wish to effect fire insurance. Building societies also hold agencies, and introduce a substantial volume of household business through their contact with mortgagors.

1.74 Anyone seeking fire insurance must disclose all relevant information (*uberrima fides*). For large properties the insurers will employ a skilled fire surveyor and the acceptance of the risk and the terms on which it will be accepted will depend on his report. Policies are usually issued for 1 year but term agreements for periods of 3 or 5 years can be effected (subject to annual renewal within the period).

1.75 Rates of premium for fire insurance are expressed as a percentage of the sum insured and vary with the nature and use of the property e.g. account is taken of the likelihood of a fire and the extent to which it could spread.

1.76 Essentially the insurer agrees to pay or make good the loss resulting from the perils insured against up to the sum insured under each item in the schedule to the policy. The perils are those referred to in paragraph 1.70. A policy is voidable in the event of misrepresentation or non-disclosure of any material particular; it is also voidable in respect of any item in regard to which there is any alteration whereby the risk of damage is increased or in the event of cessation of the insured's interest; it is also voidable if there is a fraudulent claim or if damage is caused by the insured's wilful act or with his connivance. The principle of contribution (i.e. the loss would be spread over all insurers) usually applies if there are other insurances effected by or on behalf of the insured; virtually all fire policies in respect of industrial or commercial property are subject to average, i.e. if the property is insured, for example, for only 80% of its value, only 80% of the claim is payable. Policies for domestic property are not usually subject to average but there has to be a declaration that the full value has been insured. The insured will be expected to give a warranty as to the preservation of any conditions laid down by the insurer to reduce the risk.

1.77 The schedule of the policy contains a specification of the property insured and gives the sum insured in respect of each item; it also identifies the insured, and states the period of the insurance and the premium.

Rating

1.78 The rate of premium charged for a fire insurance will depend on the past underwriting experience for the class of property and the surveyor's report as to the nature of the particular building to be insured. Factors to be taken into account include the construction, the number of floors and the area, the manufacturing processes carried on and the storage of hazardous goods and materials. Rates are reduced for approved sprinkler protection and other fire extinguishing appliances and fire alarms.

Profits insurance

1.79 The ordinary type of fire policy covers only the cost of making good the material damage. Other consequential losses, which may be substantial, such as loss of profit or extra running expenses resulting from a fire requires separate insurance.

1.80 The standard loss of profits policy was introduced in 1939. It is concerned with the business of the insured and aims to indemnify him in respect of loss of net profits, standard charges and increase in the cost of working resulting from the fire. The policy contains the formula by which losses will be measured. The fire will normally result in an interruption to the business which can be measured by the consequent reduction of turnover. The cost of raw materials will be reduced proportionately but not so the standing charges such as e.g. staff salaries. Some working costs will increase if the insured has to work in more difficult conditions while awaiting repair of the building or if he has to temporarily subcontract to another concern. The profits insurer normally undertakes to pay the insured the loss of gross profits proportional to any assessed loss of turnover *less* any part of the insured standing charges which it has been possible to reduce after the fire, *plus* any increase in the cost of working necessary to minimise the loss of turnover. Gross profit means net profit plus the insured standing charges (specified by the proposer). The policy will operate for a stated maximum indemnity period after the fire during which the insured's loss of profit will be protected; this period will be selected by the proposer and will depend on his assessment of how long a fire would be likely to interrupt his kind of business. The past trend of profits of the business and the expectation for the future should be brought into the calculation of the sum insured.

1.81 The rates of premium for loss of profits insurance are based on the average fire rate applicable to the contents which contribute the material damage risk. This is the *basic* rate and it is subject to adjustment according to the maximum indemnity selected.

Household insurance for private dwellings

1.82 The discussion so far has been of the fire risk for large buildings and business premises. The insurance of the ordinary dwelling is simpler. Buildings and contents policies known sometimes as houseowners or householders policies respectively, are combined in a single policy for owner-occupiers. The building policy covers loss of or damage to the building caused by some or all of a variety of perils: fire; explosion; lightning; thunderbolt; riot; civil commotion; strikes; political disturbance; aircraft or articles dropped from aircraft; storm or flood; subsidence; theft; escape of water from any fixed installation; earthquake; impact with any road vehicle or animal; breakage or collapse of television or radio receiving aerials, fittings or masts; leakage of oil from oil-fired heating installation; falling trees. The cover also includes loss of rent if the dwelling is rendered uninhabitable by an insured risk; accidental damage to underground water pipe, gas pipe or electricity cable extending from the dwelling to the public main supply; accidental breakage of fixed glass in windows, doors, fanlights, sky lights; breakage of wash basins, pedestals, sinks, lavatory pans and cisterns; legal liability of the insured, as owner, for damages and costs in respect of bodily injury or loss of or damage to property not belonging to or in the charge of the policyholder or members of his family or persons in his service.

1.83 The contents policy covers loss or damage to the contents arising from a similar range of perils. Cover extends to contents temporarily removed from the house up to a proportion of the total value. If the insured is a tenant the policy will cover him for his liability as a tenant (up to a specified limit) for damage to the buildings arising from some of the perils but not for example, from fire. The insured and his family are usually indemnified for occupier's and personal liability arising out of accidents to servants or members of the public and compensation is provided, up to a stated maximum, in the event of the death of the policyholder or his spouse, resulting from injury caused in the building by thieves. Loss of rent and the cost of alternative accommodation are included. The insured is required to cover the full value of his property, both for the building and the contents.

Tariff and non-tariff market

1.84 The Fire Offices Committee is an association of those companies transacting fire insurance which agree to adhere to certain minimum rates and standards.

1.85 The remainder of the U.K. market comprises independent companies and Lloyd's who together constitute a powerful competitive market capable of handling very large risks. It is normal practice for both tariff and non-tariff insurers to subscribe as co-insurers to the same insurance, although the schedule is normally but not invariably led by a tariff company.

1.86 Notwithstanding the fact that they are—in commercial terms—in competition with each other, the two sections of the market co-operate very fully in more general matters. Notable among these are the financing and operation of the Salvage Corps in London, Liverpool and Glasgow, the Fire Protection Association and the Fire Insurers Research and Testing Organisation. They also combine in representing the U.K. market in discussions with European fire insurers.

The spreading of risk—reinsurance

1.87 An insurer will prefer to operate in terms of collective rather than individual risk. He will prefer to spread his liability by taking a small share of a large number of risks rather than take the whole of one large risk which could more than exhaust his resources. We have seen how some sharing of risk is effected between syndicates at Lloyd's (para. 1.16). Reinsurance is another method of achieving this sharing of risk; it is an arrangement between the original insurer and the reinsurer under which some part of the risk accepted by the direct insurer is passed on to the reinsurer. By means of reinsurance, an insurer is enabled to accept insurance of sums substantially greater than the maximum he wishes to retain for his own account. It has no effect on the contract between the direct insurer and the insured, and the latter does not enter

NATURE OF GENERAL INSURANCE

into any contractual relationship with the reinsurer. Reinsurance business is done partly by specialist companies, which undertake reinsurance only and do not undertake direct insurances; but in addition major insurance companies and Lloyd's underwriters commonly undertake reinsurance as well as direct insurance. A substantial amount of reinsurance is placed overseas with foreign companies, frequently with a reciprocal arrangement under which foreign companies reinsure with British companies.

1.88 Most reinsurance is effected under reinsurance treaties, which are renewable annually, under which some part of the direct insurer's business is automatically reinsured. The reinsurance is either on a proportional or non-proportional basis. In proportional reinsurance, the reinsurer accepts a proportion of each individual insurance, receives that proportion of the premium and pays that proportion of all losses. In non-proportional reinsurance, the reinsurance applies to the whole portfolio of insurance and gives cover to the reinsured in excess of a negotiated cash figure or claim ratio (see Chapter 4), in respect of any one event, or in excess of a negotiated overall claims ratio.

1.89 If 'treaty' reinsurance facilities are not sufficient to enable the direct insurer to accept the whole of a risk, he might arrange reinsurance on an individual or 'facultative' basis, but most probably the risk will be co-insured. Co-insurance differs from reinsurance, in that each of the co-insurers accepts a stated percentage of the total insurance and, each enters into a direct contractual relationship with the insured. When a risk is to be co-insured, it is usual for the insured or his broker, to approach one insurer to take the lead, and to accept a substantial share of the risk, and then to approach other insurers who may be expected to follow the lead. Co-insurance plays a very important part in the insurance of commercial and industrial risks. In terms of premium income, a substantial proportion of the total business is co-insured.

1.90 There may be more than one limited layer of reinsurance of a particular risk (and correspondingly more than one layer of premium within the total premium). It is important to bear in mind that reinsured claims can rebound on the primary insurer when the top reinsured layer is broken (if it is limited). This is dealt with in Chapter 9.

1.91 For some risks, especially liability risks, it is common for reinsurance to be by means of an excess-of-loss treaty. This means that the direct insurer pays all claims up to an agreed limit and the cost of any claim in excess of that limit is met by the reinsurer. Such treaties prevent an occasional heavy claim from upsetting the profitability of the direct insurer's account for the particular class of business. Under this kind of treaty a negotiated percentage of the premium is payable to the reinsurer. Excess-of-loss reinsurance need not be restricted to an individual risk but may be extended to a whole portfolio of risks.

1.92 There is also 'stop loss' reinsurance, though rarely obtainable. Under this system the reinsurer is liable for the claims which exceed an agreed percentage of the premium income. It relates to the total experience of the direct insurer for a particular class of business.

1.93 Both 'excess-of-loss' and 'stop loss' are forms of non-proportional reinsurance.

Statutory control of general insurance

1.94 In the public interest the Goverment exercises supervision and control of general insurance (as it does of life assurance). The legislative background is dealt with in detail in Chapter 2, but we may complete this review of the market by summarising the legal situation. The governing act is the Insurance Companies Act of 1974. Only those insurance companies and other bodies including Lloyd's which are authorised by the Secretary of State for the Department of Trade can conduct general insurance. These companies must meet certain requirements including a specific margin of solvency expressed in terms of minimum net assets in relation to premium income, adequate arrangements for reinsurance and a requirement that no 'unfit person' is associated with the company. The 1974 Act imposes similar conditions for authorisation to carry on general insurance upon members of Lloyd's, friendly societies and trade unions.

1.95 The Secretary of State has power to issue regulations governing the actual conduct of general insurance e.g. in regard to accounting and auditing. These regulations also give the Secretary of State statutory access to such financial and statistical information as is deemed by the government to be necessary for the proper exercise of supervision of the industry. The statutory returns are described in Chapter 2.

1.96 In the past the government of the United Kingdom has relied on the principle of freedom with accountability and its control of the insurance industry has been less comprehensive than that of other governments in Europe. Now that the United Kingdom is a committed member of the European Economic Community some degree of harmonisation between the United Kingdom and the other member countries is already taking place although certain aspects of control will be left to the national supervisory authorities. There may therefore, be changes in the future but few people expect these to be material.

CHAPTER 2

BRITISH LEGISLATION GOVERNING INSURANCE COMPANIES

2.1 Legislation in Great Britain provides for the overall supervision of insurance business. It also provides for the protection of policyholders in the event of a company experiencing difficulties. It makes provision too for certain types of insurance to be compulsory. Furthermore there is some provision for control of premium rates, but unlike the control in some other countries this is entirely part of the Government's counter inflationary policy and is not part of the general supervision process.

A list of the relevant Acts and Regulations relating to supervision is set out at the end of the chapter. Where the Acts do not cover Northern Ireland the legislation there is similar. In the case of Insurance Companies Regulations, Northern Ireland Regulations follow the British ones but tend to be made after the British ones, so that at any time there may be minor discrepancies.

Following the entry of the United Kingdom into the European Economic Community the developing harmonisation of insurance legislation within the Community will impinge on legislation in the United Kingdom and an important distinction has to be drawn between those aspects of the supervisory system which are required by Community Directives and those which are left to national supervisory authorities.

Supervision and control of insurance companies

2.2 All companies and persons whether British or not carrying on insurance business in Great Britain must comply with the Insurance Companies Act 1974 (the Act) and where appropriate with the Regulations made under that Act or previous Acts governing insurance business. In addition companies have to comply with the more general provisions of the Companies Acts. Supervision of insurance companies is carried out by the Insurance Division of the Department of Trade on behalf of the Secretary of State. In what follows references are made to the Department for convenience and reflect the practical position, but it should be remembered that it would be more correct legally in each case to speak of the 'Secretary of State'.

2.3 Much of the Act does not apply to friendly societies, trade unions or employers' associations providing provident or strike benefits, and persons carrying on pecuniary loss business 'in the course of carrying on, and for the purposes of, banking business' (i.e. most banks and similar institutions). Therefore almost all that follows does not apply to these organisations. Under section 57 of the Act the Department may on application excuse a company from many provisions of the Act, and the application of this section is discussed in paragraph 2.38 below. The Act provides for the making of a large number of Regulations. In addition to the Regulations already made there are at the time of publication many still under discussion and the legal position will alter as these are made. The main provisions of the Act and the Regulations applying to general insurance business are described below. The description has been simplified for brevity and clarity. For exactness or greater detail the original documents should be consulted.

Segregation of long term business

2.4 If an insurance company carries on both long term business and general insurance business, the assets and liabilities of the long term business must be kept separate from those of any other business of the company. This was a new requirement in the Act and the initial identification (a 'once for all' procedure) should have been carried out by December 1975 in accordance with the Insurance Companies (Identification of Long Term Assets and Liabilities) Regulations 1973, if they were not already identified. The effect of this separation is that the two sides of an office conducting long term as well as general business can be thought of as distinct entities subject to the following provisos.

(i) There is nothing in the Act to prohibit transfers from the general business to the long term business.

(ii) Surplus may, subject to certain constraints, be transferred from the long term business to the general business, following an actuarial valuation.
(iii) A dividend may not be paid while the long term business fund is in deficit and the deficit should be added to the general business liabilities before calculating the solvency margin (see para. 2.6 below).
(iv) In a winding-up the creditors of the long term side have a prior claim on the assets of the long term business fund and the other creditors a prior claim on the general business assets, but if either side has a surplus it will be available to meet the liabilities of the other side of the company.

Classes of general insurance business

2.5 The Act defines the following general business classes: liability; marine, aviation and transport; motor vehicle; pecuniary loss; personal accident; property. There are provisions in the Act that business carried on in a class incidental to business of another class may be regarded as business of that other class under most circumstances. Personal accident business is insurance against sickness or against injury or death resulting from an accident, when the duration of the policy is less than 5 years. Pecuniary loss includes the guarantee of debts due from third parties (e.g. mortgage guarantees), contract guarantee, business interruption (e.g. consequential loss following fire), unforeseen expense and any other insurance business not included in the other classes. The other classes are fairly well defined by their titles.

Solvency margin

2.6 An insurance company doing general business must maintain at all times an excess of assets over liabilities (other than liabilities in respect of share capital), known as its required solvency margin, in its general business side. The solvency margin is £50,000 or 20% of its general premium income (net of reinsurance) in its previous financial year (whichever is greater) or, if that income is greater than £2·5m, 10% of that income plus £250,000. If the 'year' is not 12 months then the appropriate multiple of that income is used in the formula.

2.7 A company that does not maintain the required solvency margin is deemed to be insolvent. The action which would be taken in this event would however depend on how the Department applied its powers of intervention under the Act (para. 2.18 below) and also on the provisions of the Policyholders' Protection Act (para. 2.44 below), which was passed subsequent to the Act.

2.8 The Act gives the Department power to vary the solvency margin and in particular this is likely to be done in the near future to comply with the relevant European Economic Community Directive (see para. 2.52 below).

Authorisation

2.9 No company may carry on insurance business of any class unless it is authorised by the Department to carry on business of that class, or was lawfully carrying on business of that class immediately before 3 November 1966.

2.10 A company may not be authorised unless it has paid up capital of at least £100,000 and a margin of assets over liabilities (excluding liabilities in respect of share capital) of at least £50,000 and if already trading (in the United Kingdom or overseas) as an insurer of at least the required solvency margin. In practice it is understood that the Department normally requires paid-up capital and a margin of assets over liabilities of considerably higher amounts. The requirements of this paragraph do not apply if a company is to insure only a limited class of persons, e.g. employees of its parent company, or only a limited category of risk, e.g. plate glass mutuals.

2.11 A company may not be authorised until the Department is satisfied either that adequate reinsurance arrangements will be made or that it is justifiable not to make reinsurance arrangements.

2.12 A further stipulation is that if it appears to the Department that any director, controller or manager (these terms are defined in section 7 of the Act) of the company is not a fit and proper person for such position then the authorisation must be refused. The term fit and proper is not defined in the Act but the information to be given in making application to the Department is outlined in paragraph 2.25 below.

Revocation

2.13 The authorisation of a company may be withdrawn if it ceases to carry on business of a class in Great Britain or, if it is newly authorised, fails to start that business within a year of authorisation.

Valuation of assets and liabilities

2.14 Regulations may be made for the valuation of the assets and liabilities of insurance companies. At the date of publication no regulations have been made under the Act as to the valuation of liabilities but provisions for the valuation of assets are set out in the Insurance Companies (Valuation of Assets) Regulations and the Insurance Companies (Valuation of Assets) (Amendment) Regulations both of 1976. The main provisions are described below but the Regulations are very complex and must be referred to for a full statement of the position. The values laid down are maxima in the sense that a lower value should be used if appropriate, e.g. if property values have fallen since valuation. It should be noted that the Regulations make provision for the limited admissibility of certain assets (i.e. to avoid too much of the insurance funds being concentrated in any one investment certain assets may not be taken into account beyond certain limits for the purpose of calculating a company's solvency position) as well as the method of valuation. Because of their recent introduction changes are being considered in the light of experience gained in the application of the Regulations.

1. Assets given a nil value: advance commission, amounts due on partly paid shares and any asset for the valuation of which no provision is made, e.g. goodwill, raw materials (in, for example, an industrial subsidiary).
2. Assets which are subject to an accelerated writedown: computer equipment, other office equipment, motor vehicles, etc.

BRITISH LEGISLATION 39

3   Assets to be taken essentially at market or realisable value at date of valuation: debts (if not due within 12 months), land including property, life interests, reversionary interests, etc., securities issued or guaranteed by any government or public authority, building society shares, share and debenture options, holdings in a unit trust and other quoted investments, including equities.

4   Assets to be taken at the amount which can reasonably be expected to be recovered (i.e. undiscounted): debts due within 12 months, reinsurance and salvage rights.

5   Assets given a more arbitrary valuation: Dependent company (a company under the 'control' of the insurance company—one third is sufficient to give control in this context)—proportionate net asset value determined as if the dependent company were an insurance company, less any solvency margin in the case of an insurance dependent. Amounts unpaid and not due on partly paid shares—one half of the unpaid amount (if the shares are at least one quarter paid). Unquoted equity shares (other than a share in a dependent company)—average earnings times the F.T. Actuaries Price-earnings Ratio (net) relating to the Industrial Group.

6   Schedule 2 to the Regulations sets out the limits of admissibility. These limits are applied independently to the assets attributable to long-term business and to the assets attributable to general business—as we have seen these two groups of assets must be separately identified. For example, within the general business assets any one property may not be brought into account for more than 5% of the 'general business amount' (i.e. the general business liabilities net of reinsurance plus the required solvency margin) and the total of quoted shares and debentures in any one company may not exceed 5% of that amount. Outstanding premiums may not exceed 30% of the general business premiums receivable in the year immediately preceding the accounting date, reduced by the commission payable thereon.

Annual returns

2.15 Insurance companies must every financial year prepare accounts and forms containing such information in such form as is prescribed. It should be noted that there is no requirement that these accounts should agree with the Companies Act accounts and whereas this has normally been the case in the past, it seems likely that this will change to reflect the requirements of the Valuation Regulations which may not be carried through to the Companies Act returns. These accounts and forms must be submitted to the Department in quintuplicate within six months of the end of the financial year. One copy must be signed by two directors and the chief executive (or, if there is none, the secretary) of the company. In addition any report to the shareholders or policyholders of the company in respect of the financial year must also be submitted. If the Department feel that the returns are incomplete or inaccurate then they would communicate with the company to obtain corrections and additional information. Shareholders and policyholders are normally entitled on application to the company to receive copies of these returns and any supplementary documents submitted. The Department must deposit one copy of the returns with the Registrar of Companies and this will normally be open to inspection. The items to be included in the Annual Returns are set out in paragraph 2.31 below.

2.16 The prescribed form is that laid down by the 1968 Regulations as amended by the 1975 and 1976 Amendment Regulations. The amendments take account of the separation of the long term assets and liabilities and the valuation of assets regulations. New regulations are in preparation which will provide for far more detailed returns, for the most part in forms intended as computer punching documents.

Quarterly returns

2.17 Regulations may be made providing for statements of business of classes (to be prescribed) to be submitted at prescribed intervals. It is likely that regulations will be introduced providing for the submission of quarterly returns of those aspects of a company's business which would be taken into account by the Department in deciding on the company's financial soundness to continue in business, but it is probable that these returns will not be introduced until new regulations are made relating to the annual returns.

Powers of intervention

2.18 The Department has powers of intervention which it may exercise on the following grounds. The ground for the intervention must be stated to the company at the time of intervention or in advance.

1. That it is considered desirable for protecting policyholders or potential policyholders against the risk of insolvency.
2. That the company has apparently failed to satisfy its obligations under the Act.
3. That its returns were apparently misleading or inadequate.
4. That its reinsurance arrangements may be inadequate.
5. That a director, controller or manager is apparently not fit and proper.
6. That it appears that the company might be insolvent (i.e. fails to meet its required solvency margin calculated in accordance with any valuation regulations).
7. That an authorisation was issued to it or that it changed control within the preceding 5 years, whether or not any of the other grounds exist. In this case not all the powers are applicable and the requirements imposed may not continue after 10 years have elapsed since the change of control or authorisation.

2.19 The powers are:

1. A company may, subject to certain constraints, be required not to effect any new contracts of insurance or contracts of insurance of a specified description. When a requirement of this type is imposed on a company, it must be published in the *London* and *Edinburgh Gazettes* and in any other expedient way to notify the public.
2. A company may be required not to make investments of

a specified class or to realise a specified proportion of such investments.

3   A company may be required to maintain assets in the United Kingdom equal to a proportion of its domestic liabilities (which term is defined more exactly in section 31 of the Act). In addition a proportion of these assets may be required to be held by an approved trustee.

4   A company may be required to limit its premium income (net or gross of reinsurance) to a specified amount.

5   A company may be required to deposit its annual returns within 3 months instead of 6 months of the end of its financial year. This requirement cannot be imposed merely by virtue of a change of control or a new authorisation.

6   A company may be required to supply the Department with such additional information that the Department may specify at detailed intervals of time, for example of market values of assets when stock market prices are falling.

7   The Department may require the production of the books or papers of a company. This may not be imposed merely by virtue of a change of control or a new authorisation. This may also be imposed even if none of the above grounds apply if the Department feels it to be desirable in the general interests of existing or potential policyholders.

8   Finally the Department has a residual power to require a company to take any other action for protecting existing or potential policyholders against the risk of its insolvency. Presumably this would apply if it is considered that the other powers were insufficient.

Director, controller or manager

2.20   The terms are defined in the Act. In particular no person may be appointed managing director or chief executive without the company notifying the Department in advance, supplying prescribed information and obtaining its consent unless the Department fails to object on the grounds that he is not a fit and proper person within 3 months of notification.

2.21 No person may become a controller of an insurance company without notifying the Department of his intention, supplying prescribed information, and the Department either gives its consent or fails to object on the grounds that he is not a fit and proper person within 3 months of notification.

2.22 If the Department is contemplating using its powers of intervention against a company on the grounds of the unfitness of a director (other than a controller) or of a manager of a company then they must notify him in advance.

2.23 If the Department makes an objection (in the first two cases) or notifies a director or manager that he is considered not fit then within a month the person and, in the case of a proposed managing director or chief executive, the company also may make representations to the Department. These representations must be taken into account.

2.24 Within 14 days of a change of director, controller or manager the company must inform the Department supplying prescribed information. Any person becoming a director, controller or manager must within seven days supply the company with the prescribed information as must any person ceasing to be a controller.

2.25 The prescribed information is laid down in the Insurance Companies (Changes of Director, Controller or Manager) Regulations 1975. These require information, *inter alia*, as to qualification and experience, present and previous occupations, any previous convictions or criticisms by a professional body and any previous bankruptcies.

Winding up

2.26 The Department may petition for a winding up on the grounds that a company has failed to meet its required solvency margin, that it has failed to meet its obligations under the Act, or that it has failed to keep proper books of account or to produce them and that the Department cannot ascertain its financial position.

2.27 When a petition is presented for the winding up of an insurance company the Department shall be served a copy and shall be entitled to be heard on it.

2.28 Rules may be made for the winding up of insurance

companies. The current rules contained in Schedules 3 and 4 of the 1958 Insurance Companies Act will continue in force until new rules are made under the Act. In practice every attempt would be made to avoid winding up and to find some other solution to the problem of a company in difficulties.

Conduct of insurance business

2.29 The Insurance Companies (Intermediaries) Regulations 1976 require intermediaries who are connected with an insurance company to inform potential policyholders of the nature of that connection. If the insurance company is not authorised the regulations require the intermediary to so inform potential policyholders.

2.30 Any person who induces another person to enter into an insurance contract with an insurance company by means of misleading or reckless statements is guilty of an offence and regulations may be made as to the form and contents of insurance advertisements.

Accounts and forms

2.31 The current regulations provide that the accounts submitted to the Department should give a 'true and fair view' except that the value of assets shall be determined in accordance with the Valuation Regulations. Items relating to the long term business of a company must be shown separately. For a proprietary company doing general business the following must be submitted as part of the annual returns: balance sheet and profit and loss account together with an analysis by type of investments. For each class of general business and for treaty reinsurance business not allocated to a specific class, a general business revenue account and if the company does any 3-year business, a 3-year revenue statement should be attached.

2.32 For each class of general business, a premium analysis which analyses gross premiums between U.K. direct and facultative business, other U.K. reinsurance, overseas direct and facultative business, other overseas reinsurance, and any treaty reinsurance business in which U.K. and overseas business cannot be split. Reinsurance cessions should be shown and as far as possible split between U.K. and overseas business. Reinsurance recoveries and commission receivable from reinsurers should also be shown. Direct and facultative business premiums should be split by month of inception and treaty reinsurance by quarter of inception.

2.33 A number of certificates should be attached to these returns.

Aggregate value certificate—this should confirm that the value of the company's assets at the year end was in the aggregate at least equal to the amount thereof shown in the balance sheet and that such value has been calculated in accordance with the Valuation Regulations.

Domestic assets certificate—this states whether or not realisable domestic assets exceeded domestic liabilities. (*Note:* there is no requirement that they should in general. This is purely for information).

Solvency margin certificate—this should confirm the aggregate general premium income shown in the revenue account, state the required solvency margin for the following financial year and the amount by which, in the opinion of the signatories, the company's assets exceeded its liabilities (excluding liabilities in respect of share capital).

Three-year business certificate—if the company submits a three-year business revenue account this should state whether the fund carried forward for each of the three years of account is, in the opinion of the signatories, sufficient.

The part of the returns described above and the certificates are subject to audit and an auditor's report must be included stating whether or not, in his opinion, they have been properly prepared and whether it was reasonable for the persons giving the certificates to have arrived at the opinions stated therein.

2.34 In addition the returns also contain a reinsurance summary and claim frequency and claim settlement analyses. The reinsurance summary should summarise the reinsurance accepted and ceded by the company indicating the nature and extent of the cover and the size of the business covered for each treaty (or each type of treaty if otherwise the statement would be too long).

2.35 The claim frequency analysis gives the company's

exposure during the year of account and carried forward; exposure being measured by gross premiums and, for motor vehicle business, by vehicle years. It also shows the number of claims arising, distinguishing the incurred but not reported (see Chapter 10) and re-opened claims.

2.36 The claims settlement analysis shows the run off of the settlement and payment of claims occurring within each financial year of account from 1970. Figures are given by numbers (distinguishing between nil and other claims) and payments, settlements and estimated outstandings (amounts are net of salvage but gross of reinsurance recoveries).

2.37 The claims frequency analysis and claims settlement analysis are to be supplied for each risk group within each class of insurance business carried on within each country, except that they need not be supplied for countries in which less than $2\frac{1}{2}\%$ of the gross premium income was written and that classes within a country need not be included if the gross premium income is less than £25,000. Risk group is defined as risks which, in the opinion of the directors, are not significantly dissimilar by reference to either the nature of the objects exposed to such risks or the nature of cover given.

Modification of the provisions of the Act

2.38 Section 57 of the Act gives the Department power, with the consent of the company, to modify certain of the provisions of the Act (or of regulations under the Act) in relation to the company. In particular this power may be exercised in relation to the submission of the annual returns and the solvency margin and any regulations—such as the valuation of assets regulations—which are made in connection therewith. It must be presumed that the Department would wish to use the powers conferred by this section selectively, but it seems unlikely that the Department would, for example, wish to proceed to the winding up of a company solely because it appeared insolvent as a result of the valuation regulations producing an unrealistically low valuation of a particular asset.

Lloyd's

2.39 The legislation governing Lloyd's underwriters differs from that governing companies. Detailed control is undertaken by the Committee of Lloyd's and Lloyd's auditors. The Act provides that each underwriter must carry all premiums to a trust fund, in accordance with the provisions of a trust deed approved by the Department. This lays down, *inter alia*, the 3-year accounting system.

2.40 The accounts of every underwriter must be audited annually and the auditor must supply a certificate in the prescribed form to the Committee and to the Department stating whether the value of the assets is correctly shown in the underwriters accounts and whether that value is sufficient to meet the liabilities calculated on a basis approved beforehand by the Department. The Committee must deposit with the Department a summary in the prescribed form of the business done by Lloyd's members in that year.

2.41 The prescribed forms are those laid down in paragraphs 16 and 19 of the Assurance Companies Rules 1950. It is understood that new regulations will be made so that information similar to that given by companies will be supplied.

Compulsory insurance

2.42 Insurance against certain forms of liability to third parties is compulsory by law. For the purposes of this book the names of the principal Acts involved is sufficient guide. These are as follows.
    Riding Establishments Act 1964; section 1 (4A) (d)
    Employers' Liability (Compulsory Insurance) Act 1969
    Road Traffic Act 1972
    Nuclear Installations Act 1965

Price control–insurance premiums

2.43 Section 9 of the Counter Inflation Act 1973 (the operation of which has been extended up to 31 July 1977 by the Remuneration, Charges and Grants Act, 1975) placed responsibility for applying price control to insurance premiums on the Secretary of State. Control is exercised by analogy to the general Price Code so far as it is relevant to insurance business. On practical grounds restriction of premium increases is applied only to general insurance business for which insurers have scheduled rates. The market leaders in motor insurance seek prior approval for premium increases; other motor insurers and all insurers in other classes of business give prior notice of premium increases on the understanding that justification for those increases may be called for at any time. As noted above the purpose of this control is solely in connection with the Government's anti-inflationary policies and otherwise there is no control of premium rates, as there is in some other countries as part of the insurance supervisory process. It will be recognised that the need to charge adequate premiums to maintain solvency could in certain circumstances be in conflict with the Government's anti-inflationary policy.

Policyholders' Protection Act 1975

2.44 'An Act to make provision for indemnifying (in whole or in part) or otherwise assisting or protecting policyholders and others who have been or may be prejudiced in consequence of the inability of authorised insurance companies carrying on business in the United Kingdom to meet their liabilities under policies issued or securities given by them, and for imposing levies on the insurance industry for the purpose'.

2.45 The Act sets up the Policyholders Protection Board, outlines its functions and powers, and provides that the Secretary of State may, after consulting with it, give guidance to the Board providing that the guidance is approved by Parliament.

2.46 It does not apply to companies in liquidation or provisional liquidation on 29 October 1974, nor does it apply to unauthorised insurers.

2.47 The following description of the Board's functions covers only general business. It is the duty of the Board to ensure that when a general insurance company is wound up all liabilities subject to compulsory insurance under the Acts mentioned in paragraph 2.43 should be paid in full and that other general business liabilities arising under U.K. policies towards private policyholders (other than reinsurance and marine, aviation and transit) should be paid to the extent of at least 90% of the amount due providing that policies under which they arise are U.K. business.

2.48 The Board may make payments to or on behalf of policyholders or by giving an indemnity to a liquidator or provisional liquidator secure that payments are made to or on behalf of policyholders.

2.49 A company is in 'financial difficulties' if it is in provisional liquidation, if it has been proved to be unable to pay its debts (e.g. does not meet its required solvency margin) or there has been an application to the court to sanction an arrangement whereby the liabilities provided under any of the company's policies are reduced. The Board may financially assist such a company or take any appropriate action to assist the transfer of its insurance business to another authorised insurer. It may only exercise these powers if members of the company or persons responsible for or profiting from the circumstances leading to the financial difficulties would not benefit to any material extent and if it would not cost the Board less to permit the company to go into liquidation and then to assist policyholders.

2.50 The Board may make a levy on authorised insurers calculated by reference to the premium income (net of reinsurance) for the previous 'financial year' in respect of U.K. general policies (other than marine, aviation and transit). The levy may not exceed 1% and may only be imposed if the expenditure has been or will be incurred within 12 months. Each authorised insurer shall send the Secretary of State before 1 March a statement of the income subject to the general business levy for the previous 'financial year'. In this context a 'financial year' runs from April to March. The first levy may not be made before 1 April 1976.

2.51 If the Board should have surplus funds then the Secretary of State may by order require them to be distributed among U.K. authorised insurers.

European Economic Community legislation

2.52 Legislation in the European Economic Community is made by way of Directives. So far the major piece of legislation affecting general insurance companies is known as the Establishment Directive and was enacted in 1973. It provides for the conditions under which an insurer carrying on general business and established in one of the countries of the Community may establish a branch or agency in another country without discrimination—freedom of establishment.

2.53 Generally the Establishment Directive lays down that the supervision of the insurer should be the responsibility of the supervisory authorities in the country in which the head office of the insurer is situated. There are, however, certain requirements, the principal ones of which are set out below.

2.54 Countries must provide for the authorisation of insurers and in applying for authorisation an insurer must submit a 'scheme of operation' covering prescribed matters as well as providing certain prescribed information.

2.55 Each country requires an insurer to establish sufficient technical reserves for its business in that country—according to rules therein operating, or if none according to established practice—and these are to be covered by matching assets localised in that country. The latter requirement may be relaxed by each country. The method of valuation of assets is that appropriate to the country where the business is transacted.

2.56 The Directive requires a minimum solvency margin. This is to be determined as the greater one of two alternative bases, the first related to premiums and the second to claims. The premium basis is 18% of the first 10 million units of account (see below) and 16% of the excess thereover of the general insurance premiums (including reinsurances accepted but before deduction of any reinsurances ceded) for the last financial year; this amount is then to be reduced by the ratio of (i) the amount of claims payable in the last financial year reduced by the amount payable under reinsurances in respect of those claims to (ii) the gross amount of those claims, provided that this ratio may not be less than 50%. The claims basis is for most types of insurance related to the amount of the gross claims paid (including in respect of reinsurances accepted) over the last 3 years increased by the gross outstanding claims reserve at the end of the period and reduced by the amount of that reserve at the beginning of the period. The result of this calculation is divided by 3 and 26% of the first 7 million units of account and 23% of the excess thereover is then calculated. This latter result is then reduced by the same ratio as applies to the premium basis. For insurance companies writing risks relating mainly to storm, hail and frost the claims basis is calculated by reference to the last 7 years rather than the last 3. Generally speaking the premium basis of calculation would apply and it should be noted that whereas at present the solvency margin in the United Kingdom for most companies is approximately 10% of annual premium income (para. 2.6 above) this will increase to rather more than 16% when the Directive becomes operative, the latest date for which is July 1978. (The unit of account is based on a weighted average of European Economic Community currencies. For 1977, the unit of account is approximately 70p.)

2.57 One-third of the solvency margin is termed the guarantee fund (subject to certain minima only applicable to very small insurers). If the value of an insurer's assets in excess of those required to cover the technical reserves falls below the solvency margin the supervisory authority in the country of the insurer's head office will require to approve a plan for the restoration of the solvency margins. If the value falls below the guarantee fund level more stringent action will be taken to protect policyholders.

2.58 As with United Kingdom legislation the Directive is somewhat complex and reference should be made to the text.

2.59 The other Directive which has been passed specifically in relation to insurance is that of 1964 which abolished restrictions on the freedom of establishment and the freedom of services in respect of reinsurance. Freedom of establishment is described in paragraph 2.52 above and freedom of services is described in paragraph 2.60 below.

2.60 Other directives are in course of consideration. In particular the directive to provide for freedom of establishment in respect of long term business may have an impact on the legal form in which composite insurers transact their business. Insurers are not permitted to operate in composite form in France and Germany and only to a limited extent in Holland, although they are permitted in the United Kingdom, Ireland, Belgium and Italy. There are additionally draft directives dealing with insurance contract law, products liability insurance, car insurance, bankruptcy and winding-up of direct insurers, intermediaries and 'freedom of services' for general insurers. The last named will set out the conditions for an insurer established in one country to provide services freely in any other country without the need to set up a branch or agency there.

2.61 There are of course other aspects of Community legislation which will affect insurers, e.g. the various directives on company law. It is important to remember that these and the specifically insurance directives will affect a company even though it only transacts business in the United Kingdom.

APPENDIX 2.1

Legislation relating to supervision

1 The Insurance Companies Act 1974 ('the Act').
2 S.I. 1950 No. 553. The Assurance Companies Rules, 1950; paragraphs 16 and 19.
3 S.I. 1968 No. 1408. The Insurance Companies (Accounts and Forms) Regulations 1968.
4 Regulations made under the Act

1973
S.I. 2064. Insurance Companies (Identification of Long Term Assets and Liabilities) Regulations 1973.

1974
S.I. 493. Industrial Assurance (Collecting Societies' Deposits) (Amendment) Regulations 1974.*
S.I. 901 Insurance Companies (Contents of Advertisements) Regulations 1974.*
S.I. 902. (Revoked) Insurance Companies (Intermediaries) Regulations 1974.*
S.I. 1051. (Revoked) Insurance Companies (Intermediaries) (Amendment) Regulations 1974.*
S.I. 1052. Insurance Companies (Contents of Advertisements) (Amendment) Regulations 1974.*
S.I. 2203 (Revoked) Insurance Companies (Valuation of Assets) Regulations 1974.

1975
S.I. 929 Insurance Companies (Linked Properties and Indices) Regulations 1975.*
S.I. 959 Insurance Companies (Changes of Director, Controller or Manager) Regulations 1975.
S.I. 1996 Insurance Companies (Accounts and Forms) (Amendment) Regulations 1975.

1976
S.I. 87 Insurance Companies (Valuation of Assets) Regulations 1976.
S.I. 521 Insurance Companies (Intermediaries) Regulations 1976.
S.I. 549 Insurance Companies (Accounts and Forms) (Amendment) Regulations 1976.
S.I. 869 Insurance Companies (Accounts and Forms) (Amendment) (No. 2) Regulations 1976.
S.I. 2039 Insurance Companies (Valuation of Assets) (Amendments) Regulations 1976.
S.I. 2040 Insurance Companies (Accounts and Forms) (Amendment) (No. 3) Regulations 1976.

* These Regulations relate only to long term business but are included for completeness.

CHAPTER 3

THE INVESTMENT AND TAXATION OF GENERAL INSURANCE FUNDS

3.1 Insurance as a business operation is by definition a random process because the income, to a lesser extent, and the outgo, to a major extent, are composed of elements that are subject to random fluctuation. This is true even of life assurance where most elements are fairly stable but especially true of general insurance. We shall see in detail in later chapters the extent to which a general insurance office must maintain reserves which are adequate to absorb the substantial fluctuations that are likely to occur from time to time in both claim frequency and claim amount. In Chapter II in particular we shall be considering the factors involved in determining the degree of solvency of a general insurance office, i.e. the excess of assets over liabilities to allow for such adverse fluctuations. Standards are required by the supervisory authority but most insurers regard it as prudent to exceed those standards. To meet these solvency standards the insurance office must be supported by capital which is substantial in relation to its premium income.

3.2 Clearly, while this capital is held it should be used to provide an investment return. Also, as we shall see, the operation of general insurance business gives rise to funds which are held for varying periods and the office would not be acting either in its own best interests or in the best interests of policyholders if it did not seek investment return from the money it holds in this way. In particular, because of the unavoidable long delay in settling some claims, especially in the liability classes, a large proportion of the reserves in respect of outstanding claims for a particular year of origin may have to be maintained for a period of time, often several years. Though this is short term in investment potential it is not of negligible duration.

3.3 Traditionally, investment return, i.e. capital gain as well as income, has not been introduced directly into ratemaking (see Chapter 7). This exclusion of investment return does not mean that it is ignored but that it is regarded as helping to finance growth, to enhance reserves and to pay dividends. Clearly it is a source of income and takes its place with other income in helping to service capital. Investment return is indirectly allowed for in ratemaking as an implicit set-off (though not necessarily of any specific amount) against profit margins which are correspondingly reduced in the ratemaking process. There has been growing attention to investment return in recent years as the rate of inflation and interest rates have both risen.

3.4 This is not an investment textbook and we propose in this short chapter to consider only the special investment considerations that arise from the nature of general insurance business.

Investment policy

3.5 Premiums received by a general insurance company, after deduction of expenses, are held to meet claims or until the risk period expires, that is to constitute the technical reserves (see Chapter 10). These reserves, together with the capital and free reserves of the company make up the funds available for investment. In managing its business the company must have an investment policy which might reasonably be stated as the maximisation of the expected return net of taxation subject to any constraints imposed by the nature of the business of the company, which is short term, volatile and subject to Government regulations.

3.6 Despite the generally short term nature of the business there will, in a continuing business, be no need to realise investments to meet claims which may be paid out of incoming premiums. Part of the technical reserves and of the capital and free reserves is therefore available for medium/long term investment, but the extent to which this will be both prudent and possible will depend on the nature of the business being written, the extent of the capital and free reserves in relation to the technical reserves or to the premium income and the impact of the regulations for the valuation of assets (see para. 2.14).

3.7 Our definition of investment aims in paragraph 3.5 spoke of the return of investment 'net of taxation'. Clearly the effectiveness of investment policy will depend on the way in which the office manages its taxation liability and some reference is made to this problem later in this chapter.

3.8 Having regard to the effect of taxation (para. 3.18 *et seq.* below), other things being equal, the best return is likely to be achieved by buying securities which provide franked investment income (i.e. company income which carries a credit for United Kingdom Corporation Tax)—equities and redeemable or irredeemable preference shares. These securities do, however, have the disadvantage of fluctuating market value and may not be readily marketable, and in the case of holdings in a particular company are subject to limited admissibility in valuation (see para. 2.14).

3.9 Inflation, especially high rates of inflation such as those that have afflicted the United Kingdom economy in recent years, is the great problem of all financial planning. Current premiums will reflect some anticipated inflation. Presently incurred claims which may not be settled for 2 or 3 years will be related to values of property or personal liability or employer's liability at the time of settlement, which will have grown by 2 or 3 years' inflation above the values which would apply if settlement could be made immediately. Those premiums cannot, especially on a short term basis, be invested at rates of return that fully compensate for inflation even though at times of high inflation interest rates may tend to be relatively high and thus help to offset the effects of inflation. It is fair to say that there is at present no investment available to insurers that offers certain and adequate protection against inflation. Recent experience has certainly shown that in the short term at least equities are not satisfactory, nor indeed are land and buildings.

3.10 The first of the constraints on investment policy referred to in paragraph 3.5 arises from the volatility of the business because of the possibility of wide fluctuations in claims experience. This not only makes it necessary for a company to maintain substantial reserves in excess of its technical reserves (see Chapter 11) but it also means that the funds may be sharply run down in a comparatively short interval of time. It will be necessary therefore to maintain a substantial measure of liquidity, i.e. money on deposit or very readily realisable assets (realisable without appreciable loss), e.g. very short-dated government stocks. Rather than carrying large amounts of cash which might not in the event be required for a very long time it would be preferable, because more remunerative, to invest in reasonably marketable assets. However, cash and short term government stocks militate against high investment return. As stated above, the maximum return to an investor subject to Corporation Tax is normally achieved by seeking franked investment income or capital gains on which tax is not payable until realisation but these sources of high return are often more sensitive to stock market conditions and their capital value more variable and they do not generally meet the requirement of being reliably marketable at all times. Most, if not all, companies accept this difficulty and endeavour to meet it by aiming at a sufficient spread of stocks and types of assets to be able to absorb the occasional loss while still, overall, obtaining a better ultimate average return.

3.11 An examination of the amount of assets which it would be prudent to hold in very readily realisable form may be carried out by considering the amount by which claims might exceed the expected if an unusually heavy claims experience occurred. It would be appropriate to hold the amount of this excess in such short term assets. Additionally, an allowance should be made for any possible reduction in premium income, since if business falls away new premiums would provide insufficient cash flow. These calculations will have regard to the nature of the company's business—some types of general insurance are more volatile than others—and require a forward projection of the business of the company on both 'most likely' and 'pessimistic' assumptions.

3.12 A company is required to maintain a minimum solvency margin and for the purpose of assessing this margin assets must be valued according to the relevant regulations (see para. 2.14). This effectively places a limit on the holding of assets whose value is subject to considerable fluctuations, in particular on equities, long dated and irredeemable government securities, preference shares and property. Gearing is important here, illustrated by a simple example. If a company has technical reserves of 100 and capital and free reserves of 25, which are represented by assets constituted as to 50 in short term deposits and 75 in securities liable to fluctuate in value, then a fall of 20% in the variable securities leads to a reduction in the 'margin' from 25% to 10%, at which point the company might be nearing insolvency in terms of the Act (see para. 2.7). The greater the excess of the capital and free reserves over the required solvency margin the greater of course the freedom to invest other than in short term securities.

3.13 A general insurance company must pay detailed regard to the asset valuation regulations and the impact of limited admissibility applicable to certain types of asset. These regulations have been outlined in Chapter 2 and it is not appropriate to go into greater detail in this textbook.

3.14 There are also the regulations of foreign governments which often require that United Kingdom offices operating within their territories must match local liabilities with local assets and indeed must often provide a minimum solvency margin there. Local investment, if made in advance of local cash flow from premium income, may create problems of acquisition of foreign currency to pay for the investment. Clearly in regard to liabilities expressed in foreign currencies it is prudent to match with assets expressed to be payable in those currencies, although the extent to which this is possible will depend on Exchange Control Regulations.

3.15 The expected growth of the business will also have to be considered. A slowing down of the rate of growth may lead to cash flow problems. A high rate of growth may lead to problems in financing the technical reserves which have to be created and the corresponding increase in the solvency margin.

3.16 It has to be borne in mind that the office is not alone. Other companies have similar investment problems. It is therefore good policy to examine from published accounts the investment policy being followed by others; if a company is markedly out of line it should check its reasoning.

3.17 Investment portfolios held by different companies differ and it is not possible to set out a specimen portfolio but as an illustration the distribution of world-wide assets by market value of a group of leading United Kingdom companies, as at 31 December 1975, was estimated as follows:

	%
Equities	29
Property	14
Fixed Interest	37
Mortgage & loans	7
Deposits and cash	13
	100

Taxation

3.18 In the United Kingdom the taxation basis of general insurance is the same as that which applies generally to companies carrying on a trade, i.e. profit. A special feature is that any realised investment gains of a general insurance company are, in most cases, treated as if they were trading profits which are assessed to Corporation Tax under Schedule D, Case I. Another special feature is the method of assessing profits from marine business. Though the statutory basis for marine business is a one year account, a 3-year basis is normally allowed as a concession. It has a complex set of rules of its own which are beyond the scope of this book. The major points of actuarial relevance are the treatment of technical reserves for tax purposes, the effects of double taxation relief and the tax treatment of reinsurances ceded.

3.19 The composition of technical reserves (see Chapter 10) is at present governed by the Insurance Companies (Accounts and Forms) Regulations 1968 (S.I. 1968 No. 1408). Except in the case of certain marine business, a company must set up the following reserves. First, there is an unearned premium reserve to cover risks to be borne after the end of the accounting year under contracts of insurance entered into before the end of that year. Secondly, there is an unexpired risk reserve to cover risks in respect of which the unearned premium reserve is held to be inadequate on its own, e.g. where premium ratings were considered to be too low. Thirdly, there is the outstanding claim reserve to meet unpaid claims under contracts of insurance in respect of incidents occurring before the end of the accounting year, including claims incurred but not reported.

3.20 The Inland Revenue, in assessing the taxable profits of general insurance business will allow a provision to be made for notified but outstanding claims, together with the establishment of an unearned premium reserve. Moreover, in cases where the Inland Revenue is satisfied as to the need and as to the method of calculation, a provision for claims incurred but not reported may also be established from pre-tax profits. The Inland Revenue will *not* usually allow the unexpired risk reserve to be made from pre-tax profits.

3.21 Normally the maximum amount of unearned premium reserve which the Inland Revenue will allow to be established from pre-tax profits is 40% of premium income. The figure of 40% is equal to the unearned premium reserve which would arise from uniformly spread one-year business where 20% of the premium has been expended on initial expenses and commission leaving half of the remaining 80% for outstanding periods of contracts. Before the 1968 regulations it was customary to use 40% for the unearned premium reserve for the purpose of official returns. Since 1968 the regulations generally require a company to compute unearned premiums by the 24ths method (see Chapter 10). Consequently if the company's business is expanding or the bulk of the premiums are written late in the accounting period, the unearned premium reserve could be higher than 40% and the excess over 40% would usually have to be met from post-tax profits. Conversely where business is contracting the unearned premium reserve calculated on the 24ths method could amount to less than 40% of written premiums.

3.22 For double taxation relief purposes, the overseas profit is computed on a United Kingdom Corporation Tax basis (i.e. after allowance for a maximum unearned premium reserve of 40% of premium income). This may well not correspond to the bases used in other countries. Consequently, if an unearned premium reserve of more than 40% of premium income has been allowed in the overseas territory the assessable profit taxed overseas could be smaller than that in the United Kingdom. It is then possible for some United Kingdom tax to be due on the overseas profit even where the overseas rate is higher. This situation could be avoided by converting an existing branch in an overseas territory into an overseas subsidiary, although this has a potential disadvantage in that losses of a subsidiary could not be relieved against United Kingdom tax, whereas they would be for a branch. As is the case with normal companies operating overseas, the double taxation relief is subject to an overall limitation which restricts it to the company's United Kingdom Corporation Tax liability for a given year with no carry forward of unused credit.

3.23 In the taxation treatment of ceded reinsurance, the United Kingdom follows a generally accepted international principle that a reinsurer's profits are taxed in the country where the risk is taken. Australia and New Zealand and some developing countries have rejected this principle. They tax profits earned from risks arising in those countries although the risks are taken elsewhere.

3.24 Because the general case for the establishment of an unexpired risk reserve made from pre-tax profits and for the full unearned premium reserve required by the Department of Trade has never been established with the Inland Revenue there is a serious inconsistency of approach between the Department of Trade and the Inland Revenue. If new regulations are made under the Insurance Act 1974 regarding the level of technical reserves, there may be an occasion for the Inland Revenue to re-examine its approach. At some time in the future harmonisation within the European Economic Community of taxation bases may well bring about modification of the fiscal treatment of general insurers.

CHAPTER 4

DOCUMENTATION AND DATA COLLECTION

4.1 The application of actuarial principles to general insurance will depend on the analysis and interpretation of information. The mathematical theory starts from a point at which the appropriate data has been assembled. The extraction and preparation of the information, however, must first be accomplished. This is a vital stage and must be given special and prior consideration. This chapter is therefore aimed at covering the steps to be taken and the problems likely to be encountered in the creation of the requisite statistical system.

4.2 Definition and collection of data is not easy to generalise about, since much will depend upon the way in which a company operates and even the data themselves will merit different considerations for different classes of business. Bearing in mind the volume of data required and the enormous task of any manual collation of figures, the availability of computer services is essential for any statistical system to be of practical value. It is assumed therefore in what follows, that such services are available and that statistical data will be submitted to the system by a network of branches which will report new business as it is written or cancelled and details of claims and claim payments.

4.3 The primary consideration in developing a statistical system must be the purpose to which the system will ultimately be put, especially the management decisions which it is required to facilitate, and the different interests which it may be required to serve. The system will naturally be developed in close liaison with the underwriters for the respective classes of business, but the needs of other departments, such as accountants, sales and claims departments, need also to be met. In the development of the system the computer department must be closely involved, particularly in any plans for either the input or the output of statistics from the computer part of the system.

4.4 It will become apparent that a considerable volume of information will be needed in respect of policies for purposes quite apart from statistics, and bearing in mind the size of the data files which will be produced, some limitations may need to be imposed on the volume of additional space containing purely statistical information. It may be advantageous for a statistical file to be created in addition to the main data file so that the statistical system can be developed and maintained unencumbered by other information needed only for administrative purposes.

4.5 An important principle to the success of the system, and one only made possible by the use of a computer, is that statistical records should be generated automatically from day-to-day transactions. Branches advising a new policy or a change in terms will not then need to submit a special additional advice for purely statistical purposes, and the normal renewal of a policy can lead to a statistical record being created without the branch being involved at all.

Computer files

4.6 The principal use of the main file will be the regular production of renewal notices to be sent to the insured and the main data file must therefore carry the most up-to-date position on every policy. The file will effectively show a balance sheet situation of the business currently held and the information needed to generate future renewals; additionally, it may also be the basis for the accounting system of the company, either containing or being closely linked to the production of agency accounts and the monitoring of outstanding balances.

4.7 Whilst it may contain some historical information (either on past premiums or on claims), the main file is basically therefore a policy file; the statistical file on the other hand will essentially be a historical record of past premium and claim transactions and be related to a revenue experience.

4.8 In theory it should be possible to determine from the premium information on the statistical file whether or not a policy is still in force, but in practice errors, transfers, etc.

will cloud the position and instant correspondence between the two files may be difficult to achieve. A mid-term increase in policy cover for example could lead to an increase of £20 in the renewal premium held on the main file, but an entry of only £10 on the statistical file to correspond to the *pro rata* additional premium actually received.

4.9 Some policy movements will not involve any financial transaction and consideration must also be given to the need to identify lapses and cancellations for subsequent loss of business analyses. Similarly, a change in a policyholder's address may not involve any premium movement, but if area is to be a coded factor the change nevertheless constitutes an alteration in the total exposure within the particular areas, old and new.

General information

4.10 Once the general form of the system has been established, considerations turn towards the details that will be recorded on the statistical file. As a safeguard against error, as well as for analyses requiring reference to policy records such as subdivision by size of premium or claim, every transaction will need to carry full identification and there will be many general items on each statistical record—e.g. branch, agency number, policy number, claim number. It is likely that occasionally the name of the policyholder or agent would be useful to produce an easily understandable working list of policies with some characteristic, but this is not really the purpose of a statistical file, and these items are of no statistical value and records will be more concise if they are excluded. Statistical information about the agent or policyholder may have relevance on the marketing side however, and there may be other items of a general nature which may merit inclusion according to the interests that the statistical system will have to serve. In addition to the record identification there are other general details, common also to the accounting side, relating to dates and amounts of money which may need to be included.

Premiums

4.11 On the premium side, the amount of each premium transaction will naturally be recorded as should the type of transaction—new business, renewal, etc.

4.12 The date on which the premium was written into the accounts will enable a balance to be made between the statistics and the accounts if necessary, and will also provide a basis for defining data to be extracted for examining returns for a specific period, e.g. a particular month.

4.13 The period of insurance covered by the transaction must also be recorded since it is usually most useful to measure claim experience on a policy year basis. In addition, this information is needed for the correct calculation of earned premium and hence for the estimation of unearned premium reserves, preparation of Department of Trade returns, etc.

4.14 Some premiums, and in particular the additional premiums payable under adjustable policies, relate to past periods of insurance. Recording the commencement date of the period of insurance is by far the easiest method of correctly backdating these premiums to their proper policy years. A temptation to be avoided however is to submit as a single entry a premium relating to two different periods of insurance, or an additional premium (perhaps in motor insurance where there has been an exchange of a small car for a more powerful model) which has been reduced by a credit.

4.15 With only the fewest exceptions there will be little doubt about the date on which cover commenced, although difficulties can arise when the cover extends to more than one period, e.g. the cancellation cover under a holiday policy. Block policies, however, will always be an exception as any attempt to correctly allocate exposure would mean expense outweighing the saving in administration expenses which is the main reason for offering this type of policy.

4.16 Few difficulties will arise over the expiry date of the insurance, although here again there are exceptions. Many indemnity bonds have no termination date, and whilst building society indemnities are limited to the term of the mortgage very few claims are ever received more than 10 years from commencement. Equally, claims can occur after cover has effectively ceased—e.g. fidelity policies and the maintenance clause under contractors' all risks policies.

Claims

4.17 On the claims side, where regular reviews of outstanding liability will be essential statistical returns, estimates must be differentiated from payments. Companies have different practices for the recording of claims where no payment by the insurer is expected and some also use a formula system to estimate the smaller claims.

4.18 Continuity of claims records cannot be over-emphasised. Any changes in the identification of a claim (renumbering, re-opening, transferring, or even recoding) can lead to discontinuity and create exceedingly misleading figures on run-offs or 'incurred but not reported' (I.B.N.R.) returns if they occur uncontrolled to any material extent. If there is no link between the old and new claim numbers, for example, the renumbering of a claim will suggest that there have been two separate claims with a consequent distortion of claim frequency distribution. An outstanding estimate of £1,000 at the date of transfer might appear to be a nil settlement or just remain for ever more as an outstanding item, and even if deemed to be settled for its estimated amount by a nominal payment of £1,000 the difficulty is not avoided, because an ultimate settlement of only £300 will require a negative payment of £700 under the new claim number.

4.19 Defining the date of a claim is also far from straightforward. A '1971' claim might on examination prove to be one advised in 1971, occurring in 1971, relating to a period of insurance commencing in 1971 or just carrying a 1971 claim number. Both the date of advice and the date of occurrence of the claim will need to be recorded but allowance must be made for cases which will arise where the date of occurrence of the claim is unknown. Clear instructions will need to be given to branches regarding the treatment of cases which are likely to give rise to recording difficulties, and help might be given by computer validity tests to ensure, for example, that the date of occurrence of a claim cannot be earlier than the date of commencement of insurance or later than the date of notification. Special allowance will also need to be made for bulk estimates submitted or any other claims practices used.

Descriptive coding

4.20 It can be seen that there are many factors to be taken into consideration before the finer coding details for entry can be determined. The foregoing paragraphs have dealt only with the general form of the system and the information needed to obtain the financial outcome of different periods of insurance.

4.21 The final step towards the development of the statistical system is the description of the type of business to which each transaction relates. In the first place such description will be a general business classification (fire, motor, liability, etc.), influenced probably by a company's departmental structure, but further coding details refining the description will be important.

4.22 Whilst the actuary is an expert in the field of statistics, it is the underwriter who is the expert in the business being written, and in developing the statistical system his assistance is essential from the outset. Detailed discussion with him about the factors that are relevant to his underwriting will help to obtain a list of particulars that may subsequently be considered as the basis for statistical coding. It is important at this stage not to lose sight of the aim of producing a systematic definition of the main factors, and to seek to establish a simple list of items that can subsequently be broken down into appropriate codes. Policies are written on an individual basis and inevitably there will be many problems peculiar to certain types of policy; no easily workable statistical system can embrace the many exceptions that will arise and at this stage progress can more easily be made by considering what can be coded rather than what cannot.

4.23 These discussions with underwriters serve two necessary purposes. In the first place they give the actuary the opportunity to appreciate the more detailed aspects of the business under consideration, giving him an insight into the way that a risk is underwritten and the day-to-day problems that confront the underwriter. Secondly, and the importance of this cannot be over-emphasised, they draw the underwriter into the development of his own statistical system (for it is to serve him as well as others) and help to achieve a relationship in which the statistician can apply his skills for the real and direct benefit of the underwriter.

4.24 Agreeing the factors to be coded is a task involving months rather than weeks, and starting from a list of the different underwriting factors that are taken into account for a risk, searching discussion and planning must be undertaken at this early stage. It must be borne in mind that branches will have to operate on a day-to-day basis the system which is being designed, and that the longer the system remains in force without subsequent change, the more successful it will be regarded. Subsequent deletions of parts of the coding will not be popular amongst those who have spent hours recording information which turns out to be unnecessary, and it is important to avoid a common tendency to put into a system all conceivably relevant information even though not needed now on the basis that some day somebody may require it. Additions to the coding, which are much more easily made, are bound to be needed in time and a reserve of unused coding capacity will give the system a valuable flexibility for the future.

4.25 We may sum up the interest of the underwriter and his relationship to the actuary as follows. It is clear that whilst there are areas where the judgement of an experienced underwriter is the only tool available (insurance of risks where claims are few or very variable or where the statistician may not have had time to accumulate data) there are other areas where enough information is available, subject to proper analysis, to enable the statistician to give valuable advice to the underwriter. Equally the statistician must not pretend to do more than his investigations allow and must ever remain aware of such things as moral hazard, selection and the realities of a competitive commercial environment if his advice is to have any value. The underwriter must seek risks where he can obtain a premium large enough to pay the claims and other outgo. Information to help him reach such a decision will come partly from statistical analysis and partly from accounting data. The information required by the underwriters and statisticians will extend to a large proportion of the information available from the file. Jointly both the underwriter and the statistician will be particularly concerned with assessing risk premium according to the various levels of rating factors and with the relative possibilities of obtaining different types of business and will also be concerned with estimating processes which lead to calculations of risk premium.

4.26 There are other special interests as well as those of the underwriter. We may detail them briefly as follows.

(i) *Administrators and accountants* They will require information for company accounts, Department of Trade returns and for the calculation of reserves.

(ii) *Sales staff* They will be concerned with effects of advertising campaigns, the cause of lapses, sources of new business and information in regard to agents.

(iii) *Claims sections* They will or may be concerned with the progress of claims, the possibilities of measuring administrative procedures in the economical settling of claims, the expenses of paying and agreeing claims; also the making (and possibly the adequacy) of estimates, although this point will be dealt with later.

Exposure

4.27 Without detailing different types of business it is very difficult to generalise on the form in which the coding may emerge. Two principles, however, will be common to virtually all classes of business—firstly the exposure, and secondly the single main factor upon which sub-division may be planned. The use of vehicle years as a measurement of exposure for motor business is well known, but other classes such as householders business have received less attention (see Chapter 5).

4.28 A loss ratio will produce a comparison of claims against premiums, but other statistics in terms of turnover, sums insured, etc., are needed. One general practice should be stressed, namely that statistical analysis based on exposure will be less at risk of input errors if exposure is always recorded in the same position in the record for each policy, be it sum insured, car years, etc. Problems of scale may well arise in that exposure will vary from units to millions, but consistency of approach will avoid unnecessary programming on the computer side.

Main factor

4.29 Within any particular class of business there is usually one main factor having the greatest effect upon the premium charged. Common amongst these main factors are area and nature of business, and ultimate computer analysis will again be less likely to suffer from input errors if this main factor can always be recorded in the same coding position; use of a coding position to mean occupation for one class of business and area for another will cause no statistical problem.

General details

4.30 However well designed the classification system may be, exceptions will always arise. Book rates may be applied to only a small part of an account and the reasons for special treatment may vary considerably. An analysis of the experience of public liability risks for instance may include cases with special discounts, loadings for bad experience, reductions for competitive reasons, etc., and it is important that these non-standard cases should be identifiable in any analysis aimed at producing a standard book rate as a basic underwriting guide. This is not to create the impression that the ultimate claim rate given by the statistics will be blindly applied as a book rate, but to emphasise that there is little value in determining a statistical rate based on a collection of risks which are very heterogeneous.

4.31 Risks which are written on 'standard terms' will, in due course, be uprated as rates are amended, and it is likely that similar risks will be written on different rate series during a year. If all policies are renewed annually, it therefore takes a full year following the introduction of new rates for every policy to be re-rated. The point is made that the particular rate version used for a risk merits consideration as a coding factor to enable the experience of a particular set of rates to be demonstrated.

4.32 However comprehensive and well designed the statistical classification its success will nevertheless depend heavily upon the accuracy with which the system is applied by branches. Errors will always be present, perhaps through a genuine mistake, a slip of the pen, or undue haste. It has to be borne in mind that the value of a coding system and the continual need for accuracy is not easily apparent to branch personnel who may never see the results of their recording efforts. It is worth considering whether it is possible to arrange for some statistical feedback to field staff; if they *do* see some results of their efforts they are likely to feel more involved in the system and they will take more trouble.

4.33 Help is likely to come from the computer department in aiding the accuracy of records, ranging from basic validity tests of acceptable values for each code to a complete premium check from the statistical coding. There is tremendous value in the latter if it can be achieved and a decision may have to be made as to whether it is worth coding factors purely for the sake of a computer premium check. This decision may be aided by administrative considerations, such as policy and endorsement preparation by the computer, and possibly too by the extent to which manual records are retained in addition to computer records.

4.34 The interests of other departments have already been mentioned, and discussions with the claims department will be particularly valuable once the premium coding has been generally agreed. There are many considerations peculiar to the statistics of claims, for example, the establishment of reserves and the run-off of claims, but valuable criticism of the premium coding may often emerge from the claims handlers who might need to rely on the premium coding to interpret the cover under the policy (e.g. for excesses).

4.35 In addition there may be scope for claims coding on the statistical records and development of the claims coding should be treated as a continuation of premium coding. The risk of over-burdening the system must be kept in mind and since both the underwriter and the claim handler may have different need of statistical information relating to claims, care should be taken to make sure that the various codes proposed really are essential. The underwriter may be particularly interested in the cause of the claim or effect of any excess present in a claim amount, whilst the claims department may require information on adjusters' fees, etc. A danger exists, that one department may propose the coding of details which they suppose to be needed by others, but which in fact are not required for any purpose. It is a sound policy for the actuary to challenge the proposers of all additions to the coding to prove the usefulness of their proposals. The actuary should also go through the drill of challenging his own requirements.

4.36 Eventually, and probably over a period of many years, coding systems will be developed for each class of business. After the initial scheme for each class of business coding has been completed however, a pilot investigation at a branch is highly desirable. The coding must be explained in easily understood terms and comments from those who will operate the system may well bring to light elements of impracticability or ambiguity less apparent to those involved closely in the initial development. Quite apart from the comments which this pilot investigation may elicit, the opportunity to criticise and to share in a new system also plays a part in obtaining the goodwill and co-operation of the branches.

4.37 Finally, when the coding system has been fully agreed, the necessary computer programming has been completed, and the necessary instructions have been circulated to branches, some indication should be given to the underwriter as to when he may expect to derive information of value from the new system.

4.38 Periodic monitoring is advisable to ensure that the system is being correctly applied, particularly in the early stages. All new systems need time to become established and trouble free and the first usable information to emerge may well not come for a full year. By this time premium statistics will provide a detailed picture of the composition of the account, but further time must pass before the corresponding claims will be recorded. Claims with little delay to settlement such as on a household account will start to provide meaningful figures in the second year of the system's operation, but professional indemnity claims for instance will mainly be estimates to start with. A feeling of anticlimax can be avoided if the underwriter is made aware of the wait that must necessarily ensue before the full benefit can be derived from the statistical system.

4.39 Up to this point the installation of a statistical system has been dealt with in very general terms. In subsequent chapters the statistical requirements for different purposes will emerge in the context of their use but in the following paragraphs some detail will be filled in. It will be useful to do so in relation specifically to motor business since more statistical work has been done in this field than in any other. Though the illustrations are in terms of motor business it should be emphasised that the principles apply in all fields. For greater clarity one particular system is described but it will be understood that each company will have its own requirements.

The data base and statistics in motor business

4.40 One particular feature of motor business is the frequency with which amendments to policy records are required and the importance of, and difficulty in, ensuring that the intended corrections are applied to the right policy. Motor business is a short term contract which may or may not be renewed at the end of 12 months, and the contract may, and often is, changed during its currency (e.g. on change of car). Moreover the order in which transactions are presented to a statistical system may not coincide with the order in which they actually happen. Another special statistical feature of motor business is that the statistics embrace many interrelated variables. District, type of car, age of car and age of policyholder are amongst variables commonly recorded.

4.41 A major complication in motor business is that the policyholder is commonly offered a discount if he makes no or few claims. On the other hand he may find his premium loaded or renewal not invited if he makes too many claims. Whilst it is not imperative for such information to be recorded on a computer file, there are very considerable advantages in doing so.

The main file for motor business

4.42 We have already noted in our general discussion that a considerable volume of information will be needed in respect of policies for purposes quite apart from statistics and that with a view to keeping the ultimate size of the data files within bounds, some limitations may have to be imposed on the volume of space containing information required, or more likely retained, solely for statistical purposes. The division between what constitutes administrative information and what is statistical is rarely clear. Statistics are intended ultimately to assist administration; a question originally designed for a statistical investigation may subsequently become a routine of administration. The main file will need to contain information for both statistical and administrative purposes and details are likely to include the following.

    Policy number
    Branch or district office code
    Agency code
    Renewal date
    Description of cover (rating area, vehicle groups, age of policyholder and so on)
    Limitations on cover (excesses, restriction etc.)
    Claims history

4.43 The administrator may be satisfied with manual records of cover and claims, but as we have already noted in the general part of this chapter, such a system would impose an almost impassable barrier to statistical work and we must assume here that full details are recorded in the computer system. The statistician will require full details of the progress of each claim settlement, whereas the administrator might be satisfied with less. Both are likely to need to know the premium but it matters little to them whether the actual premium charged or the annual rate is actually recorded or whether the data are available to enable premiums to be calculated as and when required (a point that will arise later).

4.44 The administrator will also wish to know more about commission arrangements (and so may the statistician at times) and to have details of the name, address and telephone number of the policyholder as well as the place to which the renewal notices should be sent (policyholder, branch, broker, etc.). He may wish to have names rather than codes for branches and agents. If both a name and a code are recorded, special steps must be taken to ensure that they agree.

Processing of changes

4.45 Any item of information is liable to be changed at any time and often there will be several changes in the course of a policy or calendar year each giving rise to a new 'status' that will be in force for this period. Unfortunately, the dates when a status begins and ends may be weeks earlier than the dates of their acceptance by the computer. The file will therefore always fail to record the true insurance position. Many statuses or policies will be recorded which are no longer in force while new policies and changes that took place some time ago may not be recorded.

4.46 As time passes and the amount of information in respect of a policy accumulates, the computer file may eventually become too extensive to handle unless records are either deleted or pruned. Rather than lose statistical information in this way a separate statistical file might therefore be created in addition to the main file so that a record of all statuses that have been in force at any time within a named period can be developed and maintained unencumbered by other information needed only for administrative purposes.

4.47 An important principle in the success of the system, and one only made possible by the use of a computer is that statistical records should be generated and passed down to the statistical file automatically from day-to-day transactions. Branches advising a new policy or a change in terms will not thereby need to submit a special additional advice for purely statistical purposes and the normal renewal of a policy can lead to a statistical record being created without the branch being involved at all. It is highly desirable that all information used by the statistician be based on data maintained for business or accounting reasons as the recording cannot then be dismissed by field staff as 'only for statistics' and hence given less attention.

4.48 We shall from time to time refer to 'files' but it must be emphasised that we shall regard a file in this chapter as a logical concept rather than having a separate physical existence so that one physical data set (volume of tape or disc) may contain several logical files, either 'concurrent' or 'consecutive'. For example a file of current policy statuses and one of statuses held 'for statistical purposes' may comprise one physical file with a series of statuses for each policy covering its history during at least some stated period. Alternatively there may be two physical files, one of administrative statuses and one of statistical statuses. The latter may comprise only out-of-date statuses: if it contains all statuses, processing may be eased but problems, likely to be severe, will arise in ensuring that the 'in force' records on the administrative and statistical files correspond precisely.

The transition from writing to computer

4.49 Having now discussed the information we wish to have recorded and retained we must consider the problems of ensuring that the information is correctly recorded. We shall restrict ourselves to systems in which all information required to calculate a premium is in the computer system. The reasons for requiring the file to have information to enable the premium to be calculated are twofold. First because the statistician is likely to want to analyse the results against all the factors taken into account in the premium calculation. The other reason is to be able to apply some notional (or actually used) premium scale to all statuses and not to analyse merely the premium actually charged: the purpose of doing so will become apparent later.

The proposal

4.50 The usual originating document is a proposal completed by or on behalf of the policyholder. This asks questions relating to the vehicle to be insured, to the policyholder, to any other likely drivers, to their past insurance history, if any, and to convictions (when it is legally permissible to ask about them).

4.51 The first step is to find out whether the answers are true. Some are very likely to be true (the registration number, make and model, date of first registration). Some are at times liable to mis-statement (whether the vehicle has been modified to give better performance, whether it is used for commuting or business purposes especially where the business use is by someone other than the policyholder). Other answers are sometimes found to be wrong (driving by young persons, convictions, past insurance history, driving experience, mileage). It would be too costly to check the answers and to do so would not be conducive to obtaining business; consequently it is uncommon to reject statements unless the underwriter smells deception. A good underwriter does have a good nose. The time spent on scrutiny of a proposal must be limited since the contribution to *all* expenses (other than commission) including claim settlement is likely to be under one fifth of the average net premium of new business and this does not permit much time per policy if that time is to be spent by a senior official.

4.52 From the information on the proposals some computer records will be created either by card punching or direct to disc or tape. It may be necessary to code some information before punching (for example rating district) but much may be left to the computer. This input record will in due course be offered to the main file via some sort of validating process that will reject values that cannot (or are very unlikely to) arise. This process may also throw up suspect statements e.g. those relating to limitation on cover or type of vehicle for young policyholders or those revealing bad claims or driving histories. All these validity tests will generate a series of messages which require human investigation and intervention. Normally they will require reference to the proposal papers, occasionally to the proposer either direct or via branch or agent. This all takes time. Meanwhile, the file has no record of the existence of the policy and, most likely, the policyholder will not receive his policy. Moreover, other things may be happening. There may be a claim, or even several claims, there may be endorsements, either because of a change of address or vehicle or merely because the proposer realises he has given wrong information. None of this can be processed until there is a record on the file to alter. It is very important therefore that this stage be completed as rapidly as may be consistent with reliability.

Changes

4.53 When we deal with changes in a policy record we must begin by ensuring that we are changing the right record. Merely to quote a policy number is unreliable unless the number incorporates a check digit such as is used by banks in allocating account numbers. One of the simplest systems is to multiply the digits of a number in turn by different prime numbers, add the products and find the remainder when the total is divided by 11. For example, using three, seven and one as multipliers, the check digit for 1234567 is found to be

$$1\times 3+2\times 7+3\times 1+4\times 3+5\times 7+6\times 1+7\times 3=94;$$

the remainder $= 6$ $(94-(11\times 8))$ so that such a policy number could be quoted as 1234567/6. This system will pick up any error in a single digit and most transpositions (e.g. 1324567, but not 1567234 which is a most unlikely type of error in normal cases). There are many variations of this arrangement which the reader can try for himself. If one does not use check digits it is useful to record some information other than the policy number which can be tested by the computer against the in force records. Agency code may be useful, especially if it is not associated with batches of policies. Vehicle registration number, renewal date, policyholder's name are other possibilities. Too complicated a system may itself be liable to error and produce excessive validity rejects. It is impossible to reduce the probability of error to zero; and there is a point at which further reduction in the risk of error would not be worth the time and money it would cost.

Delays

4.54 The time taken to record information on a file depends on many factors, including:
- Method and frequency of updating
- Frequency of, and time taken to correct, errors
- Delays in notification of changes

Delays in claim notification where the effects of knock-for-knock agreements are particularly noticeable

It is important to monitor these delays.

Periods of cover

4.55 We have referred to a policy status, that is a condition which remains stable for some period. The simplest logical concept is of a status with a starting operative date and (if it is superseded) an ending operative date. The recording on the computer file may enable this information to be extracted but in some cases a change may be recorded only in the field to which it applies to avoid repeating data that are not changed.

Multi-vehicle policies

4.56 If a policy covers several vehicles problems are likely to arise. If each vehicle is treated as a separate insurance and the records can be separated into parts corresponding to each vehicle, all is probably well, and it may be possible to analyse such cases to see if they behave differently from the general body of single-vehicle policies. If, however, there are different arrangements in regard to no-claim discounts or if the policy is to be treated as a fleet and rated on an experience basis it may be necessary to identify the policies so that they can be excluded from the normal analyses.

Claims

4.57 On the claims side, where estimated run-offs are likely to be essential statistical returns, estimates must be differentiated from payments. Companies have different practices over the recording of claims on the computer, some restricting computer records to payments only, while others maintain a full claims history recording not only payments but also the various estimates placed on the claims throughout their currency.

4.58 There are advantages in maintaining up-to-date estimates and the eventual need to produce quarterly returns to the Department of Trade will reinforce this point. However there are major problems in regard to the frequency of estimating and the methods to be adopted which we shall not consider here. For the moment we must remember that at one extreme there will be estimates for every claim in which any amount may be outstanding and which are continuously updated; at the other extreme all estimating may be by statistical methods and few, even no, claims (at least for the last year or two) may have individual estimates. The treatment of these cases may range from the application of an average estimate on every open claim to ignoring them altogether on the claim record.

4.59 To record the claim payments alone will considerably restrict the scope of the system—to produce the experience of a cohort which included outstanding claims it is necessary at least that the latest estimate on a claim be recorded (see Chapter 10). Retrospective information, however, will often be required for year-end positions and can be provided for by recording on the statistical record for the claim the position at consecutive year ends. Nevertheless, to obtain a complete retrospective experience giving the position at any point in time requires only that the then current estimate should not be lost when a revised estimate has been submitted and this can be simply achieved by the addition of estimate records to the statistical file: for any claim there will be a succession of payment and estimate records, each showing the date on which it was raised and enabling the retrospective position at any point in time to be derived from records raised prior to the required date. For example:

Date	Payment Made	Estimate Outstanding
1. 6.72	—	1,000
1. 9.72	50	1,000
30. 6.73	—	10,000
1.12.73	6,500	2,500
1. 3.74	2,300	—

By reference to the date of each record a run-off of the claim can be produced showing for instance at six-monthly intervals, the current position as it then appeared.

Position At	Payments To Date	Estimate Outstanding	Total
30. 6.72	—	1,000	1,000
31.12.72	50	1,000	1,050
30. 6.73	50	10,000	10,050
31.12.73	6,550	2,500	9,050
30. 6.74	8,850	—	8,850
31.12.74	8,850	—	8,850

Two remarks should be made. The first that this sort of sequence of estimated final totals is by no means uncommon with liability claims, namely a steady rise to a maximum followed by ultimate settlement at a figure rather less than the maximum previously attained. The second is that if claims are estimated statistically it is unlikely that this process can be usefully begun before the end of the second year or so from the notification of the claim.

4.60 In practice few companies record specific estimates, (also known as 'case' estimates) on the computer for every outstanding claim. One practice is to allocate a standard reserve to every claim expected to be settled for less than a certain amount. This saves considerably on the administrative task of manually estimating every individual claim, although an additional run-off will be wanted from the statistics (affecting as it does the overall level of outstanding reserves that the company must hold at any time) namely, a review of the adequacy of the standard estimates by examination of the actual amounts for which these claims are ultimately settled. It must be realised, however, that this can only be done on a bulk basis and not on an individual claim basis.

4.61 The use of standard estimates does, however, have underwriting drawbacks for classes of business such as motor fleets where 'incidents' may be reported to the company more because of the insured's internal accident reporting procedure than because any claim payment is likely. In any event such claims, if damage only is involved, may be quite unlike claims for individual vehicle policies since rating will probably not involve no-claim discount, giving rise to many small claims. There may well also be a larger excess in such cases, causing further differences.

What is a claim?

4.62 We have been referring on several occasions to claims and payments. Unfortunately, however, it is not easy to define either. So far as a claim is concerned practice varies from one company to another, but in the United Kingdom we think it is fairly standard practice for any one incident to give rise to one claim at most for each vehicle involved, however many other vehicles, people, animals or property are involved. One car hitting a lamp post will give rise to one claim (at most) in the books of the insurer of that car. Two vehicles hitting each other will give rise to two claims (at most), one in the books of each insurer, although if one vehicle were clearly and solely to blame and there were no knock-for-knock agreements involved, the insurer of the other vehicle might not set up a claim file or give it a number. When there is a multiple collision, if all damage happened more or less simultaneously, there would probably be one claim at most for each vehicle involved.

4.63 It is, however, a normal policy condition that an insured reports any incident that *might* give rise to a claim and many such incidents are reported either direct or through brokers. Such incidents may not lead to any liability on the part of the insurer either because no claim is made by a third party or the insured merely *reports* (to comply with the terms of the policy) but does not claim in order not to jeopardise his no-claim discount. There is a third case where no payment is made, because the damage caused by the insured is settled under a knock-for-knock agreement by some other insurer and the insured is covered for third party only. It is probably essential to record such 'incidents' as claims as they will normally cause the policyholder to lose his no-claim discount exactly as if the knock-for-knock agreement did not exist and his own insurer was therefore called upon to pay.

4.64 The most important thing is to maintain consistency within a company. Whether an incident is treated as a claim immediately on notification or later is not vital although so far as the statistician is concerned, it is better to create a record as soon as possible, a view doubtless shared by the auditor.

Some companies are believed to defer counting a claim or allocating it a number until either payment is made or some estimate is raised. Some are also believed to count as a new claim one which is reopened after being 'closed' in the normal way.

4.65 This is an area where the administrator may wish to be heard, but it seems wise to require every notification to a company or to its agents or brokers to be recorded at once as a claim so that it can be counted and its progress watched until final settlement, and for any subsequent operations to take place under the original claim number.

What is a payment?

4.66 This seems simple but it is not. First if an insurer pays cash or draws a cheque relating to an identifiable claim or covering a number of identifiable claims then it should count as a payment on the claim or one payment on each claim (if more than one) of the relative amount applicable to that claim. However, difficulties at once arise with professional fees. If an insurer pays one surveyor for specific reports he can normally allocate the payment to individual claims. If, however, he pays the salary and expenses of his own staff for engineering reports or legal assistance, then it is not so easy to allocate the cost to individual claims and even if one does do so on an average cost basis it is likely to involve an amount of *unnecessary* work out of all proportion to the benefit. This applies also to payments in bulk to the engineer units maintained by the insurance industry and administered by the British Insurance Association and may apply to emergency treatment fees and police reports if they are paid in bulk out of an expense account. The effort involved in separately charging, validating and analysing all payments under these headings, other than payment to a third party's legal adviser above some minimum sum, is hardly justifiable and they could conveniently be grouped with general claim settlement expenses with little, if any, loss of information. Similar problems arise with payments under the Motor Insurers' Bureau and any other indemnity schemes. The important condition is that there should be a standard practice within the company.

4.67 Further problems arise with recoveries, but first we must dispose of a special kind of recovery, namely that from a reinsurer, whether excess of loss or, if such exist, stop loss, or in respect of treaty business. They must in every case be rigorously excluded from settlement details of any given claim. It is vital to work with gross liabilities. The fact that part of the liabilities are shared with another insurer in return for a share of the premium must not be allowed to interfere with the assessment of the full liability under a claim (although abnormally large claims may require special treatment and are considered later). Other recoveries fall into at least two categories. One comprises reimbursement of payments made for which the insurer was primarily liable but with a right to recover, or where, by concession, a payment is refunded to preserve no-claim discount. The other and more important class comprises payments received under knock-for-knock and claim sharing agreements: in the former case, the insurer may pay, but if he later discovers the insurer of a third party, and he has an agreement with him, he will claim reimbursement under the agreement.

4.68 It is desirable for some purposes to be able to separate payments and recoveries under claim sharing agreements in order that claim amount distributions may be examined at the gross and not the net level. Unfortunately, this is not possible under knock-for-knock agreements covering damage to the insured's own vehicles. In some cases an insurer may seek to recover from an uninsured party by instalments over a period, and some of these cases may involve hundreds of individual recoveries of small amounts. The treatment of recoveries is believed to vary considerably from one insurer to another but the position outlined above is thought to be the most satisfactory.

Type of payment

4.69 It is normally considered desirable to provide a breakdown of net payments by the nature of the payment or the peril in respect of which it is made; common examples are:
    Own damage
    Fire
    Theft

Third party bodily injury
Third party property damage
Legal charges
Other (mostly personal accident)
Claims sharing

This means that every payment made has to be coded. The precautions to ensure accuracy apply here as elsewhere.

CODING OF INFORMATION ON THE MASTER FILE

Descriptive coding

4.70 The final step towards the development of the statistical system is the description of the type of business to which each transaction relates. In the first place such description will be a general business classification (private car, fleet, etc.) influenced probably by a company's departmental structure, but further coding details refining the description will be equally appropriate. Taking some of the factors which might be considered for coding on private car motor business, distinction might be made as follows.

Coding possible	Coding impossible or impracticable
Use	Annual Mileage
Cover	Traffic density in area of common use
Age of policyholder	Driving proficiency
Age of car	Colour of car
Make and model	Annual salary
Rating group	Car roadworthiness
Area	Average number of passengers
Driving history	Moral hazards
(convictions etc.)	Physical and psychological conditions
No-claim discount	Extent of use for business
(present and past)	Extent to which the vehicle will have
Excesses (voluntary/compulsory)	to be used even in adverse conditions
Occupation (within certain limits)	
Whether used for commuting	
Whether garaged at night	
Membership of Institute of	
Advanced Motorists	
Number of vehicles insured	

It may well be that some of the factors in the second column have more influence on the risk than those in the first. Clearly, it is necessary to use some of the data in the first column as a proxy measure of the real risk factors though they themselves may not have any direct influence on the risk.

4.71 In addition to purely descriptive details there are other items of a general nature which have been mentioned previously and which may also be appropriate.

> Type of transaction (new business, renewal, etc.)
> Agency details
> Premium
> Date of inception of policy
> Date of accounting entry
> Period covered by risk (commencement and expiry dates)
> Renewal frequency
> Renewal date

Coding of information regarding claims

4.72 It might be thought necessary to arrange for information as to the origin of claims to be recorded on the file. However, an insurer is in business, *inter alia*, to make a profit and that profit is affected by a £100 (or £100,000) claim equally whether it arose from a right turn, a cross-roads collision, a left turn or wandering attention. If one can relate claims cost to factors that can be used in rating, either directly or by a proxy variable, then a case could be made out for analysing claim cost by type of accident. If not there seems little merit, from the insurer's point of view, in recording type of accident. But even if the association could be established clearly and certainly, it is difficult to foresee 'Are you careless when turning right?' as a question on a proposal form. The practical value to the underwriter of the recording of the type of accident is low.

4.73 The information about a claim that might be useful to an insurer is age of driver and his or her relationship, if any, to the policyholder, where the policyholder himself is not driving. The results may show the extent to which claims arise from driving by persons other than the policyholder, but if the results suggest that a high proportion of such claims arise, one cannot necessarily relate them to exposure since there is no measure of the relative amount of driving by such persons. Similar remarks apply to foreign use. If we take all vehicles for which green cards are issued and calculate the claim frequency per vehicle year of the cover we shall probably find it greatly exceeds the expected frequency for the group. But how many claims would there have been if the holiday or business trip had been in the United Kingdom and not abroad? This question cannot be answered.

4.74 Before any special coding of information regarding the occurrence of claims is contemplated, the statistician must ask himself—'What use will the answer be?'. If there is any doubt whatever, it is unwise to consider the coding; to call for codes one cannot use, will not merely result in careless completion, but cynicism is liable to be infectious and to spread to a disregard of the need for reliability on the things that do matter.

Motor data base

4.75 We have now considered the elements of a data base for a motor insurance account and outlined some of the practical problems of which the actuary should be aware. These of course will vary from company to company. Essentially, however, a sophisticated data base should allow for direct access to computer records of the recent history of all policies that have been in force at any time during a specified period. The minimum such period that is likely to give the statistician all the information he requires is about six months, but longer periods are desirable. Unfortunately, in motor insurance changes take place so frequently that if the period of record retention is lengthened the cost may become large in relation to the value of the records; this is almost certain to be so if the period exceeds about 2 years.

4.76 So far as claims are concerned, information regarding frequency should be kept for the same period as the in force data, but information regarding their settlement should be kept at least until all claims arising in a given calendar year are finally settled—that will be for between 10 to 15 years. With well designed tape systems this is not likely to pose any serious data processing problems, but if the records are used, as they should be, for the production of statutory returns, then it must be possible to reconcile them with the insurer's audited accounts.

Description of the system: the master motor tape

4.77 This file comprises a list of all policies known to the computer to be in force, together with some policies that have been cancelled prior to the normal end of the period of insurance. Each record consists of a 'status' giving details of the insured and the cover, including some required only for administrative purposes, for example, names and addresses of policyholders, and some might be used by the statistician, for example occupation, if they could be reliably entered and subsequently coded. If any information (other than no-claim discount) is altered a new status is created with a starting operative date and this date is applied as an ending operative date to the existing status which is then transferred to the supplementary master file (see below). A claim is treated as an alteration (with an ending operative date on the record equal to the accident date). The old record is given a distinctive record type (L) so that a count of type L records on the supplementary master file gives full information on the number of reported claims and their accident dates. This notification also acts as a signal to output a record (claim rating record) of the insurance position as at the date of the accident which is used to build up the motor claims master file (see below).

The supplementary master file

4.78 This contains all obsolete statuses removed from the motor master tape and they are retained for at least 9 months; provision is made for increasing this period to as much as 9 years if special investigations are envisaged. In practice it has been found that the number of records transferred to this file in a year is of the order of 50 to 70% of the number on the motor master file.

The claims master file

4.79 This file is normally opened by the claim rating record. To it are added the details of all payments and recoveries (other than for any excess of loss reinsurance) estimates, closures, re-openings and re-closures. No time limit is put on the retention, but it would seem, based on experience, to be

DOCUMENTATION AND DATA 89

unwise to drop any records for a year of notification (or accident) until the whole of that year's claims are finally settled. This is likely to be of the order of 10 to 12 years so that with a claim frequency of 1 in 7 this file would ultimately have about twice as many records as the motor master file if the portfolio is stable, although most of these records will be quite short.

Frequency of updating

4.80 In the particular system here described the *motor master file* is updated weekly with information regarding new business, lapses, cancellations, endorsements, claims, claim settlements and no-claim discount decisions. The *supplementary master* is updated monthly. The *claims master* is normally updated monthly, although the interval is more flexible, and more frequent processing is possible when necessary, often at the year end. It is emphasised that this is not the only or necessarily best system; it is used here solely for illustrative purposes. (Some other systems update daily and print out fortnightly for example.)

Transaction statistics

4.81 Transaction statistics are concerned with the measurement of changes to the insured portfolio. Such information is of use in many areas, for example:
1. *Motor Department* Transaction statistics provide basic information for the management of the motor account. They show whether the account is growing or declining, and at what rate. They shed light on the normal structure and development of the portfolio.
2. *Marketing* Here transaction statistics can be used to measure the effect of changes in premium rates, of advertising campaigns or of changes to the commission rates. This is a prerequisite to the ultimate aim of being able to predict the effect of such changes. The figures may also help the direction of advertising to the correct audience. They will help to identify sections of the portfolio where cancellation rates are very high and to show up particular

risks where premium rates are out of line with the rest of the market.
3 *Accounts* The figures may help to identify agents or types of agent who are slow to pay. The figures may also help in making projections of cash flow and by providing more accurate estimates of earned premiums and of premium reserve.
4 *General* The figures may provide information which is of help in the allocation of expenses. A knowledge of transaction volumes may assist in the design of computer or manual procedures. Finally, the figures may help in other areas of statistics, by showing how long it is necessary to wait before the majority of transactions have been processed.

Processing delays

4.82 It has already been stressed that it can take time for a company to find out that it has gone on risk or come off risk, or that a risk has changed. Such delays constitute a problem in the measurement of transaction volumes. Each company will need to investigate the pattern of processing delays within its own system and to make due allowance in the interpretation of statistics.

Lapses

4.83 It is convenient to distinguish failure to renew, which we can call 'lapses', from cancellations during the policy year. Among the reasons for drawing these distinctions are:
1 Lapses which occur in a particular period can affect only those policies which are due for renewal in that period.
2 The effective date of lapse is implicitly known.
3 Reasons for lapsing are different from the reasons for cancelling mid-term.

4.84 Ideally we should like to know the reasons for lapsing. For example the policyholder may be giving up motoring altogether or may be getting a company car. He may have been dissatisfied with some aspect of service, or he may be changing companies to get a cheaper rate. Unfortunately, experience shows that it is almost impossible to get useful information in this area.

Mid-term cancellations

4.85 It seems reasonable to suppose that all policies are exposed to the risk of mid-term cancellations; thus a reasonable measure of the mid-term cancellation rate for a particular month may be the number of cancellations occurring in that month divided by the exposure of that month. It may be, however, that mid-term cancellation rates depend upon the time of year and since last renewal. For this and other reasons we probably want to measure the mid-term cancellation rate in any particular month, on each of the 12 monthly cohorts separately. Here the need to re-group by effective date to overcome the effect of pipeline delays results in a very complex analysis.

New business

4.86 There is no obvious base to use to convert the number of new policies into a new business rate. For comparison with cancellation rates we can construct a new business rate as the number of new policies commencing in a particular month divided by the number of renewals accepted in that month. We should recognise, however, that there is no natural relationship between the number of new policies commencing in a month and the number of renewals invited or accepted in the same month. In framing the above definition it has implicitly been assumed that new business is written for an initial period of one year. This is not always the case, and cohorts should be kept distinct. There is also the problem of short period new business which will lapse automatically within the next year.

4.87 The problems of measuring new business volumes are similar to those of measuring mid-term and renewal cancellations, and in particular we need to allow for the effect of processing delays. In addition we need to consider the possibility that a policy can be added to the computer file without being treated as new business. This could be done to reinstate a policy cancelled in error, or take on the portfolio of another company in the event of amalgamation.

4.88 If new business is more difficult than lapses in one area, it is easier in another; we can establish where it came from. There may be merit in at least distinguishing between new entrants to the insurance market and transfers from other companies. Also an analysis of transfers to show the company of origin may help us to make more sense of the relationship between price and new business. It may also be that changes in the number of licences current, or the numbers of new registrations would form a suitable base for the construction of new business rates for new entrants to the market.

Growth rates

4.89 We come now to the stage of putting together the measures of new business lapses and cancellations. Once we have established, either by waiting or by estimating pipelines, the numbers of new business lapses and cancellations, we can calculate the net change in the portfolio over a defined period such as a month. (Because of delays this will not be the same as the change in the number of live computer records over the same period, and indeed these two figures can move in opposite directions.) An obvious measure of growth is the ratio of this net change, to the number in force at the start of the period.

4.90 Normally, regular monthly tabulations would be made of renewals invited (i.e. those extracted), new business, lapses and cancellations. These would be analysed by several factors including:

    Operative month (except for renewals)
    Administrative division

and for private cars, comprehensive and non-comprehensive separately:

    Rating area
    Rating group
    Age of policyholder
    Age of vehicle

In addition private car new business would be analysed according to whether it was a revival by a former policyholder

DOCUMENTATION AND DATA

of the company, a transfer from another insurer or someone entirely new to insurance.

4.91 If we now consider lapses, then for month x we issue R_x renewal invitations and in months y (where y will normally start $x-1$ and continue at least up to $x+12$) we process L_{xy} lapses. We shall ultimately have lapsed

$$\sum_{y=x-1}^{x+12} L_{xy} = L_x$$

lapses giving a lapse rate of $1000 L_x/R_x$ per thousand renewals invited. This lapse rate is a real rate since the lapses relate exactly to the renewals invited and the tabulations will show how the lapses are processed. A typical example can be set out as shown in Tables 4.1 and 4.2. Table 4.1 relates to the numbers, Table 4.2 converts the numbers into rates per thousand renewals invited.

4.92 It will be seen that in this example the number of lapses processed each month varied quite considerably. The actual numbers being:

Month	10·74	11·74	12·74	1·75	2·75	3·75	4·75	5·75	6·75	7·75
Lapses processed	9000*	6250*	3080*	2595*	4240	7385	7490	7900	6610	6005

*Allowing for columns not given in the table.

The figures given are realistic, although the variations in numbers of renewals per month and the effect of premium increases (and the subsequent approach to the old rates of lapse) are a little exaggerated.

4.93 These data which are similar in form to those given earlier are given here to facilitate the explanation that follows in regard to lapse, new business and growth rates in subgroups of the portfolio. Obviously, if we can sub-divide each sub-group by operative month we can proceed exactly as for the whole portfolio. However, this involves the output and retention of very large data volumes and in the system illustrated here this was quite impracticable when the system was originally designed. An alternative method was adopted assuming that delay patterns were uniform across the whole portfolio.

TABLE 4.1 Lapses—class: Total business—numbers of lapses

Consecutive operative month	7·75	6·75	5·75	4·75	3·75	2·75	1·75	12·74	11·74	10·74
Processing month										
10·74										350
11·74									150	3100
12·74								180	1800	900
1·75							210	1600	600	150
2·75						200	2460	1300	210	70
3·75					840	3800	2100	605	40	0
4·75				400	4900	2000	150	40	0	0
5·75			315	3400	3990	120	55	20	0	0
6·75		240	3240	2750	350	30	0	0	0	0
7·75	195	2965	2395	330	120	0	0	0		
Total lapses to date (no.)	195	3205	5950	6880	10200	6150	4975	3745	2800	4570
Renewals invited (no.)	40000	40000	45000	50000	70000	40000	30000	20000	30000	50000
Lapse rate to date per 1,000	5	80	132	138	146	154	166	187	93	91

TABLE 4.2 Lapses—class: Total business—rates per 1,000 renewals invited

Operative month	7·75	6·75	5·75	4·75	3·75	2·75	1·75	12·74	11·74	10·74
Processing month										
10·74										7
11·74									5	62
12·74								9	60	18
1·75							7	80	20	3
2·75						5	82	65	7	1
3·75					12	95	70	30	1	0
4·75				8	70	50	5	2	0	0
5·75			7	68	57	3	2	1	0	0
6·75		6	72	55	5	1	0	0	0	0
7·75	5	74	53	7	2	0	0	0	0	0
Total lapses to date (no.)	195	3205	5950	6880	10200	6150	4975	3745	2800	4570
Renewals invited (no.)	40000	40000	45000	50000	70000	40000	30000	20000	30000	50000
Lapse rate to date per 1,000	5	80	132	138	146	154	166	187	93	91

4.94 If, therefore we wish to estimate the movement rate among group r vehicles, we may wish to proceed as follows.
Let

M^r_{xy} = Movements M for group r, with operative month x, processed in month y

R^r_x = Renewals for group r, invited in month x

Also let

$M^r_y = \sum_{x=-\infty}^{+\infty} M^r_{xy}$ (Total movements for group r processed in month y)

$M_y = \sum_{r=1}^{p} M^r_y$ (Total movements for all groups processed in month y)

$M_{xy} = \sum_{r=1}^{p} M^r_{xy}$ (Total movements for all groups with operative month x processed in month y)

$R_x = \sum_{r=1}^{p} R^r_x$ (Total renewals for all groups invited in month x)

Then we calculate weighting factors f^y_x from the all-group totals by

$$f^y_x = \frac{M_{xy}}{R_x} \Bigg/ \sum_x \frac{M_{xy}}{R_x}$$

4.95 In practice, if the bulk of the movements are processed within n months of the operative date, it is adequate to calculate

$$f^y_x \text{ for } x = y-n \text{ to } y \text{ only,}$$

$\sum_x M/R$ being summed over the same range of x. (In the above example, it would be adequate to consider only the 5 most recent months for lapses.)

4.96 The adjusted rate for movement M, for group r processed in month y, (per 1,000 weighted renewals) is then given by

$$\frac{1{,}000 \times M^r_y}{\sum_{x=y-n}^{y} R^r_x \, f^y_x}$$

The movements are related to a weighted mean number of renewals, the weights being the proportions of movements relating to renewal month x to the total movements processed in month y, from the same range of x.

4.97 Calculation of the adjusted rates for new business and for lapses may be done on the above basis. For cancellations, a rather simpler calculation may be adopted because of the wider spread of cancellations over the policy year. A formula which is suitable for cancellations is

$$\frac{1{,}000 \times M_y^r}{\frac{1}{12}\sum_{i=1}^{12} R_{y+1-i}^r}$$

4.98 Depending on the definition of processing month used by an individual company, which will be affected by its own processing cycle, a variable of processing days may be included in successive months' figures. It may be necessary, therefore, to apply simple scaling factors to each of the above rates to make them comparable from month to month.

4.99 The rates for both new business and lapses brought about by this process should be reliable and sensitive. Care in interpretation is, however, needed since there are cyclical patterns. It is for this reason that figures for about 15 to 18 months are regarded as essential if the observer is not to be misled.

4.100 A typical table arising from these tabulations is set out in Table 4.3.

TABLE 4.3 Relative adjusted lapse rate—private car comprehensive

Processing month and year	A	B	C	D	All areas
	\multicolumn{4}{c}{Area weighting factors (see note below as to use)}	Lapse rate
5·74	99	100	110	80	145
6·74	100	102	109	78	160
7·74	100	98	111	79	170
.					
.					
.					
5·75	104	105	95	80	150
6·75	104	105	96	80	170
7·75	105	106	95	80	180

Note: The actual adjusted lapse rate in July, 1975, area A is $\frac{105}{100} \times 180 = 189$.

These figures would indicate a set back in areas A and B and an improvement in C.

4.101 Tables of this nature are essential to measure the effect of pricing and selling practices, but experience suggests that it is far from easy to measure cause and effect so that forecasting should be carried out with caution. But at least some insight has been gained as to what is happening.

The measurement of exposures and claims

4.102 The aim is to measure expected claim costs and to seek to establish whether there is a relationship between the levels of various factors that might seem to affect the risk and the relative expected claim costs. The factors include the traditional ones of the size and type of vehicle, the place where it is normally kept the use to which it is put and the characteristics of the policyholder or regular driver. It should be made clear at the outset that we are looking for associations between rating factors and claim costs (or 'risk') regardless of whether or not these are causal relationships.

4.103 A list of factors that can be readily examined will be limited in general to those from which reliable information is available on the master tape. If we wish to examine experience by some other factor we must make special enquiry either of the whole file or a large sample in which we can compare the levels of the factors, or, if we are able to forecast expected risks, we may select only those cases with particular levels of the factor in which we are interested. The techniques for such estimation are dealt with in Chapter 5. As indicated in paragraph 4.70 the facts which are likely to be recorded on tape and which are likely to be reasonably accurate (if only because they affect the premium calculation) are:

    Make, model and cubic capacity of vehicle (or plated weight for goods vehicles)
    Date of first registration
    Place of garage
    Class of use
    No-claim discount category and/or claims history
    Age of policyholder (and possibly some note if young

drivers other than the policyholder are likely to drive the vehicle)
Restrictions on driving
Excesses
Other covers
Special loadings

Other information which might be available, but which is likely to be difficult to verify, even after a claim, include:
Actual or expected mileage
Use for commuting
Use for business purposes, motor sport etc.

4.104 In some countries, for example U.S.A., premium may depend on the sex or marital condition of the policyholder and for the younger ones it may even depend on school or college records. Little thought is needed to realise the difficulty in updating this sort of information even if it used in rating, unless premiums are revised immediately on any change, or notification is made a condition of continued cover. As a rating factor occupation presents problems since it is difficult to define and code in a way that might seem to be related to risk. Most insurers enquire about certain occupations which are felt to be particularly hazardous, although whether these are associated with additional risk, or moral hazard is often hard to discover.

4.105 In view of the small numbers which are often involved the most we can probably hope to achieve within a single company is to see if cars loaded by underwriters whether for occupational risk or other reasons, do on the whole seem to merit the loading applied. However there are serious difficulties involved as will appear later. Some companies give special rates to members of certain professions (civil servants and teachers get lower rates, doctors and insurance outside staff higher) but a company not currently doing so will have great difficulty in testing whether the practice is justified simply through lack of information on exposure.

4.106 Finally there are characteristics that may well affect the risk but are incapable of measurement except possibly by reference to other recorded characteristics which may be representative of them. These include moral hazards, medical conditions, temperament, and so on. The amount of risk unexplained by conventional rating suggests that, collectively, factors of this nature are quite important and, for reasons explained in the paper by Johnson and Hey 'Statistical Studies in Motor Insurance' (*Journal of the Institute of Actuaries*, 1970, Vol. 97, 199), can only very imperfectly be measured by examining the claims experience.

The actual measurement of exposure

4.107 If we were examining experience by only one factor, say private cars by age of policyholder, the situation would be very close to the measurement of exposure under one class of life assurance, say endowment assurance on male lives. There is one major difference. In life assurance exposure is likely to be classified by age last birthday on the census date, whereas in motor insurance, where the premium is normally based on age last birthday at renewal, age at any point, whether on census date or the date of an accident should be taken as age last birthday at the renewal prior to the event. Other definitions, if consistent, might be used, but since, *inter alia*, we want to measure risk in relation to the premium charging process the above definition is likely to be much the best. The same rule must apply to all other factors, so that our risk measurement is in line with premium charging process.

4.108 The actual definitions will therefore need to depend on the practice of each insurer. Some companies will amend the premium rate on any change which brings the vehicle into another rating category such as change of place of garage, change of vehicle, change of use and so on. Others may continue cover for the rest of the period at the old rate. If it were the company's practice that a change in rating area is ignored until next renewal we should define rating area as that in force at the last renewal (although this involves the assumption that such changes are uniform from year to year); if the premium is altered immediately we should define rating area as that which applies at the date of any event (census or claim).

4.109 It seems that no-claim discount will be that applying at last renewal, but problems arise with adjustment of no-claim discount status some time after the claim date. Once again, so long as we are consistent, the choice of procedure is not critical, although the practice adopted by some insurers of an instant, but provisional, no-claim discount decision will help since it means that subsequent changes should be fairly few in number.

The simple case

4.110 Let us now consider the simple case of a single rating factor, namely age of policyholder. Experience tells us that the 'calendar year' type of method is appropriate. Whilst it is customary to use an actual calendar year, any period of time would be satisfactory so long as all policies are exposed to the whole of the period chosen or for such part of it as they were in force in; for example, experience can be built up quarter by quarter and can be merged into summer (May to October) and winter (November to April) which have quite different types of experience. One common method of obtaining exposure is the census method, counting at the start and end of each period (at least quarterly, if not more often) the policies in force classified by age last birthday at renewal (or inception) prior to the census date and the number of claims classified by age last birthday at renewal (or inception) prior to the accident date. If the file is counted about three to four months after the end of the quarter it is likely that most alterations and claims will have been recorded and the results will be reliable. Alternative methods are:

1 Before a status record is removed from the file it should be counted if it was in force on a census date which is going to be investigated in the future and the totals of such statuses should be accumulated and added to the count of the current statuses at the end of the quarter if those statuses were in force at the census date (this last count can be made only some time after the end of the quarter).
2 To count the number of days which each status has been in force during the period of investigation (which need not now be as short as a quarter year) by the age (or ages if it has been renewed during the period) according to which

it has been classified. This can be done either on a file containing necessary retained statuses or by the method described in (1) above.

Any of these methods will give a number of claims C_x at age x and the corresponding vehicle years of exposure at that age E_x, from which a claim frequency may be derived.

Other factors

4.111 It has long been clear that there are associations between the levels of various rating factors, some of them quite strong. For example, a 17-year-old policyholder is unlikely to have earned any no-claim discount whilst a 50-year-old is very likely to be on maximum no-claim discount. In the case of motor cycles the association between age and no-claim discount is so strong that it is almost impossible to separate the effect of the two factors. Other associations noted have included age of vehicle with cover (strong) and with rating area and age of policyholder (weak); also with age of policyholder, voluntary excess (strong) and driving restrictions (moderate). It should therefore, be clear that some steps have to be taken to deal with these associations.

4.112 The basic method for dealing with this situation is described in Chapter 5. Briefly it consists in the production of a standard table which expresses the expected claim frequencies for any policy as the sum of a number of parameters, one for each level of each factor thought to be associated with the risk. These parameters are used in two ways, firstly to estimate the expected number of claims in a group, secondly to adjust the actual claim frequency in the group so as to eliminate the distorting effects of factors associated with the one under investigation. This will give a relative claim frequency for that factor alone; these are similar to independent rates of decrement in a multiple decrement life table.

The measurement of expected claim cost

4.113 Traditional practice has been to compare claims cost with premiums collected (the claim ratio). This ratio does however have serious limitations in particular as an indication

DOCUMENTATION AND DATA

of the adequacy of premiums. The main objections to the claim ratio are:

1. A year's revenue claims are a mixture of the current year's experience and the effect of previous years' experience.
2. Unless the results are to be delayed for several years they must depend to a greater or lesser extent on estimated outstanding claim payments. This is an unreliable process and if, in order to maintain the right overall level of cost, adjustments to estimates are required then fluctuations arising from the adjustment of past errors as well as current errors in estimating are likely to produce major errors.
3. Further, the claim ratio was often computed on the basis of a stable portfolio, i.e. claims paid and outstanding in an accounting period divided by premiums received in that period. If business (i.e. premiums) is growing, this clearly undervalues the expected claim cost.
4. The premiums actually charged, even within one company, are likely to be a mixture of more than one scale and where frequent adjustments of scale are coupled with the existence of a discretion to local staff to quote special terms, then total premiums are likely to be a poor indicator of actual risk and, particularly, changes in premium may be an even worse indicator of changes in risk.
5. Except in very large groups the incidence of individual large claims is likely to cause the claim ratio to fluctuate substantially.

4.114 One way to avoid all these difficulties would be to ignore the actual premiums charged and to measure the risk in some other way. At the same time the basic process could be analysed by examining separately the probability of a claim and the distribution of the amount of the claim once a claim had occurred. This assumes that there is no correlation between frequency and amount. On the assumption that expected total claim amount (at least expected total relative claim amount, see para. 4.119) is relatively stable (apart from the effects of inflation on the actual overall average) then one can use amount data based on other more fully developed cohorts, where the claims are sufficiently developed to give a reliable picture and couple this with up-to-date claim frequencies.

4.115 If this hypothesis is justifiable it makes statistical investigation much easier. At present it is known, or at least strongly suspected, that some influences cause claim frequencies to move in one direction and the average amount in the opposite direction, giving a smaller proportionate overall movement in total cost than in either component. Whether different groups behave sufficiently differently as to upset comparison based on current relative frequencies and historic relative amounts is not clear. Where caution is most needed, however, is in making assumptions as to any relationship between claim frequency and claim cost.

4.116 Pursuing this line of investigation we may use the standard table of estimated claim costs allied to the actual number of claims occurring to calculate an expected total cost for all the claims in the group. We also have the premiums for the total exposed to risk in this group (on a selected scale which is adopted for use throughout the year) and obtain a calculated claim ratio from these two figures. Since absolute values of claims and the absolute level of premiums earned in the period are not readily available we express all our claims ratios for every group in terms of the overall claim ratio calculated on this basis and multiply the result by 1,000.

4.117 If we see a ratio so calculated that exceeds 1,000 it means that the group is being relatively undercharged whilst if the ratio is below 1,000 it is being relatively overcharged. No allowance is made in this calculation for expenses that may not be exactly or even nearly proportional to the risk premium.

4.118 We can now set out a table (Table 4.4) showing the presentation of some actual results: a *voluntary excess* for which a discount is given has been chosen as it illustrates many of the points that have been made previously.

4.119 Some comments on this table may be useful:
1. The final exposure is simply a count of the in-force as on 31 December 1974.
2. The total exposure = 1/8th final exposure + 1/8th exposure as at 30 September 1974.

DOCUMENTATION AND DATA

TABLE 4.4 Motor claim analysis for a typical quarter—breakdown by voluntary excess

Excess (£)	Exposure Final	Exposure Total	Total premium (£000)	Expected claim costs	Relative C/R	Claims Act.	Claims Exp.	A E
0	326550	82120	2784	1296	983	11449	11481	997
5	23112	5861	165	68	863	646	721	896
15	132854	33259	1055	521	1042	4733	4644	1019
30	56939	14149	507	253	1051	2178	2160	1008
Total	539455	135389	4511	2138	1000	19006	19006	1000

Excess (£)	Rates Act.	Rates Adj.	Claim costs	Av. premium	'Gross'* premium	Discount (%)
0	139	142	113	33·9	33·9	0
5	110	125	105	28·2	31·8	11
15	142	136	110	31·7	35·6	11
30	154	131	116	35·8	42·7	16
Total	140	140	112	33·3	—	

* This is the premium *before* the discount allowed for the relevant excess and gives a crude measure of the relative risk.

3   The total premium is calculated on an old scale which had subsequently been increased by flat percentages. The absolute level, in this tabulation, is of no importance so long as the correct relativities are used. This premium is 1/8th of the total of the premiums on the in-force at the beginning of the quarter which comprise the exposure.

4   The expected claim costs come from the standard table. The units are not given but may be taken as £1500. Like the absolute level of premium this figure has no effect on the tables.

5   The relative C/R is

$$1000 \times \left(\frac{E}{P}\right) \text{group} \div \left(\frac{E}{P}\right) \text{total}$$

where E is the expected claim cost and P the earned premium for the group total.

6   Under claims, Act. is the number recorded in the quarter, Exp. is the value from the standard table multiplied by

a factor to make the totals of Act. and Exp. equal to each other.

7   A/E = 1000 × actual/expected; it will be seen that except for the £5 excess the ratios are very nearly equal to 1000. The short-fall in the £5 excess is partly a random fluctuation and partly a result of the parameters not allowing quite enough for this rather unusual group.

8   Rate Act. = 1000 × actual number of claims ÷ total exposure. Rate Adj. = Act. ± an adjustment calculated from the standard table to allow for the make up of vehicles insured in this group.

9   Claim cost is an average in units of 1/1000th of those for total claim costs = expected claim cost ÷ claims Act.

10   Av. Premium = total premium ÷ total exposure.

11   It will be seen that total exposure is a little greater than ¼ of final exposure indicating a slight reduction in the portfolio over the quarter.

12   The relative claim ratio is much below 1000 for the £5 group. It is known that this follows from relative overcharging of some older policyholders or those driving older cars. For the £15 and £30 excesses the relative C/R is above normal, as a result of slight relative undercharging of younger policyholders (to whom the larger excesses have the greater appeal) and the fact that the premium scale assumes that the administrative cost is a smaller proportion of the premium than for the whole portfolio.

4.120   Tabulations of this nature provide a very satisfactory test of the performance of the portfolio, and if the claim ratios and A/E are observed over a period of years it is possible to see whether or not the situation is controlled.

The analysis of claim amount

4.121   The problems here are different from those associated with claim frequency. Getting the rating factors right, whilst important, is less essential. For claim frequencies it is absolutely imperative to make sure that the numerator of the frequency (the number of claims) and the denominator (the exposure) are calculated so as to correspond precisely. When analysing claim amounts, however, the effect of a few claims being wrongly grouped would be marginal.

4.122 There are however four major problems, namely:
1. What to do about claims not yet closed.
2. What to do about large claims.
3. What to do about associated factors which produce effects similar to but usually relatively smaller than their effects upon claim frequency.
4. What to do about inflation.

4.123 One system adopted has been to produce at the end of each quarter an analysis of average amounts of claims then regarded as settled. The treatment of claims re-opened is a matter for individual choice but it is probably best to adopt one of two possible courses.
1. To ignore altogether transactions not included in the first closure and subsequently to make a separate analysis of all such payments and recoveries. If the amounts are large enough one can investigate whether they arise in a random manner or not. Much will depend on the current practice of the office in regard to the speed of the original settlement and on the definition of 'settlement'.
2. To replace the original settlement by a later settlement, ignoring any extra payments or recoveries until the later settlement is actually recorded. This has the merit of giving a truer average settled claim and a truer claim amount distribution.

4.124 The progress of overall average settlement shows a steady rise in the average amount. The precise curve these averages follow will depend, amongst other things, on the rate of inflation and the mix of business (comprehensive cover should, however, be kept separate from non-comprehensive at all times even though the various classes of non-comprehensive can probably be treated as a single group). A typical rate of increase of average settled claims for a *yearly* cohort by date of notification, *not* by date of accident, in quarters, quarter one being at the end of March of the year of notification when only about one quarter of the cohort has been notified and less than a quarter of these notifications has been settled, and the rate of settlement for private car comprehensive, is shown in Table 4.5.

TABLE 4.5

Quarter	Average settled claim as a % of ultimate	Percentage settled by Number	Percentage settled by Amount*
1	27	6	1
2	35	19	7
3	42	36	16
4	47	59	28
5	52	78	46
6	57	86	55
7	64	91	60
8	70	96	65
12	77	98·7	78
16	85	99·4	84
20	91	99·7	91
24	93	99·8	93

* Excluding payments on claims not treated as settled. The actual amount *paid* will be greater, often much greater.

(In this table the average settlements are the average monetary amounts so that the effect of inflation has been left in. An alternative approach would be to express the settlements in constant pounds by choosing a base date and dividing each subsequent settlement amount by the ratio of a suitable price index of the settlement date to that of the base date.)

4.125 It will take many years before it can be shown that this type of table gives reliable estimates of final average settled claim. Not enough is yet known about the behaviour of the figures, although in times of increasing inflation it is likely that the figures in the second and fourth columns will decrease slowly. There will of course be fluctuations in the results but it seems reasonable to expect that unless there are major changes in the mix of the portfolio or in the rate of inflation, the relation between the second column and the third and fourth columns will be reasonably close. If this is true, then knowing:

(a) The amounts paid on claims already settled
(b) The percentage by number of claims already settled
(c) The amounts paid on outstanding claims

might be sufficient to make a reliable estimate of the amounts still to be paid on the outstanding claims. There is, however, a serious difficulty in that after the end of quarter eight the number of claims outstanding is very small ($1 \cdot 25\%$ at 3 years, $0 \cdot 5\%$ at 4 years, $0 \cdot 2\%$ at 6 years) whilst the amount unpaid is still large (22% at 3 years, 15% at 4 years and 7% at 6 years) so that small errors in the number settled can cause large errors in the estimates of the percentages paid. It would also be extremely difficult to detect by statistical methods any artificial distortions in the pattern of settlements.

4.126 An office is principally interested in the assessment of ultimate claim amounts for two distinct purposes. The first is for setting future premium scales and here abnormal fluctuations in the contribution of large claims or other abnormal features (such as a surge of minor or major claims arising from exceptionally bad weather) should be ignored, except to the extent that they need to be spread over several years. For this purpose an estimate of claims cost can best be made after two or three years. Any benefit from waiting longer and thus having more settlements is offset by the additional waiting time and by the disturbing effect of large claims.

4.127 The second purpose is for reserving and solvency. Here, abnormal features have to be taken into account in the year of occurrence. The problems of solvency estimating, outstanding claims and large claims are inextricably mixed up with each other.

Statutory statistics

4.128 The regulations call for returns in respect of each of the statutory classes of business namely liability, marine, aviation and transport (MAT), motor, personal accident, pecuniary loss and property. Returns are required not only in respect of each class of business but also in respect of each country in which risks are undertaken. Companies are further required to sub-divide the classes in each country according to the type of risk within the class (for example private cars and motor fleets would usually be two separate 'risk groups'). The number of risk groups is currently between one and five for any class and country but this is likely to increase under revised regulations now being considered by the Department of Trade. There are provisions to exclude small returns, but whilst they apply to small class or small country, they do not extend to small risk groups within the class. The rest of this section of the chapter relates solely to motor business.

Claim frequency statistics

4.129 A return is prepared in respect of each group; this should show:

Gross premium and the number of vehicle years of cover granted during the year
—that were brought forward from the previous year
—that were commenced during the present year
—that were carried forward to the next year.
Number of claims in the year that
—were in respect of incidents in earlier years
—were old claims reopened
—were in respect of incidents in the current year
—the estimated number that occurred in the current year but which will not be reported until next year.
Claim frequency for the year.

An example of a claim frequency return is shown in Appendix 4.1.

Claim settlement analysis

4.130 A return is prepared in respect of each risk group for years of claim from 1970 onwards giving a historical record of the claims settled, and outstanding. These schedules show for the year of claim and each year up to and including the year of account the following figures:

Number of claims closed without cost
Number of claims closed with payment
Number of claims outstanding at the end of the year
Amount paid in the year
Cumulative amount paid in respect of the years to date
Amount reserved at the end of the year
Total amount and reserve at the end of the year

An example of a claim settlement analysis is given in Appendix 4.2.

The Motor Risk Statistics Bureau

4.131 The Motor Risk Statistics Bureau was formed in 1966–7 as a department within the British Insurance Association with a main objective of producing market statistics which would provide useful management and underwriting information to those B.I.A. members who subscribed to the running of the scheme. It has always been a principle of the Bureau's operation that only 'raw data' on policies and claims, submitted to the Bureau by member offices on computer media, should be accepted for analysis. This has enabled several important changes in the scope or type of analysis to be introduced without the need to continually re-approach members for additional information. At present, 22 offices supply data in respect of their private car portfolio, and from each of these the Bureau receives two computer files each quarter. The first contains details of all policies in force at the end of the quarter, and a comparison by the Bureau of this file with that submitted 3 months earlier allows the estimation of exposure to risk during the quarter, sub-divided by any combination of risk factors for which information is available. The second file contains information on claims currently outstanding, or which have recently been closed, and the Bureau uses this to build-up a master file on claims and their development. From these two data bases, the Bureau attempts both to establish relative claims experience between different levels of risk factors, and to consider trend movements in both frequency and size of claim.

APPENDIX 4.1

Claim frequency analysis (Year of account ending 31 December 1974)

Country:	Class:	Company ref	Country	Class	Risk Group	Year
United Kingdom	Motor vehicle insurance business	100				

Risk group: Private cars

		Gross premiums 1	Units of exposure 2 vehicle/years
A	Exposure during year of account:	£000	
	(a) under contracts commencing during the previous financial year	1 800	25,000
	(b) under contracts commencing during the year of account	2 950	27,000
	(c) total (a) + (b)	3 1750	52,000
B	Exposure carried forward to financial year following the year of account in respect of contracts commencing during the year of account	4 850	26,000

			Number of claims
C	Number of claims:		
	(a) originated in earlier financial years and first notified during the year of account	5	500
	(b) closed in earlier financial years and reopened during the year of account	6	200
	(c) originating during the year of account and notified before closure of the records for that year	7	6000
	(d) estimated number of claims originating during the year of account but not notified before the closure of the records for that year	8	300
	(e) estimated total number of claims attributable to the year of account (c) + (d)	9	6300

Per cent

APPENDIX 4.2

Claim settlement analysis (Year of account ending 31 December 1974)

Country: United Kingdom	Class: Motor vehicle insurance business		Company ref		Risk group: Private cars				
For DOT use			300						

Year of origin: 1970

Year	Number of claims closed in year		Number of claims outstanding at the end of the year	Amount of payments made in the year in settlement or on account	Aggregate payments made up to the end of the year	Claims outstanding at the end of the year		Total number of claims attributable to the year of origin 8000	Total amount paid and outstanding at the end of the year (Total of columns 6 and 8)
	at no cost	at some cost				Payments on account included in column 6	Estimated payments remaining to be made		
1	2	3	4	5	6	7	8		9
				£000	£000	£000	£000		£000
Year of origin 1970	1500	3500	3000	350	350	350	350		700
Year of account 1971	500	1700	500	165	515	50	125		640
Year of account 1972	15	180	300	55	570	40	90		660
Year of account 1973	5	60	200	80	650	30	60		710
Year of account 1974	2	60	100	70	720	30	30		750

CHAPTER 5

THE RISK PREMIUM

5.1 As we have already stressed, general insurance operates in a market and is governed, as is any other service offered for sale in a free market, by a price mechanism. The insurer if he wishes to remain in business, and especially if he wishes to expand his business, must offer to cover risks at a competitive price. While the insurer would be at peril if he ignored competition, he would be equally at peril if he were to ignore the expected cost of providing the service offered. The insurer must know whether he *is* charging a premium below the expected cost, in what classes of business, in what particular groups of insured and over what period so that the trading strategy can be conscious and calculable. Otherwise the insurer is running his business like a car being driven with all the windows and windscreen blacked out.

5.2 So, while we shall consider in a later chapter the basis of the market premium which is actually charged, we shall first consider the estimation of the pure premium which would exactly meet the expected cost of the risk covered (analogous to the net premium in life assurance). The term 'expected' is used here in its statistical sense, i.e. as the mean value of a probability distribution function; in this case a compounding of two functions, the *number* of claims in the period of insurance and the *amount* of a claim. We shall consider the two elements separately. While it would be possible to calculate a rate of claim by total amount per unit exposure (similar to the traditional 'claim ratio' i.e. the ratio of claims to premiums) this would not be a reliable basis for prediction. The two probability distributions are different and need to be examined separately. Especially in a time of inflation, claim amount distributions may be far from stable. Furthermore, to examine the two elements together as one cost distribution would add greatly to the problem of delays. To have to wait for most claims to be reported before investigating claim frequency is bad enough since the rates are not then fully up to date; to have to wait for most claims to be settled would exacerbate the problem.

The frequency of claims

5.3 We have already considered briefly, in Chapter 4, the estimation of the number of claims and we may now consider the problem in greater detail. The concept of a rate of claim in general insurance is not as clear as the concept of the rate of mortality in life assurance. In the latter case the object of exposure is the insured person and the unit of exposure is the person-year (when an annual rate is to be derived). The numerator of the rate is the number of deaths during the investigation period and the units of exposure, to form the denominator of the rate, are calculated by multiplying each person by the time exposed during the period of the investigation and within the category to which the rate is to apply. (In exposed-to-risk formulae some group averaging may be used.) In subsequent experience, multiplication of the number actually entering a category, by this derived rate provides an estimate of the number of deaths to be expected during the year. Since the main object of the exercise is to obtain this estimate any consistent combination of unit of exposure and multiplier could be used; consistent, that is, in using the same unit in the denominator of the multiplier (or rate) and as the multiplicand for estimating deaths. Premiums could be used as the unit of exposure but since this would give greater weight, within the age or other category, to those with larger sums assured, the efficiency of the multiplier as an estimator would be at risk of changes in the mix of sums assured from time to time. The life happens to be the easiest, as well as the best, estimating unit to use.

5.4 In general insurance the best estimating unit of exposure is not necessarily the insured object weighted by the time for which it is exposed to risk of a claim-originating incident. For example, in fire insurance, one policy may cover a number of sites, each site comprising a different number of buildings each with different insured values. The building itself is unsatisfactory as a unit not only because of different monetary values attaching to different buildings, but also because of the different types, sizes, designs and uses of buildings. In motor insurance the time spent off the road represents time at minimal risk; time on the road, or, even better, mileage covered would be a better measure of exposure than time insured. It would however, be impracticable, certainly too costly even if possible, to record mileage covered.

Exposure

5.5 The units of exposure used in practice are those which are possible rather than those which might be desirable. The following are examples of possible units of exposure.

Class of insurance	Unit of exposure
Employers' Liability	Turnover; no. of employees; payroll; premium
Marine	No. of voyages; ship-miles; sum insured; premium
Aviation	No. of take-offs; plane-miles; passenger-miles; sum insured; premium
Motor	Vehicle-years; vehicle-miles; policy-years; premium
Pecuniary Loss	Sums insured; full value; premium
Personal Accident	Person-years; premium
Property	
Fire	No. of buildings; sum insured; maximum expected loss; premium
Householders	No. of buildings; sum insured; premium
Reinsurance	Premium—of reinsured —of reinsurer

5.6 One disadvantage of using a convenient proxy unit of exposure (e.g. vehicle-years) instead of a more specific measure (e.g. vehicle-miles) is the submerged heterogeneity which is then introduced (some vehicles travel much larger mileages). This may be largely overcome by standard statistical procedures, i.e. separate claim rates (the multipliers of para. 5.3) may be computed for different categories within a particular class of insurance, the categories being such as to separate the different sources of heterogeneity. For example, in motor insurance different levels of mileage may be separated by classifying policies according to class of use (especially if used for business purposes or for commuting) or location of garage (town users have different average mileages from country users), age of policyholder (old drivers tend not to drive so far as younger drivers), and these axes of classification are of interest in themselves as sources of differential exposure. We shall return to the problem of multivariate analysis later.

5.7 A disadvantage of using the premium as a unit of exposure, is that premiums are relative to a rating structure which may change from time to time. It is therefore desirable to adjust premiums to a common reference structure otherwise heterogeneity arising from structure changes will be introduced into the data. Furthermore, premiums incorporate loadings for commission and expenses, and these may vary between class and also between risks within a class of insurance, and this will introduce additional bias unless it is avoided by the use of the net risk premium. (It is stressed again, that claim ratios, that is, total claim amounts divided by premiums, though extensively used in general insurance, are very crude measures. Though the inherent distortions referred to above may be relatively stable within a single company, sufficiently to allow their use for the approximate monitoring of experience, it would not be safe to make comparisons between insurance offices on this basis.)

Calculation of rates

5.8 When the unit of exposure has been chosen and defined (so that the office data files can store and retrieve it, as described in Chapter 4) the calculation of the total amount of exposure, to form the denominator of the claim frequency, is straightforward and employs the same counting principles as are used in mortality investigations for life assurance. [See Chapter 19 *The Analysis of Mortality and Other Actuarial Statistics* by Benjamin & Haycocks 1970.] Both policy-year and calendar-year aggregation is used in general insurance. The basic principle is that whatever aggregation is used for units of exposure must also be used for claims.

5.9 The calendar-year or calendar-accident-year method groups together all units of exposure and all claims within the calendar year or years under investigation (and within any specific categories, e.g. age of driver in motor insurance). The policy-year method allocates units of exposure and claims to the policy years commencing within the calendar years, and this allocation requires a little more data processing to achieve. It is claimed as a disadvantage of the policy-year method that the information is more out of date than in the calendar-year method because of the need to await the ends of the policy years. However, any trend in rates can be projected unless the experience is changing too rapidly or violently for this to be a reliable procedure, and in the latter case the calendar-year method would also give results that would be unreliable for future use. Moreover, there is in both methods a delay in processing because of the need to allow for the delay in reporting claims.

5.10 The calendar-year method is on the whole simpler because only premiums (if used as a unit of exposure) have to be apportioned for the parts of the policy years divided between two consecutive calendar years, and it is to be preferred unless there are reasons for requiring a reference to the policy year. It is possible that in employers' liability and third party policies, the total premium is sometimes not known until the end of the policy year; this happens when a deposit premium is paid at the beginning of the year on an estimated basis and an adjustment is made at the end of the year when the exact turnover or wage roll is ascertained. It will be frequently found in reinsurance that the premium is not fully received for perhaps three years.

5.11 In both the calendar-year and policy-year methods account must be taken of any changes in effective exposure during the policy year. There are not often cancellations during a policy year but there may be endorsements increasing sums insured, adding items to the schedule of insured properties or changing the vehicle covered by the policy. These kinds of changes have already been discussed in detail in the previous chapter (especially paras 4.45–4.49, 4.52, 4.124–4.125).

5.12 Where, as in most modern offices, the statistical system is computerised, each policy can be given an exact period of exposure within the year of investigation. If a computer is not available then it is possible to use an approximate method of aggregating periods of exposure. Methods generally in use are given below.

(1) *8ths basis*
If it is assumed that the annual policies written in a quarter are uniformly distributed over the quarter (with no bias in location according to size of premium etc.) then it may also be assumed that these policies, as a group, commence on average at the midpoint of the quarter. Thus, policies written in the consecutive quarters of the calendar year contribute $\frac{7}{8}$, $\frac{5}{8}$, $\frac{3}{8}$, $\frac{1}{8}$ years respectively to the exposure within that calendar year and $\frac{1}{8}$, $\frac{3}{8}$, $\frac{5}{8}$, $\frac{7}{8}$ respectively to the following calendar year. Endorsements which are effective for a fraction of a policy year are either ignored (on the assumption that they balance out) or some estimate of their overall effect must be made.

(2) *24ths basis*
The principle here is the same as for the 8ths basis, but a month rather than a quarter is used as the operative counting unit of time. Policies written in the month of May are assumed to contribute $\frac{15}{24}$ years to the current year and $\frac{9}{24}$ years to the following year. On the assumption of uniform distribution of policy dates this will give a closer approximation to the exact exposure count than the 8ths basis. If the assumption of uniform distribution does not hold then the 24ths basis may not be more accurate. Both methods will give biased results, the bias depending on the actual distribution of policy dates over the year. In order to conform to the insured's financial year, many commercial policies are renewed at 31 March or 31 December. To take an extreme example, a distribution of policies equally shared between these two dates would, on the 8ths basis lead to overstatement of exposure, in the year in which the policies were written, by $\frac{1}{8}$ year for each policy; and on the 24ths basis by $\frac{1}{24}$ year for each policy. In practice such an extreme case would not arise but it would nevertheless be a necessary precaution at least to examine the renewal date distribution of a random sample of policies in each category of exposure so that more appropriate approximation formulae can be designed to reflect these distributions.

(3) The census method

As in mortality investigations, a weighted average of counts of policies in force at terminal and intermediate dates can be used to calculate the total exposure. In general the census method is the simplest and quickest to use. The greater the number of censuses the closer the approximation to exact measurement, but the law of diminishing returns applies and there is usually insufficient gain of accuracy to justify the cost of carrying out censuses more frequently than quarterly, i.e. one at the beginning and end of each quarter giving equally spaced censuses over each calendar year with weights of $\frac{1}{8}, \frac{1}{4}, \frac{1}{4}, \frac{1}{4}, \frac{1}{8}$ in averaging. The census method has the advantage of implicitly taking due account of the effect of endorsements and also cancellations.

5.13 As an example of the calculation of exposures by the different methods, consider the following four motor policies.

	A	B	C	D
Renewal date	9.1.76	1.5.76		3.12.76
Inception date			23.9.76	
Claim date		15.2.76		
No-claim discount status:				
1976 renewal	2 years	2 years	1 year	2 years
1975 renewal	1 year	4 years	—	1 year

5.14 All other factors are assumed to be the same for each policy and unchanged throughout. The total exposure for the four policies in 1976 for each no-claim discount level and for all other factors together is shown in Table 5.1 for each of the four methods of calculation, exact, 8ths, 24ths and 5 quarterly censuses.

TABLE 5.1

Method	Exact	8ths		24ths		Census	
	days	years	days	years	days	years	days
No-claim discount level							
1 year	444	$1\frac{3}{8}$	502	$1\frac{7}{24}$	471	$1\frac{3}{8}$	502
2 years	630	$1\frac{5}{8}$	593	$1\frac{15}{24}$	593	$1\frac{5}{8}$	593
4 years	121	$\frac{3}{8}$	137	$\frac{9}{24}$	137	$\frac{3}{8}$	137
All other factors	1195	$3\frac{3}{8}$	1232	$3\frac{7}{24}$	1201	$3\frac{3}{8}$	1232

5.15 As might be expected, quarterly censuses give the same result as the application of the 8ths rule in straightforward cases (no endorsements and cancellations); as might be expected also the 24ths rule is more accurate than the other two approximations. The four cases have been deliberately designed to strain the accuracy of the approximate methods (even so the largest error is only 3%). In practice with a large number of policies and renewal dates well spread over the year, the errors in the approximate methods would be relatively insignificant. Nevertheless, given computer availability and proven software, exact counts would be quicker and more reliable especially if the risk group classification is at all complicated.

Claims

5.16 The risk classification is an important aspect when we come to consider the numerator of the claim rate. As in mortality investigations, it is a fundamental rule that the numerator and the denominator used in the calculation of the claim frequency should correspond. The coding used for claims must be the same as that used for exposures. We have already considered in Chapter 4 the precautions which ought to be taken to ensure this correspondence, e.g. the derivation of exposure and claim data from the same file. We have also stressed the need to have a firmly established definition of a claim and its reference date (normally the date of the incident giving rise to the claim). This definition must be consistent throughout the office statistical system and consistent with the use to which the calculated claim frequencies are to be put. Application of these rates in future experience will reproduce any errors or bias in the identification of past claims for the numerators of claim frequencies. Bias can arise from delays in notification and in processing into the filing system of claims, new policies, endorsements, cancellations and we have already discussed this difficulty in Chapter 4 (para. 4.61 and following paragraphs). It has been stressed that the input to the statistical system should be directly derived from day-to-day transactions as these take place so as to minimise the delay in recording policies, changes of status, claims, etc. It is also necessary to see that sufficient historical detail is retained on the file for each policy in order to ensure that it is possible to refer back to the true insurance position as it existed at an earlier date. This will make it possible to be sure that all contributions of the policy to exposure in different statuses (especially no-claim discount status in motor insurance) have been correctly counted.

5.17 This last point is important because in measuring claim frequencies according to no-claim discount category we require to classify the claims according to the no-claim discount category at the renewal date (or entry date) preceding the date of the accident, and, if using the census method, to classify the policies in force according to no-claim discount category at the renewal date (or entry date) preceding the census date.

5.18 In considering what to do about delays it is certainly not safe to ignore them on the assumption that the same proportional error will be introduced into both exposures and claims.

Delays in claim reporting

5.19 Delays in reporting claims can be very long—dependent on the class of insurance—so that claim frequencies cannot in the ordinary way be reliably estimated until sufficient time has elapsed to encompass this delay; at least until a date at which the number of incurred but not reported claims is likely to be a negligible proportion of the total incurred claims. While motor claims may nearly all be reported within three months of being incurred, employers' liability and products liability claims may not be reported until years after actual incurrence. Reinsurers suffer from delays in reporting claims because the direct insurer may initially expect settlement within his own retention, but may eventually have to call upon the reinsurers because the final claim amount proves to be greater than the initial estimate (either from monetary inflation prior to settlement or because injuries prove to be greater than initially diagnosed).

5.20 If allowing sufficient time to pass to encompass these delays means that the claim frequency analysis (counting all claims related to exposures) is too out-of-date to be relevant to current experience, then an attempt must be made to project the eventual total of claims for a particular year of origin from the durational distribution of those which have already occurred. The process is analogous to the use of the d_x column of the life table (up to age t) to estimate the value of l_0. The radix of the table l_0 (births in the life table) is the total claims in the origin year and the decrements d_x are the numbers of claims (incurred in year 0) but reported in development year x, $l_0 - l_x$ of claims $= \sum d_x$ being the total number reported by year x. The unit of time may be smaller than a year for shorter term classes of insurance. For motor insurance the unit may be a week.

5.21 Given a delay table, based on recent experience, of this form, the total claims N_0 to be expected when N_x have been reported in x units of time is

$$N_x \left(\frac{l_0}{l_0 - l_x} \right).$$

5.22 Table 5.2 is an example of the use of the method.

TABLE 5.2 Delay table

Unit of time (months)	l_x	d_x	Month of occurrence	Reported by December	Estimated total no. of claims
0	1000	556	January	974	974
1	444	284	February	964	964
2	160	53	March	955	955
3	107	37	April	1040	1044
4	70	28	May	1023	1033
5	42	15	June	969	986
6	27	10	July	937	963
7	17	7	August	989	1032
8	10	6	September	965	1038
9	4	4	October	893	1000
10	0		November	880	1047
			December	535	962
				11,124	11,998

The total claims arising from September (for which we have $N_4 = 965$) will be

$$N_0 = N_4 \cdot \left(\frac{l_0}{l_0 - l_4} \right) = 965 \cdot \left(\frac{1000}{930} \right) = 1038.$$

It will be seen that the estimated total claims arising from the year, at 11,998, is some 8% above the total reported by the end of the year.

5.23 The delay table would be monitored regularly to see that it continued to be appropriate. One way of doing this is to estimate from the table the number of later notifications which should follow from any month of origin. For example, if the 937 claims arising in July and reported by the end of the year represents

$$\frac{1}{l_0} \sum_{x=0}^{5} d_x$$

of the total, then the numbers of late reports arising from July, in the months of January, February and so on of the next year, would be expected to be d_6, d_7, d_8, etc. multiplied by ·963 or 10, 7, 6, 4. Obviously with such small numbers there would be large sampling deviation from expectation. To increase the size of the numbers the test would probably be of *all* late notifications in January, February etc. arising from the preceding year, against expectations. The total expectation for January (which the reader should check) will be 437 (s.e. 21 approx. if d_x is binomially distributed). A figure outside the range of two standard errors either way, i.e. 395–479 would suggest another look at the delay experience.

5.24 The calculation of the 'life table' for claim reporting is itself a straightforward mortality type investigation. Given a statistical system that can readily relate claims to their period of origin, the only problem is the choice of a unit of time which is neither so long that the table is too short for reliable prediction (i.e. inadequate subdivision so that all reports are exhausted in d_0 or d_1 for example) or so short that there is unnecessarily detailed arithmetic in the application of the table.

Multivariate analysis

5.25 Actuaries have always had to be acutely aware of the danger of trying to predict on the basis of mixed probability distributions, i.e. probability distributions derived from heterogeneous data. The danger is that the nature and extent of the heterogeneity may vary as between the populations from which the probabilities are derived and those to which they are applied. The oldest and simplest cautionary tale is of the danger of applying a crude death rate (all ages) derived from a retirement area like Bournemouth to a New Town area like Peterlee with relatively few older people outside the working age range. Even when age has been taken into account by the use of age-specific rates of mortality there is, in life assurance, the difference between the 'select' rates applicable to new entrants who have been recently medically examined and the 'aggregate' rates applicable to the generality of policyholders of larger duration in respect of whom such selection may be assumed to have lost its force.

5.26 In general insurance, especially motor insurance, there are many possible sources of heterogeneity with regard to risk of claim; we refer to these as risk factors. Some examples of risk factors have already been discussed in Chapter 4 and we have mentioned them earlier in this chapter (para. 5.6). If there are risk factors attaching to policies each at defined levels of intensity which differ from policy to policy, then an aggregate claim rate derived from one period of experience will not be applicable subsequently, if, as is likely, the mix of levels of the risk factors in the total portfolio of policies were to change. In the following paragraphs we shall refer specifically to motor insurance to illustrate methodology.

Motor insurance as an illustration

5.27 What we need therefore is a sub-division of the portfolio into a matrix of numbers $P_{i,j,k,...}$ of policies subject to risk factor 1 at level i, risk factor 2 at level j etc. and a matrix of claim frequency rates $f_{i,j,k,...}$ applicable to each combination of levels of risk factor. To derive this matrix of rates, standard methods of multivariate analysis may be used. These methods are treated fully in the statistical textbooks and can be dealt with only briefly here.

5.28 The first problem is to decide upon the extent of subdivision of experience that is necessary. The true risk factors are not all known and some that are thought certainly to be significant are not directly measurable because it would be impracticable to record the necessary data (e.g. actual mileage travelled). It would be necessary to consider the likely risk factors and to, then, decide whether their levels can be recorded on policy files or whether some other factors which are directly recordable can be used to indicate their levels. The experience of underwriters will be invaluable in these considerations which are largely empirical. The larger the number of risk factors to be investigated, the more complicated the investigation, the smaller the numbers in individual cells of the matrices (so that broad groupings required may defeat the object of analysis) and the less the predictive reliability of the results. As in similar statistical exercises in other fields this is the stage when hard thinking in concert with experienced underwriters can bring valuable dividends in simplicity and practicality. Possible candidates are given in para. 4.120 of Chapter 4.

Levels of risk factor

5.29 Even when the number of factors has been reduced to the minimum considered to be essential, there is a further problem. Unless a particular risk factor is capable of being graded (and measured) at increasing levels of intensity, its use in a rating structure will be limited to a 'present' and 'absent' role. There will be an unknown element of heterogeneity in either group; to put it another way, the factor is unlikely to be more than a rather crude discriminant of risk (this does not mean that the differences between the two groups will be small). The following paragraphs may make this need for 'levels' of risk factors clearer.

A model of risk variation

5.30 To provide as much information as possible to enable the variation of risk associated with the different factors to be fully taken account of in rating, it would be desirable to construct a model of the risk process which expresses the departure of the claim frequency of a specific group from the overall mean frequency as a function of the quantified intensity of presence of the risk factors that are identifiable. Such a model may be *additive*:

$$f_{i,j,k,l,m,\ldots} = \mu + a_i + b_j + c_k + d_l + e_m \cdots \quad (5.1)$$

where $f_{i,j,k,l,m,\ldots}$ is the claim frequency for the subgroup of policies at levels i,j,k,l,m, etc. respectively of risk factors A, B, C, D, E, etc., and a_i, b_j, c_k, d_l, e_m, etc. are the values of the parameters associated with the factors and expressing the departure of $f_{i,j,k,l,m,\ldots}$ from μ, a base frequency when no risk factors are operating; or it may be *multiplicative*:

$$f_{i,j,k,l,m,\ldots} = \mu \cdot a_i \cdot b_j \cdot c_k \cdot d_l \cdot e_m \cdots \quad (5.2)$$

(the parameters having different values from those of formula 5.1 above).

The multiplicative model means of course that $\log f$ is expressible as an additive model. Johnson & Hey (1971) have used an additive model while Bailey & Simon (1960) and Mehring (1964) have used a multiplicative form.

5.31 The usual procedure for fitting such a model to the values of $f_{i,j,k,l,m,\ldots}$ derived from experience, is to apply multiple regression techniques. These are set out in standard statistics or econometric text books. The first step is to derive a matrix of the zero order correlations between each pair of the risk factors A, B, C, D, E, etc. This enables the degree of independence of the factors to be assessed. Clearly there would be no point in introducing the further complication of a fifth factor E if it is so highly correlated with B as to be adequately represented by B; b_j would account for the greater part of the influence of E, and since the 'free' variation of E (undetermined by B) would be small, e_m would be of little significance. This first step then is a precaution against unnecessary complication of the model.

5.32 The next step is to fit the model by least squares, i.e. by minimising $\sum (C - n \cdot f)^2 / n$ where n is the exposure, and C is the number of claims and the summation is carried out over all $i, j, k, l, m. \ldots$ This gives rise to a set of normal equations which may be solved to yield values of the parameters a, b, c, d, e. Standard computer programmes are available for the necessary matrix inversion. It is then possible to produce a standard table to give expected claim frequencies for different combinations of the various risk factors. In practice as Johnson & Hey (*loc. cit.*) point out it is advisable continually to refine the model by comparing actual with expected claims and adjusting the parameters to conform to experience. Johnson & Hey also point out that having obtained the parameters it is possible to increase all the a_i and decrease all the b_j simultaneously by the same constant without affecting f. They found it convenient to introduce the constant parameter μ and to make it equal to the overall claim frequency of the portfolio, and to adjust the values of a_i, b_j etc. so that the total contribution from each factor is approximately zero. This is likely to remain true unless the composition of the portfolio changes markedly.

5.33 Up to this point we have been talking of the total claims frequency of a particular group without considering whether the claims are produced by a number of policyholders having one claim each, or a few policyholders having several claims, i.e. we have not considered the possible heterogeneity of a group which might be a mixture of groups with different underlying claim risks.

5.34 The mixture would not be a problem in itself provided that its constituency remained stable and the average experience thus remained also stable. No group however well defined in terms of the separation of known risk factors is ever pure. We may use our model to reduce heterogeneity but we cannot entirely eliminate it. The problem lies in the likelihood that the heterogeneity may change from year to year thus gradually invalidating the claim frequency model.

5.35 Johnson & Hey (*loc. cit.*) have suggested that heterogeneity can be examined by looking at the relative frequencies of 0, 1, 2, ... etc. claims by an individual policyholder during a defined interval of time. As might be expected, such a distribution is highly skew. The following figures are taken from the paper by Johnson & Hey:

Number of claims in year	Frequency among those exposed throughout the year
0	370,412
1	46,545
2	3,935
3	317
4	28
5	3
All	421,240
Mean	·1317
Variance	·1385

This distribution fits closely to a negative binomial with the same mean and variance. This might also be expected since in early work on what was then supposed to be accident proneness, the negative binomial was developed as the appropriate distribution for the relative frequency of accidents to an individual person given that the risk varied from person to person but for an individual person remained constant over the period of observation (Greenwood & Yule 1920). The concept of accident proneness has largely been abandoned but the concept of a risk distribution remains. It has been shown that the risk distribution associated with the negative binomial claim number distribution is of the Pearson Type III form (also highly skew).

5.36 Examination of the multiple claim distribution from which the risk distribution can be inferred (Delaporte 1964 and 1965, Beard 1968) will show the way in which heterogeneity is changing over time. One difficulty in British experience is that since the frequency of multiple claims is very low there is considerable error in the estimation of the variance of the claim distribution even from a large portfolio. For this reason recondite mathematical treatment would not be justified. It is probable that superimposed plotting of the observed distributions would reveal significant changes; at least sufficiently to indicate whether mathematical analysis would be of practical value.

Claims amount distributions

5.37 We must now consider the second of the two components of cost referred to in paragraph 5.2, the average *amount* of claim. Reliable estimation of the average amount of claim depends upon the adequate exploration of the claim amount distribution—also an awkward skew distribution affected by delay in claim reporting.

5.38 Knowledge of the shape of the claim amount distribution is not only necessary for the calculation of the true cost of insurance but it has important subsidiary applications. Examination of the lower tail will enable calculation to be made of the appropriate deduction for 'excess' restrictions for which the policyholder has opted; examination of the upper tail is necessary for decision about retention before reinsurance.

5.39 There is an immediate problem of heterogeneity. In motor insurance the distributions of claim size arising from own damage, third party property damage and bodily injuries respectively, are different. The claim for serious disablement may be many times the cost of replacement or repairs of a car. Digressing for a moment to other classes of general insurance, it is obvious that the distribution of fire claims in commercial insurance will have a much larger upper tail than in householder comprehensive insurance. If the mix of types of claim is likely to be changing it may be necessary to subdivide the claim frequency by type of claim and to combine claim frequency specific for type with the approximate claim amount distribution for the specific type of claim. Apart from the extra work there are no additional theoretical problems. We shall return later to the claim amount distributions in other classes of insurance but for the present we shall continue to consider motor insurance.

5.40 At this point the reader should refresh his knowledge of the data considerations set out in paras 4.61–4.68 and in some later paragraphs of Chapter 4, especially the caution about consistency of treatment of data.

5.41 While for cost purposes interest lies in the average claim amount, it will be clear, when we come to discuss technical reserves in Chapter 10, that we also need to know the amount of dispersion of claim amounts about the average. It is therefore necessary to establish the shape of the claim amount distribution. Since this distribution is a right-skewed distribution* of money amounts a number of distributions, in common use in financial statistics, suggest themselves.

Types of claim amount distributions

5.42 *The log Normal distribution* has been found to be appropriate in many general insurance claim amount distributions. If the cost of a claim be x, the log Normal distribution arises where $\log x$ is Normally distributed with mean μ and standard deviation σ

$$f(x) = \frac{1}{\sigma\sqrt{2\pi}} \frac{1}{x} \exp \frac{-(\log x - \mu)^2}{2\sigma^2}$$

where $x \geq 0$, $\sigma > 0$ and $-\infty < \mu < \infty$ (clearly in practice the mean must always be greater than zero).

5.43 This Normal distribution may be derived theoretically from a situation in which the variable x is dependent on the *additive* effects of a number of factors; it follows that the log Normal distribution implies that $\log x$ depends on factors with additive effects or that x depends on a number of factors the effects of which are multiplicative. The log Normal distribution is skew to the right. It has a single mode at $x = e^{\mu - \sigma^2}$ a mean of $e^{\mu + \sigma^2/2}$ and variance $e^{2\mu + \sigma^2} \cdot (e^{\sigma^2} - 1)$. It has the disadvantage that it does not lend itself easily to mathematical development (Aitchinson & Brown 1959).

5.44 The fitting of a log Normal distribution is most easily accomplished by graphical methods. The cumulative frequency function $F(x)$ if plotted on log-probability paper is effectively a plot of $F(\log x)$ on a probability scale and since $\log x$ is Normally distributed this must be a straight line. If therefore the observed cumulative frequency is plotted on log

---

* This statement is generally true but in some instances where the range of claim amount is limited, e.g. glass claims under a householder's policy, a fairly symmetrical distribution might emerge and a Normal distribution might be a convenient and adequate approximation.

probability paper then if the points appear to lie about a straight line it is likely that the log Normal distribution applies. The parameters of this distribution may then be quickly derived by drawing a straight line through the data. A more rigorous fit may be obtained either by using moments in the usual way or by fitting a Normal distribution to log x and transferring back to frequencies of x. Examples are given in Beard (1959 and 1964) for motor insurance and in Ferrara (1971) for fire insurance.

5.45 *The Pareto distribution*, $f(x) = a \cdot c^a \cdot x^{-a-1}$ where $0 < c \leqslant x < \infty$ and $a > 1$ is commonly used in distributions of income and wealth and therefore suggests itself for claim amount distribution (since claim amount is to some extent correlated with wealth as represented by the sum insured). The Pareto distribution is also skew to the right and even more skew than the log Normal distribution; it is sometimes preferred for that reason. The moments are readily computed but it has to be remembered that the nth moment exists only if $a > n+1$.

$$\text{The mean} = \frac{ac}{(a-1)} \text{ so that } a > 1$$

$$\text{and the variance} = \frac{ac^2}{a-2} - \left(\frac{ac}{a-1}\right)^2 \text{ where } a > 2$$

The distribution can easily be fitted therefore by the method of moments. Examples in fire insurance are given in Anderson (1971) and Benckert & Sternberg (1957). The constraint that a must exceed 2 is sometimes a real difficulty. Although arithmetical results for example, in reinsurance, are not greatly affected by taking $a > 2$, more use in recent experience is made of truncated distributions (see below).

5.46 *Other distributions* The log Normal and Pareto distributions both have the disadvantage of having infinite range and this is not appropriate for all data. In the real world there is a finite limit to the size of a claim, certainly in motor insurance and, except in catastrophe, for most other classes of general insurance. Fitting a curve with an infinitely long tail

THE RISK PREMIUM 133

to data which represents, in reality, a truncated distribution (even if extended at the tail) means some distortion at the early part of the tail where claim sizes are large so that the distortion may be important. Some work has been done and is being done with truncated distributions but mathematically such distributions are difficult to handle. Attention has turned to other distributions of a log type but with finite range; for example Beard (1957) has used a log-Beta distribution for fire claims and has compared the fit obtained with that of the log Normal.

Simulation

5.47 The possible applicability of a particular claim amount distribution to the experience of a company can be tested by computer simulation (Benjamin 1966). In effect the distribution is stored in the computer and sampled randomly (the random number generation being also performed by the computer). In this way the computer can produce a large set of realistic claims data, representing several years of experience, in a few minutes of central processing time. The results may be compared with actual experience. It is also possible, using simulation methods, to see the effect of making changes in the basic parameters of a given distribution possibly to make some provision for known changes in the portfolio. This procedure is also a way of fitting a distribution, i.e. the parameters are roughly estimated, perhaps from mathematical work on earlier experience and are then successively adjusted to achieve closer correspondence with current experience.

Large claims

5.48 The numbers of claims occurring in the upper tail of the claims amount distribution are small even within a large experience so that there is the likelihood of fluctuation from year to year. In any one year the occurrence of a large claim (so large as to be likely to occur once in a period of several years) will make the average claim differ considerably from expectation. To put it another way this means that in a group experience of moderate dimensions (and it has to be borne in mind that the total experience is divided to take account of various risk factors), the estimation of mean claim will have low precision. Some method has to be found to improve the precision by reducing the effect of the chance bunching of large claims in a small cell of the claims frequency. It would be possible to avoid the problem by calculating the overall average claim amount over the whole experience and applying this average within each risk factor group. Apart from casting away important information, this ignores the known fact that some risk levels are associated with a relatively high incidence of large claims. Distributing large claims proportionately according to numbers of claims in each risk level would not do because a chance low claims frequency would attract too few large claims (large claims would be defined as above a certain size). The normal approach to this kind of problem in statistical practice is to weight the data with factors that are inversely proportionate to the sampling errors associated therewith (commonly the reciprocal of the standard error is used). Hey (1970) has made experiments in which large claims are weighted by factors which get smaller as the claim amount increases; this also has the effect of weighting inversely to the error though not necessarily on a one to one basis. The results are encouraging. Reference might also be made to Flack *et al.* (1971) for a method which concerns itself with excessive claims (i.e. $> \mu + 2\sigma$)

Delays in claims settlement

5.49 We have already discussed in relation to claim frequency the problem of delay in reporting of claims. There is a further element of delay in that claims are not settled instantly on being reported. The damage may take some time to assess; perhaps only weeks in motor own damage claims, but possibly years in liability claims from motor or employers' liability policies. For personal accident capital payments and glass payment, the delay may only be counted in days. Where the delay is short, the statistical analysis of claim amount can safely be deferred for a short while until all claims have been settled without risk of the results being out of date. Where the delay is long it is not possible to defer statistical analysis without the results becoming too out of date to be applicable to current experience. Unfortunately, it is, not unexpectedly, the larger claims which are the most delayed in settlement. The figures in Table 5.3 are provided by Scurfield (1968) in respect of comprehensive policies on private cars.

TABLE 5.3 Average cost of claims settlement in 1967

Year of occurrence of claim	Own damage payments (£)	Third party payments — Property damage (£)	Third party payments — Bodily injury (£)	All payments combined (£)
1967	70	38	26	61
1966	80	52	72	75
1965 or earlier	108	190	323	218
All years	74	51	78	72

5.50 As well as showing the increase in average payment with increasing delay, these figures also demonstrate the need to distinguish different types of claims in motor insurance.

5.51 For the limited purpose of considering relativities between risk levels it might be possible to limit the analysis to claims settled within a specified period. This is tantamount to assuming that, if it were known, the grossing factor to estimate the amount of total settlements from the amounts of those made in the period, would be the same for each risk level; there would be some error in this but within the stated limited objective it might be acceptable. For fixing the absolute level of premiums however (and this is what we are considering in this chapter) we need to know the grossing up factors and this method would not yield the factors. It may be possible as suggested by Scurfield (*loc. cit.*) to assume that the payments made within the year of claim incurrence as a proportion of the total amounts in respect of all claims originating in the year, is constant and to derive this proportion from earlier experience, but this assumption would not be justified if the portfolio were known to be changing significantly from one year to another or if the rate of inflation were changing.

5.52 It is possible to use a 'life table' approach as for the delays in claim reporting. The claims incurred in a year are treated as 'births' and the settlements of claims as 'deaths'.

If N = total number of claims incurred in the year
d_t = proportion of claims settled t years after incurrence
c_t = estimated average cost of claims settled t years after incurrence

then the total expected claims cost is

$$N . \sum_{t=1}^{\infty} d_t . \bar{c}_t .$$

The values of d_0 and $\bar{c}_0$ will already be known and are not estimates as are the other terms in the summation. In estimating $\bar{c}_t$ from past experience some allowance must be made for inflation and for any other secular factors affecting the claim amount, e.g. court awards.

5.53 The treatment of the run-off of claims from an accounting standpoint is dealt with fully in Chapter 10 on technical reserves.

Time trends

5.54 In making estimates of both claims frequency and claim amounts from past experience it is important to look for evidence of changes in experience over time especially if these show a persistent trend which should then be projected forward. Inflation is one such trend which has already been referred to. Economic conditions affect the level of industrial output and the dimensions of stocks so that fire claims may be affected both in frequency and amount. Changes in the portfolio are also important. If the portfolio is growing it will be essential to keep all statistical analyses on a year (or period) of origin basis since each year's generation of claims could be larger than that of the previous year. The gross average of amounts of settlements in a given period would be depressed by the larger generation of recently incurred claim settlements which are smaller than the more delayed payments arising from earlier and smaller generations of claims. The reverse is true if the portfolio is declining. As indicated in paragraph 5.52 above there is also the influence of court awards. In the discussion of the Johnson & Hey paper (*loc. cit.*) Beard referred to an annual upward drift of motor claims (apart from that due to monetary inflation) of 5% in the period 1963-9, a large part of which was attributable to the rise in legal awards as the courts endeavoured to adjust to current monetary levels.

The risk premium

5.55 We are now in a position to calculate the risk premium for a particular type of claim at a particular risk level in a particular class of insurance by multiplying together the specific claim frequency and the specific average claim cost.

BIBLIOGRAPHY

AITCHISON, J. & BROWN, J. A. C. *The Log-Normal Distribution*, Cambridge University Press, 1957.

ANDERSON, H. An Analysis of the Development of the Fire Losses in Northern Countries After the Second World War. *The ASTIN Bulletin*, 1971, **6,** Part 1.

BAILEY, R. A. & SIMON, L. J. Two Studies in Automobile Insurance Rate-Making. *The ASTIN Bulletin*, 1960, **1.**

BEARD, R. E. Analytical Expressions of Some of the Risks Involved in General Insurance. *Transactions of the 15th International Congress of Actuaries*, 1957.

BEARD, R. E. Some Statistical Aspects of Non-life Insurance Statistics. *Journal of the Institute of Actuaries Students' Society*, 1959, **13.**

BEARD, R. E. Some Statistical Problems arising from the Transaction of Motor Insurance Business. *Journal of the Institute of Actuaries Students' Society*, 1964, **17,** 279.

BEARD, R. E. Some Observations on No-claim Bonus Schemes in Motor Insurance. *Transactions of the 18th International Congress of Actuaries*, 1968, **II,** 345.

BENCKERT, L.G. & STERNBERG, I. Distribution of Fire Damage Amount. *Transactions of the 15th International Congress of Actuaries*, 1957.

BENJAMIN, B. & HAYCOCKS, H. W. *The Analysis of Mortality and other Actuarial Statistics*, Cambridge University Press, 1970.

BENJAMIN, S. Putting Computers on to Actuarial Work. *Journal of the Institute of Actuaries*, 1966, **92,** 134.

DELAPORTE, P. J. Principes de Tarification de l'Assurance Automobile par la Prime Modelée sur la Risque. *Transactions of the 17th International Congress of Actuaries*, 1964, **III,** 560.

DELAPORTE, P. J. Tarification du Risque Individuel d'Accidents d'Automobiles par la Prime Modelée sur la Risque. *The ASTIN Bulletin*, 1965, **III,** 251.

FERRARA, G. Distributions des Sinistres Incendie selon leur cout. *The ASTIN Bulletin*, 1971, **6,** Part 1.

FLACK, D., SCHLUNG, J. & STRAUSS, J. An Analysis of German Fire Loss of Profits Statistics. *Blatter der Deutschen Gesellschaft für Versicherungsmathematik*, 1971, **10,** Part 2.

GREENWOOD, M. & YULE, C. U. An Inquiry into the Frequency Distributions of Multiple Happenings. *Journal of the Royal Statistical Society*, 1920, **83,** 233–79.

HEY, G. B. Statistics and Non-life Insurance. *Journal of the Royal Statistical Society "A"*, 1970, **133,** Part 1.

JOHNSON, P. D. Actuarial Aspects of Motor Insurance. *Journal of the Institute of Actuaries Students' Society*, 1968, **18,** Part 3.

JOHNSON, P. D. & HEY, G. B. Statistical Studies in Motor Insurance. *Journal of the Institute of Actuaries*, 1971, **97,** 199.

MEHRING, J. Die Versicherung von Kraftfahrschaden in der Bundesrepublik Deutschland. *Transactions of the 16th International Congress of Actuaries*, 1960, **B1,** 5.

MEHRING, J. Ein Mathematisches Hilfsmittel für Statistikund Tariffragen in der Kraftfahrtversicherung. *Blatter der Deutschen Gesellschaft für Versicherungsmathematik*, 1964, **VII.**

SCURFIELD, H. H. Motor Insurance Statistics. *Journal of the Institute of Actuaries Students' Society*, 1968, **18,** Part 3.

CHAPTER 6

EXPENSES IN GENERAL INSURANCE

6.1 By the nature of the business, expenses account for a relatively high proportion of general insurance premiums. The work involved in underwriting, paying claims and in servicing is high—proportionately much greater than in life assurance. In many classes, claims are fairly frequent but liability is not always clearly defined and this leads to heavy claims expenses. In other classes, the likelihood of a claim may be slight but the sum at risk is large leading to extensive underwriting costs. Servicing the insured is expensive especially when the risk is often altering during the year. This can lead to frequent endorsements to the policy together with appropriate premium revisions though there is a tendency to make changes coincide with the renewal date if possible. At the renewal date for contracts, such as those in motor insurance, which provide indemnity with no fixed monetary sums insured, a regular revision of premium rates is necessary to match inflation and experience. For other policies, e.g. fire, written on the basis of a maximum sum at risk, endorsements are necessary from time to time to increase the amount of cover and a revision of rates will occasionally be needed here too if claims costs outpace the rate of inflation. With most of the contracts on an annual basis and particularly when insurance costs are rising with inflation, there is a tendency for the insured to look around the market at renewal each year. This means considerable additional expense to the industry as a whole both in the transfer of risks and with abortive quotations, without any real increase in the total business written by the market.

6.2 Since expenses form such a high proportion of premiums, it is clear that a proper subdivision of expenses is essential both for considering the profitability of different sectors of the individual company's portfolio and for incorporating expenses as a factor in premium rating. Although much work has been undertaken in respect of detailed consideration of underwriting statistics, it is only in recent years that the allocation of expenses to individual classes of insurance has been considered in detail. Where companies allocate expenses to classes in proportion to premiums it may give a false appreciation of the profitability of different classes and also give opportunities to other companies to gain profitable business by charging lower premiums for those risks which were over-priced by the market as a result of the false expenses allocation. The analysis of expenses by class, by type of risk and by size of risk has not been fully developed and much work remains to be done in this area—this is probably as true of long term business as it is for general insurance. In addition, considerable further attention needs to be paid to both the theory and practice of pricing policy, including marginal costing and its implications for incorporating expenses in premiums.

Types of expenses

6.3 The general insurance industry is normally considered to be labour intensive. Notwithstanding the use of computers the major part of expenses arise from salaries and other staff costs. It is generally accepted that of all the management expenses approximately 50% is incurred in salaries, wages and similar payments whilst up to another 20% arises from other benefits made available to staff, including pension schemes, house mortgage schemes, etc. and such items as national insurance contributions. Approximately 10% of expenses is absorbed by property costs. The balance is split amongst other expense headings such as computers, postages, telephones, general management expenses, etc. It is clear, therefore, that any allocation of expenses to individual classes must concentrate in the first place on the allocation of staff costs since a small error here is much more important than a similar error in other expense areas. (The percentages quoted in this paragraph are reasonably realistic for the major composite offices with large branch networks but patterns could vary for companies operating on a different basis.)

Allocation to classes

6.4 The first objective is to split the total expenses incurred in such a way that the office can ascertain the past profitability of each individual class of insurance. Premiums, claims and commission should all be known specifically for each class of insurance and thus the allocation of expenses is needed to complete the picture. As well as providing a year-by-year picture of underwriting results of the different classes of business, the figures can be used as a basis for forecasting future results. Allocation of expenses to classes of insurance is also essential as a step in the determination of the loading of future premiums.

6.5 If we consider the operations of an insurance office whether it is on a branch system with many staff employed around the country or on a centralised system with only a limited number of staff mainly at head office, it will be clear that the majority of staff will be directly concerned with the undertaking of insurance business. The first need, therefore, is to analyse the time they spend on each class of business and thus obtain a suitable allocation of their salaries to the different classes. For some staff, e.g. motor engineers, fire surveyors, it may seem relatively clear that the whole of their time is spent on a particular class of business though even here problems can arise since, for example, motor engineers' time needs to be allocated between private car insurance and commercial vehicle insurance. For staff working in departments dealing with several classes of business, individuals can be asked to estimate the proportion of their time spent on each class and these figures can be used to apportion all the expenses between classes. A sampling procedure can be devised whereby the staff are asked to record the time spent on each job over a short period. Some weighting system will be necessary to take into account the different grades of staff employed on these various parts of the business and obviously the sample needs to be checked to see that it is reasonably representative between branches of the company's operations and that the time is reasonably representative of the year's work. Such time sheets not only give an analysis of salaries which can be used in allocating other expenses such as pension fund contributions which are directly related to salaries (though usually allocated separately according to sex), but can also be used for allocating expenses directly related to the individual and the time he or she spends on each class of business, e.g. national insurance contributions. Furthermore, property expenses can be apportioned to the individual in proportion to floor space occupied and the individual's time sheets can be used to allocate this to different classes of business.

6.6 Problems arise with off-line departments, e.g. postal, investments, staff and marketing which act as service departments to the whole company. There are two approaches which can be used in dealing with these departments. The first is to exclude them from the allocation of expenses and to consider the 'contribution' of each class of business defined as 'earned premium less incurred claims and commission and direct costs clearly associated with the particular class' (see para. 6.15). Any positive 'contribution' will help to meet the expenses of such departments. However, the whole of these overheads must be met somehow and the danger is that each class will be expected to make a 'contribution' based on the size of the class—size being traditionally considered as equivalent to premium income—which is tantamount to allocating such expenses to classes in proportion to premium income. This can be taken as one acceptable method of looking at overheads but an alternative method is to allocate these expenses to different classes on an arbitrary basis that appears reasonable and commands general agreement.

6.7 There will always at the end of the day be some expenses which it is not possible to allocate other than arbitrarily but the following gives examples of bases which may be appropriate to some of these departments.

1 *Postal department*—the number of policies should be a reasonable measure unless certain classes of business generate a great deal of correspondence per policy.

2 *Staff department*—numbers of male/female staff in each class of business may provide a basis. One might want to treat each sex separately as the staff turnover of females is usually the greater.

3 *Data processing*—it is likely that machine usage (including depreciation) can be directly costed; if not numbers of policies (renewals) may be used. Salaries of staff and other expenses could then be spread by machine usage but the cost of special projects such as setting up a new system ought to be known and should be directly allocated.

4 *Investment department expenses and general management expenses*—the expenses incurred in the investment department are clearly directly attributable to investments and it is, therefore, reasonable to charge these expenses against investment income. General management expenses will be partially in respect of work in the investment area and partially in respect of controlling the organisation—in some companies a large proportion of management time is spent on investment work. An allocation between the time spent on investment matters and the rest is probably best obtained by an *ad hoc* assessment of how the management are spending their time. The breakdown of the balance of general management expenses to individual classes of insurance can only be on a completely arbitrary basis, although it is important to maintain consistency from year to year.

Functional costing

6.8 The method described above of allocating expenses to classes can absorb a considerable amount of effort by staff and, therefore, becomes difficult to undertake on a regular basis. In addition, if repeated, say annually, it is quite likely that there will be variations between the results obtained which would be too large to be acceptable for practical purposes. Such variations can arise from sampling errors and regularly repeating the costing process can be expected to lead to a falling off in the level of importance attached to it by staff which in turn can produce inaccurate results. An additional problem is that staff will tend to round off estimates of time. This practice has a significantly distorting effect where small amounts of time are involved and this generally leads to an over-estimate of the expenses for the smaller classes.

6.9 In order to avoid these problems a system of functional costing can be used which will ensure reasonable stability in the allocation of expenses from year to year. The objective is to express the various costs in total, by a function of one or more easily monitored parameters. As a first stage the expenses of the off-line departments are split among the line departments in accordance with agreed percentages which would remain unaltered unless the company's structure has been changed radically. The total estimate of expenses for the department becomes E_ℓ. This bulk total must then be allocated between the classes of business written by the line department.

6.10 To accomplish this an index system is set up incorporating such items as number of renewals, new proposals, claims paid, endorsements, enquiries, etc. Each constituent would be weighted in some agreed manner which may well vary between classes and the share of the expenses borne by any class of business will then be $E_\ell \cdot I_c / \sum I_c$ where I_c is the numerical value of the index for class of business c, and the summation is over all classes.

6.11 The construction of the index, including the weightings, may be somewhat subjective but will be based on a full investigation of expenses incurred by classes as indicated above. Once set up the subjectiveness will not change in character from year to year. The machinery to monitor the business and build up the index will generally be available from a centralised computer system which in most offices is used for providing renewal notices, recording claims payments, endorsements, etc.

Pricing

6.12 In considering expenses so far we have looked at how they should be allocated to the different classes of insurance in ascertaining the profitability of those classes. We now turn to consider how expenses can be included in the premiums to be charged for different risks and a number of different concepts arise.

6.13 One conceptual problem which arises in pricing is probably best illustrated by considering in the first instance pricing of a consumer product. An industrial firm in deciding the price to be charged for the product before the addition of the wholesalers' and retailers' margins needs to consider the cost of producing the goods and the price the market will bear. In looking at the cost of producing the goods he will normally split his expenses between fixed and variable expenses; the latter being defined as those which vary directly with the volume of the product produced whilst the former are those made up of all other expenses which vary little with the volume of the product (unless there are major changes in volume). Raw materials are clearly variable expenses and in most branches of industry the costs of the labour force directly involved in producing the goods are also variable in view of the traditional practice of laying off men at times when production is low and increasing the labour force level when high production is required. On the other hand, buildings, machinery and employees in 'staff' positions are normally considered to be fixed expenses.

6.14 The significance of this becomes important when consideration is given to how the price should be built up to maximise profit. In business economics generally, price less the variable expenses is normally defined as contribution. The aim in pricing policy is to produce the maximum contribution and this may mean that the best result can come from a high price and a relatively low turnover, or from reducing the price and thus taking a lower contribution per item but increasing the turnover sufficiently for the total contribution to be higher. The contribution itself must meet all the expenses of a fixed nature and the balance after meeting these expenses is available for the profit of the company. It should be clear that since the fixed expenses will not vary during the year, irrespectively of the volume of the business, maximising contribution contributes to the maximisation of profit.

6.15 Translating these terms to apply to the insurance field it is clear that claims and commission are variable expenses. Advertising expenses can also be considered as variable costs—to the extent that the money spent results in a proportionate increase in business. However, it is not the normal practice to vary the labour force in the short-term in line with movements in business written. Indeed, a number of conditions militate against this. Firstly, the labour force is in most cases spread round the country; secondly, the amount of training necessary before a person can play a useful part is considerable, and thirdly, most insurance companies can write a significant amount of additional business (in 'real money' terms) without any need to increase the work force (and correspondingly if they wrote less business would not necessarily vary the work force). It will be seen from this that expenses as normally considered in insurance are virtually all in the category of fixed expenses for pricing policy purposes. Thus the aim of pricing policy in insurance should be to maximise contribution taken as earned premiums less incurred claims and commission, subject to the constraints imposed by the other aims of the organisation, e.g. market share.

6.16 The problem in insurance must, of course, be to decide what price to charge in the light of market conditions for each individual class and type of risk to produce the maximum contribution from the business. It is assumed that the expected value of claims is known and that the risk premium required to cover this would be charged. It is also assumed that commission will be charged directly in relation to the premium and the only other element in pricing is in respect of expenses and the profit margin. The decisions involved here will be crucial in operational terms and need to take into account the price-flexibility of the market and the likely action of competitors. At the same time account will be taken of the knowledge obtained from costing of the allocation of expenses to classes which shows how, in the past, staff time has been absorbed in handling the business. This will be a guide for the future in view of the high proportion of business which is renewed each year.

6.17 The overall pricing policy must be, as stated, to maximise the contribution (taken as earned premiums less incurred claims and commission) over all the classes. In addition, it is clearly necessary for the ruling rates in the market for each class of insurance to be considered to ensure that the rates produced are competitive and if, for example, a rate is too high for one individual class of insurance, it may be necessary to reduce the rate to market level subject to the need to obtain some contribution from that class towards meeting overall expenses. The company in deciding its pricing policy must ensure that overhead expenses are met and must produce a reasonable margin of profit from the operation of the total portfolio. In the marketing strategy it may be willing to take a lower contribution from some classes than others in order to maximise the overall profit.

Claims expenses

6.18 The expenses incurred in handling claims need separate consideration. The practice adopted by the individual company in handling claims will vary depending upon its method of operation and also by class of business. It is traditional within the general insurance market for most of the larger claims in the fire and consequential loss market (including the fire section of household business) to be handled by independent loss adjusters and it will thus be normal for their expenses to be included as part of claims. Similarly, legal fees incurred in connection with claims in any class of business will be treated as part of claims. Where companies depend on services provided from outside the company the expenses thereof will again naturally be charged to claims. Companies will, however, employ their own claims staff, including motor engineers, and most now consider it appropriate to make a transfer to claims of all expenses incurred in handling claims so as to put them on a comparable basis between classes. The estimation of the right claims expense transfer to make is usually derived from costing exercises referred to above in paragraph 6.16.

Pricing at class level

6.19 Whilst the overall policy for pricing is to maximise contribution, at the individual class level account will be taken of the expenses allocated to the class in the past. Naturally the direct expenses have to be covered by the premiums before any margin is available to meet overheads and profits from the class. It should be realised, however, that the direct expenses allocated to the class in the past are only a guide in deciding upon the amount of expenses which will be allocated in the future.

6.20 In looking at an individual class of insurance it may seem obvious to consider in the first place the expense ratio. This is normally defined as the ratio of the expenses incurred during a financial period to the net written premiums in that period. It is an apparently simple step to assume that the same expense ratio applies to each section of a class and indeed to each individual risk. In practice this has been the traditional method of taking into account expenses in the general insurance field though it is quite clear that such an approach which ignores the effect of the size of the risk or the level of the risk premium is unlikely to be very accurate. It is necessary, therefore, to consider what part of the expenses can be directly related to the size of the risk and thus should vary with the sum insured and what part should be fixed for each policy. For those expenses which increase with the risk it is possible if the variation is linear to produce a formula based on number of policies and sums insured which produces the right expense element for such items. Even if the variation is non-linear it will normally be possible to use a formula of this kind which is sufficiently accurate for practical purposes.

6.21 Stating the problem, however, is only the first stage and it is necessary to provide some solutions. The problem is well illustrated in relation to private car insurance, most of which is written on a premium per vehicle basis. It might be thought that in this case it would be relatively easy to incorporate the expenses into the premiums on a per policy basis but real difficulties arise in respect of no-claim discount. It will be clear that a considerable part of the expense is incurred irrespective of whether no-claim discount is being allowed on the policy and therefore, should be outside the no-claim discount calculation but so far no company is known to have a premium calculated in this way. In addition, the expense cost which is incurred on some of the lower rated cars in the lower rated geographical areas would look to be a very high proportion of the premium which could be unacceptable in market terms—indeed, one could be completely priced out of the local market and thus obtain a nil 'contribution'.

Incorporation into premium structure

6.22 The pricing approach shows us that the premium received for a risk must cover claims and variable expenses and also provide a contribution towards fixed costs. The total of these contributions must exceed fixed charges for the business to be profitable. (Note that for the present discussion the return from investment is ignored.) How then do we fix the premium to take account of these factors?

6.23 For any risk the cost of claims cannot be known at the time the risk commences. The underwriters will need to obtain an estimate of the cost to be expected—from statistics and/or general intuition. In the expressions set out below the phrase 'claims cost' is used to mean this expected claims cost plus a loading for risk fluctuations. This loading may be based on the standard deviation of risks though in practice this is difficult to estimate and the loading will be based on more general considerations. If the claim cost for a certain risk is R and the variable costs, proportionate to the premium, take up a fraction k of the premium, P, and if the costs, proportionate to the number of policies, are j per policy then the contribution will be $P - R - (k \cdot P) - j$. Suppose in total we have N such risks and the fixed costs are F, the 'break even' situation occurs when

$$N[P - R - (k \cdot P) - j] = F$$

or

$$N \cdot P = \frac{R \cdot N + j \cdot N + F}{1 - k}$$

6.24 This formula is correct for the total premium for the risk group. If we divide through by the number of policies N, the individual premium for any risk is given by

$$P = \frac{R + j}{1 - k} + \frac{F}{N(1 - k)}.$$

On this basis each risk will contribute an equal amount F/N towards the fixed costs. There is no real reason why all the risks should contribute equally though in total an amount

150   GENERAL INSURANCE

F must be recovered for the fixed costs. For marketing reasons we may decide that a certain risk should not contribute at all, in which case the other risks must obviously provide more than F/N.

6.25 Suppose we decide to make the contribution for a certain risk equal to E. We can equate the premium to the risk and expenses thus:
$$P = R + f \cdot CE + k \cdot P + j + I + E$$
Where P = premium to be charged
  R = risk premium
  f = claim frequency
  CE = average claims expenses per claim
  k = the fraction of premiums represented by costs dependent on the premium (including commission)
  j = expenses dependent on number of policies (per policy)
  I = the additional expenses incurred in setting up a new contract
  E = contribution towards fixed costs.

Initial expenses

6.26 It is not the usual practice to make any extra charge for new business expenses in premium rates. Although companies in the motor field are becoming increasingly concerned about the tendency of the insured to transfer his insurance every year to take advantage of the cheapest premium rates offered in the market at that time, in the following paragraphs it will be assumed that initial expenses have been spread over the years in such a way that $I = 0$.

Claims expenses

6.27 The above equation incorporates an amount $[f \cdot CE]$ for expected claims expenses. Since the risk premium R will be of the form $[f \cdot CA]$ (where CA = average claim incurred) we can rewrite the term $R + f \cdot CE$ as
$$R\left(1 + f \cdot \frac{CE}{R}\right)$$

or
$$R\left(1+\frac{CE}{CA}\right)$$

This shows that claims expenses can be covered by applying a loading to the risk premium.

6.28 The complete formula can now be expressed as

$$P = R \cdot \left(1+\frac{CE}{CA}\right) + k \cdot P + j + E$$

$$P = R \cdot \frac{\left(1+\frac{CE}{CA}\right)}{1-k} + \frac{E+j}{1-k}$$

or $\quad P = R \cdot a + b$

writing a for

$$\frac{1+\frac{CE}{CA}}{1-k}$$

and b for

$$\frac{E+j}{1-k}$$

6.29 The first term represents a loading of the risk premium for those expenses dependent on the premium whilst the second term, essentially a flat expense fee per contract, provides for the expenses dependent on the number of policies and the share of the fixed costs to be borne by that risk.

Effect of loadings/discounts on these formulae

6.30 For those classes of business where the basic premiums are reduced for features in the risk a further problem arises. If the expense loadings are incorporated in the basic premium as they stand the effect of the discounting is to reduce the amount the company actually receives to cover expenses. One possibility is to up-rate the values of E and j by the average rate of discount granted

$$\text{i.e. } P = R \cdot a + \frac{b}{1-d}$$

where d is the average rate of discount. However, anomalies will arise if the rate of discount becomes too large. In motor business young drivers are commonly loaded by perhaps 100% whilst the average (mature) policyholder will probably have earned say 60% no-claim discount ($d = \cdot 6$). If b is numerically equal to £4 the basic premium formula will be $P = R \cdot a + £10$ and young drivers will, after loading, be effectively charged a policy fee of £20. In the interests of simplicity this may well be acceptable, particularly if accompanied by a reduction of the young drivers loadings, but a better method is to charge an explicit policy fee which is added on after the discounting has been done. Unfortunately the expense fees necessary are fairly large as a percentage of the premium.

6.31 Many companies now calculate their motor premiums using numerical rating (points) systems. Under such systems numbers of units (points) are allotted according to the various risk characteristics and the total points scored determines the size of the premium. A points/premium table is generally derived using a simple mathematical formula perhaps assuming a multiplicative basis for the risk factors. In some systems the problem of expense fees can be solved by building them in as an integral part of the premium formula. In this way the policy charges are made much less explicit. It is possible to incorporate the flat expense charge in the premium structure in such a manner that the loadings/discounts are not applied to it. If N is the numerical rating or total points scored then the premium table can be drawn up as

$P = R \cdot a(1+c)^N + b$ where c is the fraction increment in the premiums per unit of numerical rating.

On this approach the loadings have been applied to the risk premium and the expense structure has not been altered.

Minimum premiums

6.32 What is the minimum premium which should be charged to cover expenses? A general branch policy is essentially an annual one, though since most of the contracts are renewed, we can regard new business expenses as being incurred in the first year only. Since we cannot rely on the policy being renewed, the premium must be sufficient to protect the office against early lapse or cancellation. Some estimate of the costs involved in writing a policy can be obtained from an investigation on the following lines. We shall assume that we have a figure for the total expenses allocated to the class of business involved (say £500). Commission and claims expenses will be ignored in the analysis as these items are best dealt with separately.

6.33 Suppose we classify the main operations on our class of business into lapses, cancellations, endorsements, new business and renewals. We can estimate, perhaps on a sample basis, the relative times spent on each single operation and the frequency of such operations. Hence the estimated cost of lapses, cancellations, etc. can be arrived at (Table 6.1).

TABLE 6.1

Operation	Relative time spent (t)	Frequency per policy (f) (%)	Relative cost (t × f)	Absolute cost £500 (t × f) 5·0 (£)
Lapses	1	10	0·1	10
Cancellations	2	5	0·1	10
Endorsements	5	40	2·0	200
New business	10	20	2·0	200
Renewals	1	80	0·8	80
			5·0	500

6.34 If we know the number of policies currently in issue (say 100), we can calculate the cost per movement as the absolute cost/$100 \times f$. To calculate minimum premiums we need to know how much of this cost is independent of the premium charged (per-policy cost). This will obviously be a lower limit for the minimum premium, applicable to risks where the premium is negligible. Clearly for lapses all the expenses will be independent of premium whilst new business expenses will be partly dependent on the premium as the more risky cases are more expensive to underwrite. Here the underwriter may be able to provide an estimate of the amount of time spent on the various types of risk with which he deals. By comparing these estimates with the premiums he charges it should be possible to form a view of how much of the expenses incurred on new business are per-policy costs. Table 6.2 shows the per-policy cost per movement derived by multiplying the total cost per movement by an estimate of how much of the cost is per-policy.

TABLE 6.2

Operation	Absolute cost	Total cost per movement	Percent of cost fixed (estimated)	Fixed cost per movement (c)
Lapses	10	1·0	100	1·0
Cancellations	10	2·0	80	1·6
Endorsements	200	5·0	50	2·5
New business	200	10·0	60	6·0
Renewals	80	1·0	100	1·0

6.35 We can now draw up a table showing the way in which the (fixed) cost arises for any one policy. The expected cost of any operation will be the product of the frequency and the fixed cost per movement (i.e. $c \times f$). Table 6.3 is drawn up on the assumption that new business costs are to be charged to the first year only.

TABLE 6.3

Operation	Cost in first year	Cost in subsequent years
Lapses	0·10	0·10
Cancellations	0·08	0·08
Endorsements	1·00	1·00
New business	6·00	—
Renewals	—	0·80
	7·18	1·98

6.36 It may be thought that this type of calculation leads to excessive expenses for new business in the first year. As the lapse and cancellation rate is effectively 15%, the life time of a policy is about 6 years. If we write the new business expenses off over this period (i.e. £1 per year), then the total cost in the first year will be £2·18 as opposed to £2·98 in subsequent years. Clearly it is unwise to write these costs off over six years, as there is no guarantee that policies will stay on the books for as long as that, and in any case it is unrealistic to have a higher cost in subsequent years than that incurred in the first year. A possible solution would be to assume £1.84 of new business expenses to be incurred in the first year, and to spread the remaining £4·16 over the next four years (i.e. £1·04 per year). This would produce a level total cost of about £3 per policy over the first 5 years.

6.37 This example shows that basic expenses amount to £3 per policy, so clearly this is the minimum premium which should be accepted. In practice a higher minimum premium would be required to cover any risk involved, commission and other expenses dependent on the premium.

CHAPTER 7

THE OFFICE PREMIUM

7.1 We considered, in Chapter 5, the calculation of the pure risk premium, i.e. the cost of meeting likely future claims arising from a policy. In doing so the allowances to be made for both interest and expenses, and in loading for profit were deliberately ignored. Some reference was made to inflation but only as a factor to be taken into account in estimating future claims costs. The main practical factor to be ignored in Chapter 5, though its paramount importance was stressed, was the price mechanism; a company, if it is to survive let alone prosper, has to sell insurance in a competitive market. However refined and precise the statistical estimation of the risk, its value, in the last resort, is, as in all other price mechanistic situations, what the customer thinks it is worth.

7.2 It was stressed in Chapter 5 that, however competitive the market, the insurer cannot afford for long to operate in ignorance of true costs; that there must be prior knowledge of the level below which a fall in price will result in loss instead of profit. No company can continue to operate at a loss for long. Indeed a loss situation is self-deteriorating since bad results undermine confidence and this affects not only investors but also customers. The company must try to win on both counts and as Ratcliff (1976) has put it, must deal, *inter alia*, with the problem of 'establishing premium rates on which business can be *obtained* and written with a *profitable* result'.

7.3 Ratcliff admits that in the past (and to some extent in the present) the theoretical gross premium rate has been 'a somewhat academic measurement; comforting if exceeded by the market rate but conveniently forgotten if undercut'. He stresses the importance however of the theoretical minimum premium rate arrived at by loading the pure risk premium with expenses (but not with contribution to fixed costs or the return on capital). 'If the market rate is below this level then every insurance written increases the potential loss, whilst every piece of business shed reduces it. Even at this rate, ... the insurance is not making its proper contribution to fixed costs which will then have to be made up elsewhere, where market pressures may be less, if an overall loss is to be avoided.'

7.4 This last sentence is a reminder that in general insurance one class of business has to be taken with another and one risk with another. If, for the protection of the company, yielding to market pressures in one sector of business is to be compensated by taking advantage of a lack of pressure in other sectors it is obviously necessary to know what are the losses and profits which are likely to emerge from such a differential pricing strategy. How much is a quoted premium below or above the theoretical break-even rate? Is the margin in an individual quotation significant as being beyond the likely random error associated with the estimation of the break-even point?

7.5 These questions emphasise that the development of a successful market strategy must begin with a structure of pure risk premiums consistently embracing all classes of business and all risk groups (including groups of one where *individual* risk quotations are made). The structure must convolute not only the claim frequency and claim amount expectation but also the margins of fluctuation in these essentially random quantities.

The basic rating routine

7.6 We may now consider the basic rating routine in the normal situation of an existing office which has been carrying on business for some time, i.e. we are not considering a new office without a prior rate structure. For this example we will assume the existence of a homogeneous block of business of adequate size in terms of numbers of claims, i.e. providing fully credible data for one year's experience. We assume that a rate is required for a standard risk and not for a group that is experience-rated or 'adjusted' from basic rates. It is also assumed that we are producing a premium to be paid for one year's risk. For the present, interest earnings will be ignored as will also taxation and any changes in the volume of business though this might affect costs per policy of those expenses that are fixed and charged in the line of business independently of volume.

7.7 The following information is required.

1. Midpoint of base claims data period
2. Date of proposed introduction of new rates
3. Period of months for which new rates are to be in force $\ldots x$

   (2 and 3 are management decisions based upon knowledge of market trends and pressures.)

4. Claims cost in the base period $\ldots c$

   (This is the cost of all claims so far reported that have a date of incurrence in the base period.)

5. Anticipated annual claims inflation rate $\ldots \inf_c$

   (This is the annual rate of inflation expected for the claims within the category considered.)

6. Anticipated annual claims incidence change $\ldots \text{inc}$

   (There may, from study of claims frequency trends, be expectations of an increase or decrease in the claims expected for each unit of exposure.)

7. Anticipated annual expense inflation $\ldots \inf_E$

   (The expenses of this category of business will be subject to inflation. The items to be looked at include staff salaries, pension fund contributions, rents and rates.)

8. Anticipated annual inflation of 'sum insured' per unit of exposure $\ldots \inf_s$

   (This is premium income, rather than sum insured, inflation. It is intended to take account of the fact that the premium charged for some classes of business is based on wages or turnover and if these are increased by inflation more revenue is received, automatically, without the risk changing.)

9. Commission rate $\ldots B$
10. Profit level (as a fraction) $\ldots F$

    (9 and 10 are management decisions each involving different considerations; the former is concerned with competition, the latter needs much theoretical study [see Chapter 12].)

11. Pure premium information

(a) average settled claims in first year, i.e. for those claims notified *and* settled by end of year of incurrence

(b) average incurred cost per claim
(This is the total incurred cost, i.e. settled costs plus payments made to date on claims still outstanding plus estimates of further likely payments on these claims, for all claims notified in year Y, this also being the year of incurrence of event, divided by the number of such notifications.)

(c) claims per unit of exposure
(The choice of unit of exposure has already been discussed in Chapter 5.)

12 I.B.N.R. factor ...I
(This is the I.B.N.R. reserve expressed as a proportion of the claims costs c (item 4 above).)

13 Re-opened claims factor ...R
(A similar factor to I, to allow for claims which having been thought to be settled have to be re-opened, e.g. because an additional third party appears.)

14 Deficit factor ...D
(This allows for the writing up or down of the estimate of eventual costs of outstanding claims. The term deficit is used because more often than not the estimate revision is upward, placing the reserve in deficit. The factor is positive for a deficit and negative for a saving.)

15 Proportion of expenses attributable to claims ...S

7.8 From items 1, 2 and 3 we calculate the period from the midpoint of the base period to the average date of event of a claim in the new rating series, t in years.

7.9 We calculate also the earned exposure (in units of cover) E. This is calculated in a similar manner to the calculation of earned premium (or even more precisely as in Chapter 5) and if not directly available may be estimated as

$$\frac{[\text{Written exposure}] \times [\text{Gross earned premiums}]}{[\text{Gross written premiums}]}$$

'Written exposure' gives each policy written a whole unit of exposure in the base year of investigation.

7.10 In order to break down expenses we need the following items.

	In sub-line for rating	In total account
Number of claims	n	N
Claims cost (incurred cost on all year's claims in base period)	m	M
Number of policies	p	P
Gross written premiums	g	G
Expenses charges to total account for base period		W

7.11 We need to split W and allocate appropriately to the sub-line using the items in the above paragraph as weights. We attach a weight of a on the number of claims, $(1-a)$ on claim cost, b on policies and $(1-b)$ on gross written premium, where a and b are both <1 and are provided by the expense analysis (Chapter 6).

Expenses for sub-line V

$$= WS\left[\frac{an+(1-a)m}{aN+(1-a)M}\right] + W(1-S)\left[\frac{bp+(1-b)g}{bP+(1-b)G}\right]$$

7.12 The premium rate per unit of exposure is thus:

$$P_{new} = \frac{c(1+I)(1+R)(1+D)(1+\inf_c)^t(1+\text{inc})^t + V(1+\inf_E)^t}{E(1+\inf_s)^t(1-B-F)}$$

and a comparison of P_{new} with the current rate indicates the percentage increase to achieve profitability in the forthcoming period.

7.13 The following is a typical calculation using realistic but hypothetical figures. This is for the motor private total amount, and the comprehensive cover sub-line. All policies cover only one vehicle. It is assumed that there has only been one rating table operative during the base period and that it is the current rating table.

    Midpoint base period is 1 July, 1974
    New rates to be introduced 1 January, 1975
    New rates to be in force 12 months
    Claims cost in base period £2,000,000
    Claims inflation 15% per annum

THE OFFICE PREMIUM

Claims incidence change $+1\%$ per annum
Expense inflation 20% per annum
Sum insured inflation—not applicable
Commission rate 10%
Profit level $2\frac{1}{2}\%$
I.B.N.R. factor $0 \cdot 12$
Re-opened claims factor $0 \cdot 05$
Deficit factor $-0 \cdot 02$ (i.e. a saving normally emerges)
$\%$ of expenses attributable to claims is 25%
$t = 3/2$ (from 1 July, 1974 to 1 January, 1976)
Earned exposure 100,000

	Motor Private Comprehensive	Total
Number of claims	15,000	17,500
Claims cost	£2,250,000	£2,500,000
Number of policies	105,000	140,000
Gross written premium	£4,200,000	£4,850,000

Expenses of total Motor Private $= £1,125,000$

Assume $a = \cdot 75$ and $b = \cdot 75$ (see para. 7.11) then expenses attributable to the Comprehensive section of the account

$$V = 1,125,000 \times \cdot 25 \frac{(\cdot 75 \times 15,000 + \cdot 25 \times 2,250,000)}{(\cdot 75 \times 17,500 + \cdot 25 \times 2,500,000)}$$

$$+ 1,125,000 \times \cdot 75 \frac{(\cdot 75 \times 105,000 + \cdot 25 \times 4,200,000)}{(\cdot 75 \times 140,000 + \cdot 25 \times 4,850,000)}$$

$$= £975,748$$

Then calculation of required premium rate is

$$\frac{2,000,000 (1 \cdot 12)(1 \cdot 05)(\cdot 98)(1 \cdot 15)^{3/2} (1 \cdot 01)^{3/2} + 975,748 (1 \cdot 2)^{3/2}}{100,000 (1 \cdot 0)^{3/2} (\cdot 875)}$$

$$= \frac{4,167,962}{87,500} = £47 \cdot 63$$

The present premium rate is $\frac{4,200,000}{105,000} = £40$

Hence the required rate increase is $\frac{7 \cdot 63}{40} = 19 \cdot 1\%$

[The comprehensive section of motor private could of course be subdivided further such as to individual level of no-claim discount.]

The statistical and underwriting concepts of credibility

7.14 We may pause here to consider the statistical problems raised in paragraph 7.5. When we consider margins of fluctuation and the reliability of measurement we must bear in mind a certain lack of definition that appears to exist in much that is written about credibility. When an underwriter speaks of 'credibility' and a 'credible' premium he is less concerned with reliability of statistical estimation from limited experience as such, than with the fact that a mistake with a large amount insured is more expensive than with a smaller amount. Thus in the following chapter we shall be discussing experience rating, i.e. the adjustment of individual premiums (or group premiums) to take account of apparent changes in the risk level of the insured (or groups of insured). By 'apparent' we mean that recent experience shows a different claim frequency or amount from that on which current premiums have been based. The credibility theory approach to making any indicated adjustment of premium considers just how 'apparent' the change in experience is, i.e. it endeavours to determine the weight to be given to the relatively less voluminous and therefore less reliable recent claims data as compared with the more extensive and more reliable past data. The new premium rating is assessed as a weighted mean of the loss ratio previously expected on past data (given a weight of $1-Z$) and the actual loss ratio of recent data (given a weight of Z) where Z is a measure of credibility on a scale from 0 to 1. If Z is equal to 1 the recent data are fully accepted and the past is ignored. More detail of the application of this approach to experience rating is given in paragraphs 8.6 to 8.11 but in the present context we need only to state that in practice the credibility factor Z, i.e. the weight attaching to the new experience, is required to increase with the absolute value of the expected losses. Hence the reference at the beginning of this paragraph to the underwriter being more concerned about an expensive 'error' in the estimation of recent claim risk. In fact the absolute expected losses may or may not be directly related to the total exposures in the limited experience; it depends upon the choice of unit of exposure for the calculation of expected losses. The statistician will take a different view; he will instinctively be inclined to measure credibility in inverse proportion to the sampling error in the estimation of claim frequency and claim amount. The sampling error can be calculated from a knowledge of exposures, claims, claim amounts and the nature of the frequency distributions. It is more likely that, for him, credibility will be related to the number of claims involved in deriving an estimation of the claims frequency since this determines the variance of the estimated claim frequency.

7.15 The purely statistical approach would be as follows (Mayerson, 1964). It is usual to assume that the claim frequency is small and therefore follows the Poisson distribution, i.e. the probability of r claims during a given time period is

$$\frac{m^r \cdot e^{-m}}{r!}.$$

The expected number of claims is m and the variance of the number of claims is also m. For purposes of simplicity in calculation it is next assumed that the Poisson distribution may be approximated to by the Normal distribution (mean and variance still being assumed to be equal). The probability P that the number of claims will lie within $m \pm Km$ is then given by the formula

$$P = \frac{1}{\sqrt{2\pi}} \cdot \int_{-K\sqrt{m}}^{K\sqrt{m}} e^{-x^2/2} \cdot dx$$

Note that the standardised deviate is

$$\frac{K \cdot m}{\sqrt{m}}.$$

Many of the credibility tables used in the U.S.A. for automobile liability insurance are based on the choice of $P = \cdot 90$ and $K = \cdot 05$ as giving the expected number of claims to which full credibility is given (i.e. unity on a scale from 0 to 1). In this case for $P = \cdot 90$, tables of the Normal distribution indicate a standardised deviate of 1·6449 and this has to be equal to $\cdot 05\sqrt{m}$ whence the expected number $m = 1082$ claims.

7.16 It should be noted that this relates credibility to the total number of claims irrespective of the time over which they occur, i.e. 5000 cars insured over 1 year provide data as credible as 10,000 cars insured for 6 months, if the underlying claim frequency is the same. It should also be noted that the claim amount has not yet been brought into the calculation, i.e. implicitly claim amount has been assumed to be invariant.

7.17 For the credibility of the pure premium we have to consider the error of estimation attaching to the product of m and M where M is the mean claim amount having a standard deviation of S. The formula then becomes

$$P = \frac{1}{\sqrt{2\pi}} \int_{-K \cdot Mm/\sigma}^{K \cdot Mm/\sigma} e^{-x^2/2} \cdot dx$$

where σ is the variance of Mm. If the two variables can be regarded as independent which, whilst not strictly true in insurance, is a reasonable assumption for simplicity of treatment, the variance of Mm will consist of two parts—the within claim variance of S^2 for each of m claims together with the between claim variance of $(m^{1/2} \cdot M)^2$, the M being introduced to give the correct money dimensions. This gives a standard deviation of

$$\sqrt{mM^2 + mS^2} \text{ or } Mm^{1/2}(1 + S^2/M^2)^{1/2}.$$

The standardised deviate then becomes

$$\frac{Mm}{Mm^{1/2}\left(1 + \frac{S^2}{M^2}\right)^{1/2}} \text{ or } m^{1/2}\left(1 + \frac{S^2}{M^2}\right)^{-1/2}.$$

If $S = 0$, then the standardised deviate becomes $m^{1/2}$ as in paragraph 7.15 where M was assumed to be invariant. It follows that for the same value of P and K we need a new number of claims m_1 such that

$$m_1^{1/2}\left(1+\frac{S^2}{M^2}\right)^{-1/2} = m^{1/2}$$

or
$$m_1 = m\left(1+\frac{S^2}{M^2}\right)$$

i.e. we need to increase the number of claims for full credibility in the proportion $(1+S^2/M^2)$ for pure premium purposes. It is found in practice that S/M lies between 4 and 6. If we take $S/M=5$ we have to increase the number of claims derived in paragraph 7.15 with invariant claim amount to a number of the order of 27,000.

7.18 If the number of claims observed, n, is less than that required, N, for full credibility, the statistician would normally reduce the credibility in inverse proportion to the variances, i.e. by the factor n/N. However, in insurance the practice has become established of using reciprocals not of variances but of standard deviations. Credibility is reduced in the proportion $\sqrt{n/N}$. This would be the factor of Z to be used in experience rating (see para. 7.14 above and para. 8.6) and for weighting the most recent year's experience in rate-making generally, i.e. if A is the actual claims cost and E the expected claims cost on earlier experience, then the base claim cost is taken as $ZA+(1-Z)E$.

7.19 We shall see however in Chapter 8 in dealing with experience rating that where full credibility can not be accorded it is common practice to derive $Z<1$ by the formula $P/(P+K)$ where P is the premium volume in the particular risk class and K is a normalising constant. The statistical justification is as follows (Bailey 1950). x is the true but unknown claim probability with a probability density of $f(x)$. $E(x)=\mu$ and $E(x-\mu)^2=\sigma^2$. The event H is observed consisting of h claims from an exposure of n giving an observed claim frequency of h/n. Let $g(H|x)$ be the conditional probability that H will be observed given a true claim probability of x. We would like to use an estimator of x, $E(x|H)$. From Bayes theorem,

$$E(x|H) = \frac{\sum_x x \cdot f(x) \cdot g(H|x)}{\sum_x f(x) \cdot g(H|x)}$$

If we take $f(x)$ as a gamma density function

$$f(x) = \frac{a^r \cdot x^{r-1} e^{-ax}}{\Gamma(r)} \text{ for } x \geq 0$$

where $$a = \frac{\mu}{\sigma^2}, \text{ and } r = \frac{\mu^2}{\sigma^2}$$

i.e. r/a is the mean and r/a^2 is the variance of $f(x)$. We assume that $g(H|x)$ is the Poisson probability

$$\frac{(nx)^h e^{-nx}}{h!}.$$

Then $E(x|H) = Z \cdot h/n + (1-Z)\mu$ where $Z = n/(n+a)$. Multiplying the numerator and denominator of the expression by the premium for a single exposure we have $Z = P/(P+K)$ where P is the premium volume for the n exposures, in the particular class studied. If P is large relative to K, the credibility is very close to 1 and this means that the ratio may be, for all practical purposes, based on the statistical results of the particular class. [*Note*: For those unfamiliar with the gamma function it should be explained that $\Gamma(r)$ is defined as $\int_0^\infty t^{r-1} \cdot e^{-t} \cdot dt$. For $r > 1$, $f(x)$ as defined above follows a skew bell-shaped curve which is typical of claim frequency distributions.]

7.20 At the present time credibility theory is not much used in U.K. experience possibly for the reason that except in some new classifications, e.g. airbuses, the amount of data available brings credibility close to unity, but there is wide appreciation of the need for a sound statistical base in rating.

The commercial decision

7.21 In the preceeding paragraphs it has been assumed implicitly that the office has sufficient information from its own experience to enable it to develop a credible premium scale. If there are classes of business for which the office does not have enough information then it must look elsewhere for guidance. This means that for individual insurances the office would follow the market, i.e. adopt premium rates not very different from the tariff (for example, for commercial fire) or the former tariff (for example, employers' liability), or follow the market leader.

7.22 Alternatively a practical method of adjusting rates can be adopted which implies that the main structure is correct but that the level needs to be adjusted. The following is an example of the use of this method.

	Premiums	Claims	L/R (loss ratio)
1972	1000	650	0·650
1973	1050	700	0·667
1974	1260	882	0·700
1975	1575	1134	0·720

Premiums increases		Price index	
2½%	1.1.73	1972	100
5%	1.1.74	1973	103
7½%	1.1.75	1974	107
		1975	110

If today's premiums had been in force throughout and claims are adjusted for the price index, we get:

	Premiums		Claims		L/R
1972	1000 (1·075) (1·05) 1·025	=1157	650 (110/100)= 715		0·618
1973	1050 (1·075) 1·05	=1185	700 (110/103)= 748		0·631
1974	1260 (1·075)	=1354	882 (110/107)= 907		0·670
1975	1575 (1·00)	=1575	1134 (1·00)	=1134	0·720

It is clear that the loss ratio on adjusted 1975 values is deteriorating and a revision is needed. The new rates must be adjusted to an effective point say 2 years ahead and a rough projection based on recent history suggests a L/R at the time of 0·85. The rates must allow for expenses, commission and profit of 35% so that rates need to be increased $(0.85 - 0.65) = 0.20$ or 20%.

7.23 Even when the office has enough information to develop a sound basis for a rate-making structure, the application of this structure must be conditioned by market conditions. The office may well have to consider adjustments to this structure so that in individual classes of business (especially those which it wishes to expand) it may remain competitive while over the total account it continues to earn sufficient profit to service its capital and maintain its reserves.

7.24 The office, before applying new premium scales, will need also to consider the effects of any changes on its portfolio. We saw in Chapter 4 the kind of statistical investigations that would be needed. Certainly in the period following a change in premium scales, lapse rates and new business statistics will be studied very closely. Doubtless there will be past experience of premium change to refer to; the office will already have an indication, for example, of the number of motor policies it will be likely to lose after a 10% rise in the premium scale. It will also bear in mind that the policyholders who leave are often the lower risks and that the residual body of policies will show a higher claim experience than would otherwise have been expected.

7.25 For commercial as distinct from personal insurance the premium eventually charged will be decided by bargaining between the insurer office and the insured and it may well be different from the premium indicated by the rating manual. Nevertheless, as we have already stressed, bargaining without reference at all to the base premium would be perilous, and no office is likely to ignore either the manual or the underlying pure premium.

Motor fleets

7.26 For motor fleets and other experience rated business (see Chapter 8) the incurred claims cost over 3 years is projected forward (effectively for 2 years) and grossed up for expenses and commission.

Domestic policies

7.27 These policies used to be determined by a tariff agreement. Recently there have only been minor changes from the old tariff, with one major exception, namely 'replacement' rather than 'indemnity'. Practice has always been to relate premiums to sum insured on a strictly proportionate basis, although in recent years minimum premium rates have been imposed. Premiums have been loaded in a few cases, for example, contents of houses in London and Glasgow and non-standard buildings, whilst cover has been restricted in cases where properties are unoccupied by day or left unfurnished. At present, the main effort is being directed to an attempt to bring sums assured more in line with current values rather than to alter premium rates per cent of sum insured.

Medical expenses

7.28 The market in the U.K. is specialised and is largely operated by two 'mutual' insurance companies and a number of organisations which operate on a small and mainly regional basis. An important feature of the background of this business is the availability of 'free' health care services from the National Health Service, and this has to be taken into account in premium rating proposals.

7.29 For individual and small group risks a large number of rating factors are currently in use. The list includes the following.

Current age (sometimes of the oldest person covered by the policy)
Age at entry to scheme or insurer
Family status (e.g. single, married, family, number of children)
Country of residence
Scale of cover
Membership of previous or other schemes
Membership of professional or trade organisations
Membership of credit card organisations
Medical history (rarely used for rating, sometimes used for policy restrictions)
Registration of parent with previous or existing schemes
Type of group membership (employee or, employer paid, or a mixture)

Size of group
Payment by direct debit
Payment by instalments

7.30 As in other classes of general insurance the financial objectives in practical premium rating are generally to aim for an acceptable overall contribution to surplus, without too much regard for the profitability of each risk group. Although the business is annual, many policyholders seem to regard their insurance cover as a long term proposition; perhaps in the light of their own expected deteriorating health with increasing age. There is thereby a large amount of office loyalty. It seems to be an accepted market fact that the highest risk groups (e.g. the oldest age groups, those in poor health) cannot afford cover at a realistic price, and that it is appropriate to subsidise these risk groups by contributions from the more profitable risk groups. In other countries (e.g. the U.S.A.) other devices such as age limits or partial self insurance are used to avoid quoting the highest risk groups seemingly 'exorbitant' premiums.

7.31 In view of the accepted cross subsidies between risk groups the approach to premium rating is generally concerned with an acceptable overall contribution to surplus; a sophisticated claims frequency and claims amount analysis is not always appropriate for practical premium rating. A close monitoring of the profitability of the financially significant risk groups is, however, invaluable for effective product and financial planning.

7.32 For large group risks one approach to this business is to offer large discounts and individual negotiations. The premium rating is similar to that for individual risks but the discounts are larger, the justification being less adverse selection, younger lives and less use of medical facilities. There is also some profit from lapses; staff turnover results in lapses as few exercise the option to effect an individual policy. The other approach is experience rating. Various formulae have in the past been used, usually based on the previous two or three years' experience. These formulae are either retrospective (e.g. $a(bP-C)$, where a and b are constants) or prospective (e.g. estimate outstanding claims and apply a formula

THE OFFICE PREMIUM

which attempts to steer the future claims experience towards a desired loss ratio).

7.33 The rationale of the formula $a(bP-C)$ may be set out as follows.

Let P_1 = Gross premiums earned in period 1
C_1 = Claims incurred in period 1
$1-b$ = Expense loading, directly proportional to gross premiums
a = Proportion of 'surplus' to be distributed to the insured

Retrospectively, the 'surplus' earned in period 1 is given by (bP_1-C_1) and so the 'surplus' to be distributed to the insured $= a(bP_1-C_1)$.

Thus, premiums payable in period $2 = P_2 - a(bP_1-C_1)$. In other words the above formula is simply a retrospective 'profit' distribution. The factor 'a' could depend on size of the portfolio, and therefore be some kind of credibility factor. Consider the 'pure risk' premium for period 2, i.e. bP_2, reduced by the retrospective surplus distribution $a(bP_1-C_1)$. The actual pure risk premium payable in period 2 is given by

$$bP_2 - a(bP_1 - C_1)$$
$$= bP_2 + a(C_1 - bP_1)$$
$$= bP_2 + a\frac{P_1}{P_2}\left(C_1\frac{P_2}{P_1} - bP_2\right)$$
$$= bP_2\left(1 - a\frac{P_1}{P_2}\right) + C_1\frac{P_2}{P_1}\left(a\frac{P_1}{P_2}\right)$$
$$= bP_2(1-x) + C_1\frac{P_2}{P_1}(x) \quad \text{where } x = a\frac{P_1}{P_2}$$

and this can be interpreted as a 'credibility' type formula with

bP_2 = portfolio pure risk premium

$C_1\dfrac{P_2}{P_1}$ = individual claims experience adjusted for inflation

x = 'credibility' factor $\left(= a\dfrac{P_1}{P_2}\right)$

7.34 Recently, reasonably effective experience rating methods have been developed with the aid of computer simulation techniques. In one case the constraints imposed on the experience rating method were as follows.

Over a long period of time (say 10–20 years) the claims paid should be reasonably close to a percentage of the premiums paid.

Premiums paid (per person) in consecutive periods should not be too divergent, even for the smaller groups. In any contract period there should be stop loss cover (community rated) for abnormally high claims.

The system should be able to handle small groups (size 50, say) as well as large groups (size 5,000, say).

Employer's liability

7.35 The premium rating factors commonly in use are the employer's payroll and the trade classification. (Trade classification is, however, not entirely satisfactory because of the lack of homogeneity within trade classes.) Considerable problems arise when rating this class of business, apart from that of the classification of the risk. The average payroll for the contract period for which the premium is set is obviously unknown at the time of the quotation. The premium is usually set on a current or near current payroll and an adjusted premium collected after a payroll declaration following the end of the policy year. The other major factor affecting this class is the length of time over which claims are settled (up to 10 years).

7.36 An accurate measure of exposure can only be derived some time in arrears, although exposure can be developed in a similar way to claims by inflating the original estimates as more data becomes available. Claims may take a considerable time to develop and inflation affects the level of claim until the claim is settled. A reliable experience is, therefore, not available until some time after the period of insurance. When projecting the claims to the future the effect of inflation on current claims experience has to be removed and then built back in again at projected levels. When setting this projection against payroll, the payroll must also be adjusted for inflation.

7.37 The statistics will provide a premium rate for a given trade class. A further difficulty lies in the fact that rating for a class is usually quoted as a range of rates per classification, the final rate being set by the underwriter. The premium rates which have in the past been charged (after the underwriter's decision) can also be tested against the projected claims experience.

7.38 Because of the long tail in the claim payments, investment earnings are more important than for most other classes. These are often used to reduce the premium charged, although because of high uncertainty in the level of claims a wider margin for profit and contingencies is usually required.

7.39 Many large businesses are experience rated. The experience, as developed over the past 3 or 5 years, is taken and projected, allowing for changing risk, inflation, etc. The premium rate is set in a similar manner to commercial motor fleets (see Chapter 8) using a unit rate per £100 payroll. The problems are, however, much worse in that the claims are unlikely to have reached their ultimate level and considerable adjustment (using grossing up factors) may be necessary. Some companies ignore the latest year's claims experience. The usual practice is to set the rate by grossing up, i.e. by dividing by a factor based on a required loss ratio. This factor adjusts the desired ultimate loss ratio for the effects of future inflation and future investment earnings.

Public liability

7.40 The majority of claims under this class of business are of a property damage type. This means that although liability for the claim is under dispute for a considerable time, the possible amount of the claim is quickly settled. This is very different from the class of employer's liability (mainly bodily injury) where inflation affects the claim throughout the period until settlement.

American experience

7.41 In the U.S.A., insurance premiums are subject to far greater control than in the U.K., although the degree of control varies considerably from State to State. These vary from one extreme where the State Commissioner makes the rate, to the other extreme *viz.* States where the office sets its rates, uses them and merely files them with the State Commissioner. In between these extremes, there are States where an office files proposed new rates with the Commissioner and then has to wait for his approval before using them. There are other States where the office may file its new rates with the Commissioner and start to use them in the knowledge that if the Commissioner rejects them it may have to make refunds to policyholders.

7.42 Rate making in the U.S.A. largely follows what has been outlined above but in rather greater detail. Experience over the previous 5 years is updated and projected forwards for inflation. There is fairly general use of credibility theory. The credibility factor approach is also used for experience rating and credibility factors have to be filed with the Commissioner in certain States.

7.43 In the U.S.A. insurance experience is available from all offices reporting to the Insurance Services Office (I.S.O.). Thus a large body of data exists. No such overall experience exists in the U.K. for each line of business.

Investment income

7.44 As indicated at the beginning of this chapter, the rating process will often not allow directly for investment income, although in the U.S.A. and certain European countries interest on technical reserves may be taken as a direct item in the calculations. However, even when an office does not allow for interest directly it does not mean that the fact that technical reserves will earn interest is ignored, but rather that it is implied by the level of underwriting profit—or profit margin—built into the rates. In particular the profit margin will differ between different classes, to have regard to the contribution to investment income, dependent on the differing length of time to settle claims. Larger profit margins on the other hand will be required for more 'risky' business, e.g. for employers' liability business, as explained in paragraph 7.37.

7.45 Two approaches appear appropriate. The first would

be to adjust the pure risk premium to have regard to the mean time between payment of the premium and settlement of the claim. The second would be to consider the interest earned on technical reserves, expressed as a proportion of the premiums. These reserves (see Chapter 10) are in respect of unearned premiums, outstanding claims (including incurred but not reported claims) and any additional reserves required, but allowance must be made for the fact that not all assets, in particular the item appearing on the balance sheet as agents' balances, are such that they may be invested. In this way allowance would be made for differences in the interest income contributed by different classes because the reserves for classes where claims take longer to settle would, other things being equal, be a higher proportion of premiums than for those classes where claims are settled shortly after they occur.

7.46 In a typical large company transacting business internationally the technical reserves might well be 125% of written premiums and agents' balances, etc., due to the company might be 15% of written premiums. The net result is that interest on 110% of premiums can be considered as available to underwriting. If we assume the rate of interest earned net of tax is 5% two alternatives under the second approach discussed in paragraph 7.44 are to:

1 allow for interest on reserves and build in a profit margin of 10% say; or
2 ignore interest and build in a profit margin of 4.5% which together with net interest of 5% on 110% of the premium gives a total profit margin of 10%.

The first method enables the interest to be applied separately for each class of business whilst the second method assumes that the mix of business is reasonably constant.

7.47 An example of the first approach of paragraph 7.45 is given by Sidney Benjamin (1976). He quotes a typical run-off, from a past year, of claim amounts for U.K. comprehensive private motor business according to delay in months from accident to payment (not settlement) as shown in Table 7.1. Allowing for an average of a further six months from the premium date to the date of claim incident, the discounted present value of these payments at 6% per annum is £92·80

Table 7.1

Delay (months)	£	Delay (months)	£	Delay (months)	£
0	2·9	6	3·2	12	0·4
1	18·8	7	2·3	13–24	7·9
2	21·6	8	2·0	25–36	3·9
3	13·0	9	1·5	37–48	3·3
4	7·6	10	1·1	49–60	2·0
5	4·9	11	0·8	over 60	2·8
					100·0

so that if a proper allowance for all factors in the run-off (including inflation) has been made, a pure premium of £100 would contain a profit margin of 7·2%. If the loss ratio is, say, 70% then this profit margin represents 5% of the office premium. For non-comprehensive business one would expect the effect to be greater because the delays to payment are greater. Although this example illustrates the approach, the reader is warned that a 6% rate of interest may not typically represent 5% profit on motor insurance generally.

BIBLIOGRAPHY

BENJAMIN, S. Profit and Other Financial Concepts in Insurance. *Journal of the Institute of Actuaries*, 1976, **103**, 233.

MAYERSON, A. L. The Uses of Credibility in Property Insurance Rate-Making. *Giornale dell' Instituto Italiano degli Attuari*, 1964, Anno **XXVII**, No. 1, 197.

RATCLIFF, A. R. N. Some Market Limitations on the Application of Mathematical Research to Insurance Management. *Proceedings of the 20th International Congress of Actuaries*.

CHAPTER 8

EXPERIENCE RATING

8.1 We have already (specifically in para 5.34) introduced the concept of a risk distribution; that within a particular class of insurance, the risk of a claim varies from one policy to another over a wide range from an insignificant level to near certainty. The distribution of numbers at differing levels of risk is in most classes of insurance bellshaped, i.e. with a pronounced central tendency and, on either side of the modal value, diminishing numbers tailing off to zero. The distribution is unlikely to be symmetrical; because all those seeking insurance have a risk which they feel is worth insuring, the distribution is more likely than not to be skewed towards the higher level of risk. The range of the distribution is an expression of the heterogeneity of the total body of policyholders and methods of reducing heterogeneity are aimed at reducing the range and hence increasing the precision of estimating the expected claim frequency. We have shown that by taking account of factors which have been found to affect risk (see para 5.26 and following paragraphs) policies may be allocated to more homogeneous groups for this purpose. In effect the overall range of the risk distribution is split up into a number of overlapping bands reflecting broad levels of risk and policies are allocated to these levels of risk by reference to levels of the known risk factors. This is what the model referred to in paragraph 5.30 is attempting to make possible. The broad (but not specific) location of an individual policy in the risk distribution is thus imputed, by reference to the risk factors, from past experience of similar policies (the risk factors are themselves a matter of experience). [It is worth bearing in mind that an experienced underwriter, though rightly arguing that he is operating non-statistically, is actually following a similar method of using his experience but referring to his own intuitive unverbalised 'model'.]

8.2 It has been assumed, if the analysis of past experience which forms the basis of the statistical model has been thorough, that once a policy has been allocated to a particular risk class, that allocation is unchanged. It has been assumed also that we know only that the policy has risk factor attributes which make it a member of a particular group for which the past average claim frequency has been measured. (Although the policy is a present member of the group [for premium purposes] it may not have been represented in the recent records on which the claim frequency is based.) The risk factor attributes, e.g. in motor insurance—use of vehicle, type of vehicle, etc. do not normally change on renewal and so the group allocation does not change.

8.3 An alternative procedure suggests itself, i.e. that the allocation to risk group should not be fixed but should be adjusted to accord with the experience of the individual policy as it emerges. This is the concept of experience rating and the operation of no-claims discount in motor insurance which we discuss later in this chapter is a particular example of experience rating. In broader terms Bühlmann (1970) defines experience rating as 'a system by which the premium of the individual risk depends upon the claims experience of this individual risk'.

8.4 In applying this concept we need a somewhat different model of risk variation. We need to apply multivariate analysis to establish the possible different levels of risk, i.e. of claim frequency. A new policy is rated by reference to the expected claim frequency to which, from the risk factor information available on the proposal, it appears to be subject. The expected loss ratio in the ensuing year, i.e. expected claims as a proportion of premiums, will then be known. On renewal the actual loss ratio will be known and the renewal premium will be up-rated in some proportion to the excess of actual over expected loss ratio. In theory the policy is given the loss ratio to which it has shown itself to be subject.

8.5 The actual operation of the system depends upon examination of what is implied by 'shows itself to be subject'. If we up-rate in direct proportion to the excess loss ratio, we are assuming that the excess of the past year will be repeated, i.e. that the experience of 1 year is a sufficient basis on which to reallocate the policy to a higher risk level.

Credibility theory considerations

8.6 How much weight can we give to the experience of 1 year? The question leads to the suggestion, underlying so-called credibility theory, that we might assess the new premium rating as a weighted mean of the previously expected loss ratio and the observed actual loss ratio for the individual policy. The basic formula for the premium modification M then can be written as

$$M = \frac{(Z \cdot A + (1-Z)E)}{E}$$

where A = actual loss for the risk
E = expected loss for the risk
Z = credibility (on a scale from 0 to 1)

8.7 It is usual to arrange for Z to rise hyperbolically to unity by writing

$$Z = \frac{E}{(E+K)}$$

where (i) K is a constant designed to regulate the speed of increase of credibility with increase in the absolute size of the risk, and (ii) it is also usually required that the percentage charge for any given loss should decrease as the size of the risk increases. The conditions are

for (i) $0 \leqslant Z < 1$ and $\dfrac{dZ}{dE} \geqslant 0$ (which implies $K \geqslant 0$)

for (ii) $\dfrac{d}{dE}\left(\dfrac{Z}{E}\right) < 0$ which must follow from $K > 0$

since the differential $= \dfrac{-1}{(E+K)^2}$

8.8 As Z in the above expression only approaches unity asymptotically it is necessary for practical purposes to select a value of E for which Z is required as $=1$. This is known as the self rating point, S.

$$E \geqslant S,\ Z = 1$$

The hyperbola is distorted to connect to the self rating point (see Fig. 8.1) by a straight line from S tangent to Z at a point $E = Q$.

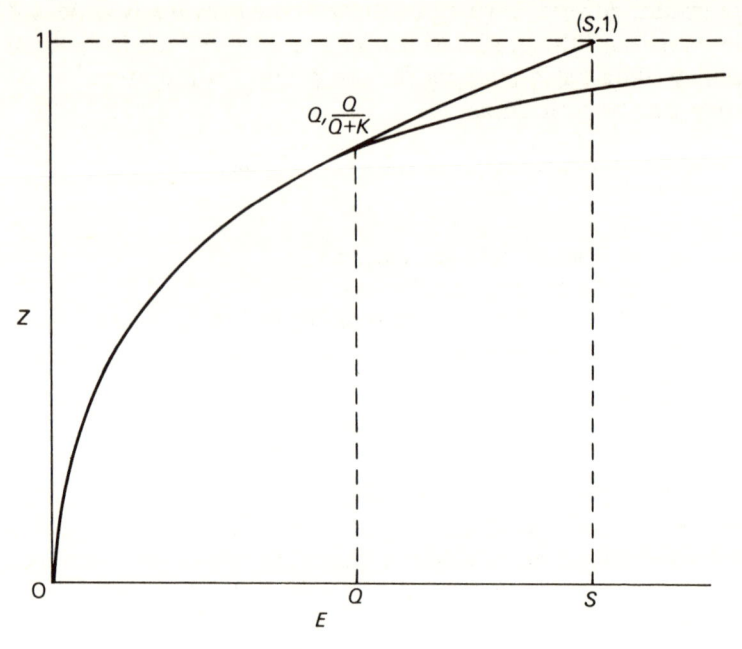

FIGURE 8.1

8.9 The equation for the tangent line may be derived in the following way.

Since $\quad Z = \dfrac{E}{(E+K)},\ \dfrac{d}{dE} \cdot Z = \dfrac{K}{(E+K)^2}$

so that at $E = Q$, the slope is

$$\frac{K}{(Q+K)^2}$$

and the line must pass through $(S, 1)$

This means that $\dfrac{1-Q/(Q+K)}{S-Q}=\dfrac{K}{(Q+K)^2}$

whence $Q=\dfrac{(S-K)}{2}$

The equation of the line may be written

$$\frac{1-Z}{S-E}=\frac{K}{(Q+K)^2}$$

and substituting for Q we have

$$Z=1-\frac{4K(S-E)}{(S+K)^2}$$

8.10 If it is considered that the hyperbola should be less distorted, a higher degree curve can be used to join the hyperbols tangentially from the point $(S,1)$. However, bearing in mind the other practical assumptions which have to be made, this appears to be an unwarranted refinement.

8.11 Credibility theory is widely used for experience rating (as indeed is experience rating in general) in American practice but it is not much used in U.K. practice at the present time. American practice is also developed to a degree of complexity at which distinction is made, in so called 'split plans', for dividing losses into primary and excess elements. The primary element reflects loss *frequency* and is given major weight in the experience rating formula; the excess element reflects loss *severity* and is given minor weight in the formula.

NO-CLAIM DISCOUNT

Background

8.12 The idea of giving a discount to a policyholder who has not made a claim is almost as old as motor insurance itself. Up to about 1928 the discount was quite small, perhaps 10% if no claim had been made in the previous year. It appears to have been intended as an inducement to a policyholder to renew his policy with the same company, and as a credit for not calling upon the services of the claims department, but the custom of offering discount to a transferring policyholder quickly developed and so nullified any advantage in discount to policyholders who stayed with the same company. For a long time the discount was termed a bonus even though it was not an appropriation of profits; the term 'no-claim discount' (N.C.D.) became established in the 1960's. 'No-claim discount' is a rather anomalous expression, for, as is explained later, both 'no claim' and 'discount' are not always strictly appropriate.

Experience rating in the U.K.

8.13 As we have seen, an experience rating system is a system by which the premium for an individual risk takes into account the claims experience of that individual risk. N.C.D. systems constitute a form of experience rating used in private motor insurance in the U.K.; the practice is to consider the number of years since the last claim, subject to some important qualifications which are considered later. It is as a form of experience rating that N.C.D. would now probably be defended. It does have to be defended since it is not offered to other classes of insurance, it operates against the principle of spreading costs (those with bad experience pay more than they otherwise would pay) and it costs money to operate if only in terms of arguments with policyholders who feel disgruntled over the loss of their N.C.D. (perhaps as a result of a claim sharing agreement between insurers). On the other hand N.C.D. does discourage small claims (see 8.34). Most U.K. private motor policies are subject to N.C.D. Those which are not, are mainly fleet risks and special policies for the mature policyholder with a good insurance record at the time that his policy was taken out.

Claims

8.14 One of the conditions of most motor insurance policies is that the insurer must be notified within a specified period of time 'upon the happening of any accident or the occurrence of any loss or damage'. Using a strict legal interpretation this condition implies that every incident, no matter how trivial, must be reported to the insurer. In practice many policyholders do not bother to report minor incidents. However, even if a policyholder does report an incident he will not lose any of his entitlement to N.C.D. if he elects to bear any liability himself. If the policyholder does not elect to bear the liability himself, the insurer will treat the report as a claim, and as a general rule this will result in loss of discount.

8.15 There are important exceptions to this general rule.

1. Many policies contain a provision whereby payments of emergency treatment fees and claims for damage to a windscreen only (with an upper limit of cost) are not taken into account, and if no other payments are involved no discount will usually be lost.
2. If the insurer is able to recover the whole of his outlay no discount will be lost. If the insurer would have been able to recover the whole of his outlay but for the operation of a claim sharing or knock-for-knock agreement between the insurers concerned, the discount may not be lost. There are occasions however where as the result of a claim sharing agreement, the insurer takes the view that there has been some outlay and that discount must be lost. Such hard decisions cause much ill feeling. A knock-for-knock agreement is a form of claim sharing agreement under which each insurer pays for the insured damage to his policyholder's own vehicle. It is a private arrangement between the insurers concerned, and should not operate to affect the rights or liabilities of the policyholder himself. Thus, a payment made under a knock-for-knock agreement that would otherwise have been recovered from another insurer ought not to be treated as affecting entitlement to N.C.D. Conversely, the absence of a payment where one would have been made had there been no agreement should not prevent loss of discount by the policyholder.

8.16 It is customary to talk of 'allowed' claims and 'disallowed' claims according to whether they are ignored or counted in assessing N.C.D. The experience of one company is that the proportion of 'allowed' claims varies from about

30% for high risk policies (e.g. young policyholders insuring sports cars) to well over 50% for low risk policies. However, these percentages can be expected to vary from company to company, not only because of differing practices in allowing N.C.D. following a claim but also because of variation in the types of incident which are recorded as claims.

8.17 Whether or not N.C.D. is allowed depends on considerations of recovery of outlay, not of attribution of blame. It cannot be safely assumed that the discount will automatically be allowed even if a car was, for example, run into from the rear or hit whilst parked in a sensible place.

8.18 The practice of different insurers in allowing N.C.D. after claims varies considerably. Some insurers have an 'instant allowed' scheme whereby claims of particular kinds are 'allowed' without delay provided certain conditions are satisfied. Such a scheme can produce considerable administrative savings which may more than compensate for the comparatively generous treatment it affords some policyholders.

8.19 The question could be asked, 'Why have allowed claims at all?'. (It is supposed to be a no-claim, not a no-blame system which is being operated.) It could be argued that the number of claims (allowed or disallowed) incurred under a policy over a period of years is related to the extent to which a vehicle is exposed on the road during that time. If this reasoning were accepted, then disallowing all claims would appear to offer more scope than at present for distinguishing the high risks from the low risks. On the other hand it would seem to the policyholder so obviously unfair if he were to be penalised even after a claim in which the insurer had recovered his outlay that it would be bad business to try to operate a system in which N.C.D. entitlement is lost after every claim.

8.20 N.C.D. is expressed as a percentage of 'basic premium'. The basic premium is an amount which is dependent on the cover provided by the policy and on certain facts about the vehicle, the policyholder and the persons entitled to drive. Among the factors used in rating are the type and age of the car, where it is kept, the age of the policyholder, and whether a voluntary excess is required (whereby the insurer is not liable for the first £X of every claim for damage to the policyholder's own vehicle). When basic premiums are set, an allowance needs to be made for the effect of N.C.D. in each group, since, few policyholders will pay as much as the basic premium, perhaps not more than 5%–15% in most N.C.D. scales. (Young policyholders will pay more than older policyholders since they will not have had time to earn so much discount.) So the basic premium must be set high enough to prevent the insurer running at an overall loss after allowing N.C.D.

8.21 Until 1966 it was normal to lose all entitlement to discount on making one claim and to have to work one's way back to the top of the scale. In 1966 most U.K. insurers increased their maximum rate of N.C.D. from 40% to 60% and consequently if the old rules had been retained the loss of discount for making a single claim could have been very severe. The practice was therefore introduced of providing that on making one, or perhaps even two, (disallowed) claims in one policy year the policyholder did not necessarily lose *all* his entitlement to N.C.D., but merely moved to a lower level on the N.C.D. scale. (Later in the chapter, moves to a lower (intermediate) level of N.C.D. are referred to as fallback.) This shows why it is, strictly, inappropriate to regard each level of discount as representing a specific number of claim-free years.

8.22 There are many N.C.D. scales in operation in the U.K., differing from each other in the number of steps in the scale, the rates of discount and the rules for moving up and down the scale. A survey in *Money Which?* in December, 1969 described 54 such scales, but a subsequent survey in September, 1972 showed that the number of scales had been greatly reduced.

8.23 In order to provide quotations it is necessary for offices either to tabulate all the levels of net premium for each basic premium or to calculate each premium net of discount as and when required. The latter method is virtually unavoidable if the manual of basic premiums is very extensive. The former method is most convenient where a points rating system is in operation.

8.24 A points rating system is a simple means of calculating basic premiums. Points are allocated for each value of each rating factor. For a particular policy the appropriate values of the rating factors are selected, and the corresponding points are added together. The total number of points obtained is looked up in a table giving, for each total points, the basic premium and the premium net of each rate of N.C.D. Usually the scale of premiums is multiplicative, i.e. the premium for $T+1$ total points is $(1+k)$ times the premium for T points.

8.25 An even simpler method of obtaining net premiums when using a points system can be introduced if it is considered acceptable to approximate to the rates of discount previously allowed. Consider, for example, points scales in which an increase of 1 in the number of points corresponds to an increase in premium of $2\frac{1}{4}\%$ and 6% respectively. Some values of v'' are given in Table 8.1.

TABLE 8.1

\multicolumn{3}{c}{$2\frac{1}{4}\%$}	\multicolumn{3}{c}{6%}
v''	$(47-n)$	n	v''	$(18-n)$	n
1·00000	47	0	1·00000	18	0
·80051	37	10	·79209	14	4
·74882	34	13	·74726	13	5
·70047	31	16	·70496	12	6
·59944	24	23	·59190	9	9
·50169	16	31	·49697	6	12
·40161	6	41	·39365	2	16
·35142	0	47	·35034	0	18

8.26 The above table shows values of n for which, at the given rate of interest, $100(1-v'')$ approximates to rates of N.C.D. of 0, 20, 25, 30, 40, 50, 60 and 65%. Thus, it will be seen that if the basic premium is given by T points the premium net of N.C.D. may be given by $(T-n)$ points. However, it is preferable for the premium calculation to involve points additions only. For example, assuming 65% to be the maximum rate of N.C.D., we can *add* $(47-n)$ in the first scale to the total number of points already obtained for the other rating factors, or *add* $(18-n)$ in the second scale, to give the premium net of N.C.D. This method has the advantage that only a single premium is tabulated for each total number of points.

Reasons for an N.C.D. system

8.27 The first reason for applying an N.C.D. system is to reduce heterogeneity within each rating category. The categories used in group rating are not sufficient to eliminate all heterogeneity, since it is not possible to identify and measure all factors which may influence the risk. There may be other factors which cannot be identified or measured and cannot therefore be used as an axis of classification. The operation of an N.C.D. system is a means of reducing the residual heterogeneity within each group of policies by reference to the actual experience of the individual members of the group. (This is another way of describing the experience rating principle.)

8.28 Johnson and Hey (1971) have described the use of a simple mathematical model to study the influence of a single risk factor after largely eliminating the effects of other risk factors represented in the model. This can be done for N.C.D. If the portfolio is grouped according to N.C.D. category we can calculate for each group the claim cost per vehicle year, having largely eliminated the effects of the rating factors, other than N.C.D., which are used as a basis for the model. (We should also try to eliminate the effect of knock-for-knock, since this will vary from one N.C.D. category to another, but only guesswork can be employed here.) Such an exercise will show, for a given scale of fallback and after making an appropriate allowance for expenses, the discounts which should theoretically be allowed for each N.C.D. category. This will indicate whether the discounts actually allowed are reasonably equitable among the different N.C.D. categories.

8.29 It should be borne in mind that any N.C.D. scale will probably be applied to all private car policyholders and all types of cover. It could be expected that different N.C.D. scales would be appropriate for different groups of policyholders and types of cover, but a number of factors encourage the use of a uniform scale, as we shall see later.

Numerical example

8.30 Statistics from the experience of one large U.K. insurance office over several years give frequencies and average costs (roughly in terms of 1972 money) of claims as in Table 8.2.

TABLE 8.2

N.C.D. category*	Frequency per 1000 vehicle years	Average amount of claim (£)	Approx. claim cost per vehicle year (£)	Estimate of claim cost if knock-for-knock eliminated (£)
0	210	132	27·5	30·0
1	180	128	23·0	25·0
2	160	125	20·0	21·0
3	150	123	18·5	18·5
4	140	119	16·5	16·5
5	135	116	15·5	15·5
6	132	115	15·0	15·0
7	127	115	14·5	14·0
8	120	115	14·0	13·0
9	110	115	12·5	11·5
combined 4–9	125	116	14·5	14·0

* Subject to the earlier qualification, this can be regarded as 'claim-free years', category 9 comprising 9 years and over.

Note: The figures have been adjusted in respect of other factors so as to represent the effect of N.C.D. category only, unaffected by any other factor (for example age of policyholder) which is associated with N.C.D.

8.31 The effect of knock-for-knock agreements is a net transfer of claim cost from the high risk categories to the low and on a true assessment of liability the range of claim cost might be from £30·0 to £11·5 with a mean for the 4–9 category of about £14·0. It follows that if the 0 group pays basic premiums, then 60% discount does not seem to be earned until one approaches category 9. After eliminating the effect of knock-for-knock, a discount scale giving net premiums in proportion to claim cost might be roughly as follows:

N.C.D. category   0   1   2   3   4   5   6   7   8   9

Discount (%)   0 17 30 38 45 48 50 53 57 62

8.32 It is interesting to note that if a points scale were used it would not be satisfactory to have the same number of points difference between successive positions on the scale. For example, using the 6% points scale referred to in paragraph 8.25 the above rates of discount could be approximately reproduced by the following points values for N.C.D.:

N.C.D. category	0	1	2	3	4	5	6	7	8	9
Points	15	12	9	7	5	4	3	2	1	0
Discount (%)	0	16	30	37	44	47	50	53	56	58

8.33 Offices do not in practice use discount scales with so many steps, one reason perhaps being the difficulty of establishing entitlement to N.C.D. on transfer from another insurer. The office referred to above uses a scale in which 25% discount corresponds roughly to 0% in most other scales, and in which the highest rate of discount is 65%; adjusting the office's discounts to be consistent with 0% N.C.D. for the basic category, the rates of discount actually allowed are:

N.C.D. category	0	1	2	3	4	5	6	7	8	9
Discount (%)	0	13	27	40	47	53	53	53	53	53

8.34 The second reason for applying an N.C.D. system is to discourage small claims and so keep claim costs and management expenses at a lower level than they would otherwise be. A policyholder contemplating whether to make a claim will usually recognise that claiming may well result in a penalty through loss of future discount. The total penalty is often somewhat arbitrary; it depends on the features of the particular N.C.D. system and the current position of the policyholder on the discount scale. A loss of £50 to £100 over a period of 3 to 5 years is by no means unusual, so that making a claim of say £20 to £50 might well result in a greater total net cost to the policyholder than if he had not claimed at all. Penalties are considered in detail in paragraphs 6.84, 8.43 and following paragraphs.

8.35 Many comprehensive policies provide cover for the contents of vehicles (personal belongings, rugs, etc.) up to a fixed amount. This extension of cover is of much less value than might be apparent, since contents claims will usually be less than the resulting loss of discount.

8.36 The third reason for an N.C.D. system is that it may enable an insurer to charge premiums more closely reflecting the individual risk. This object is hardly achieved in practice. If one postulates a policyholder with a true disallowed claim frequency p (assumed constant) it is simple to calculate for a given N.C.D. scale the expected premium he will pay over a period. For more detail the reader should refer to the papers by Beard (1964 and 1968) and Johnson and Hey (1971). The Johnson and Hey paper showed that a much higher than average risk produced, over a period of years, an expected net premium which was little above the average for all policyholders. This was for a particular N.C.D. scale, although other scales are likely to produce similar results. It would appear then that in U.K. practice the claims history of an individual policy does not enable the insurer to go very far towards correcting the premium for a policyholder for whom the risk differs materially from the average for the group in which he has been placed. Whilst this seems unsatisfactory, it may be regarded as inevitable in conditions in which there are only about 90 disallowed claims per 1,000 vehicle years. But one can readily understand why members of the motoring public may claim that an N.C.D. system penalises unlucky motorists rather more than reckless or careless ones.

8.37 The fourth reason for an N.C.D. system is that it may induce safer driving. It could be argued that the existence of a financial penalty on claiming may induce safer driving but there can be no evidence to support this and it seems unlikely that the amount of potential penalty could have any significant effect. It is possible that the potential heavy penalty involved in the loss of N.C.D. might make policyholders reluctant to allow driving by others, particularly by young or inexperienced drivers.

Determining the rules for moving up and down

8.38 Consideration must be given to setting appropriate rules both for moving up and for moving down an N.C.D. scale. Let us take a new entrant with no previous claim experience. We can classify the risk according to the available information (rating area, car group, etc.) and charge what seems an appropriate initial premium. At the end of the first year we have more information, since we know what the claim experience has been. We can use this information to modify the original premium since claimants can be expected, as a result of heterogeneity, to be on average higher risks than non-claimants. It is the extent of the heterogeneity which we should wish to determine.

8.39 Delaporte (1964 and 1965) has approached this problem by using observations of numbers of vehicles having 0, 1, 2, ... accidents in a given period. He found that these observations corresponded closely to a negative binomial distribution (a skew distribution with a long tail that is commonly applicable to accident frequency studies), and hence he derived the parameters of such a distribution for the underlying risks. He showed how this distribution could be used to produce a table of premium adjustments related to the number of claims made on an individual policy. He appeared to visualise that the premium adjustment table would vary from one rating category to another.

8.40 The concept underlying Delaporte's approach seems quite attractive but its practical application appears to have significant drawbacks:

(i) In order to obtain reliable estimates of the parameters for the initial distribution, large numbers of policies must be brought into observation.

(ii) Observations based on policies exposed for a period of several years relate to a select group because of movements into and out of the group of policies being studied.

(iii) Over a period of several years the underlying risk distribution may change and thus invalidate the original published tables.

(iv) Finally, the introduction of a scale of experience rating where none has existed before may be expected, because of the deterrent effect, to alter the pattern of claims for the future.

8.41 There are clearly severe limits on the extent to which the underlying risks can be assessed on the basis of the information which we are likely to have at our disposal. An approach which is less ambitious than that described by Delaporte would be to examine the claims experience according to the number of claim-free years (ignoring allowed claims) at the previous renewal and whether or not a (disallowed) claim arose in that year. In practice we should probably have to use N.C.D. category rather than the number of claim-free years for the lower categories. Also, we should wish largely to eliminate the effects of rating factors other than N.C.D.

8.42 This process would give a good guide to the increase or decrease in premiums required according to whether a claim has or has not arisen in the year. It would still have to be borne in mind, however, that a change in the levels of discount and fallback arrangements could affect penalties and hence affect the subsequent pattern of claiming. Although in principle the increases and decreases could vary from one rating category to another, it seems likely that in practice one would seek to adopt a system of uniform percentage adjustments in premium.

The penalty on claiming

8.43 The first effect of making a disallowed claim is that the next year's premium is higher than it would otherwise have been—often much higher. For example the loss of all discount when 60% was expected would result in the premium being $2\frac{1}{2}$ times that which was 'expected'. This may mean a very substantial increase in expenditure. Moreover, a penalty will also be incurred in each subsequent year until the policyholder reaches his maximum entitlement. It will be seen that in general the longer the period to maximum entitlement, the larger the penalty in total for a given initial penalty.

8.44 If the rules for an N.C.D. scale have been determined using statistical methods of the kind previously described in paragraphs 8.39–8.41 the penalties on making a claim will already have been fixed in such a way as to take specific account of the rating category change implied by the claim. Often though, the rules for an N.C.D. scale are determined on a somewhat arbitrary basis, and this can lead to an inappropriate range of penalties.

8.45 It is a widely held view that it is desirable to make the total penalty, i.e. increase in premiums, much smaller for the policyholder who has reached maximum discount than for

EXPERIENCE RATING

the new or inexperienced policyholder. It is difficult to see why this should necessarily be so. In the absence of statistical evidence to the contrary it would seem to be preferable to make the penalty roughly the same for policyholders in all N.C.D. categories.

8.46 It is an interesting exercise to experiment with different scales and fallback arrangements, taking care to compare what *will* be paid with what *would have been* paid had there been no claim. In the following examples, penalties in future years have not been discounted to the present, and no allowance has been made for future increases in premium rates or the possibility of more than one claim.

8.47 *Example A: (A typical N.C.D. scale)* Discounts of 30%, 40%, 50% and 60% after 1, 2, 3 and 4 claim-free years, with 2 years maximum fallback following a claim. Comparisons of penalties for policyholders now on 40% and 50% N.C.D. are given in Table 8.3.

TABLE 8.3

Year after claim	Current rate 40%			Current rate 50%		
	Discount after claim	Discount if no claim	% loss	Discount after claim	Discount if no claim	% loss
1	0	50	50	30	60	30
2	30	60	30	40	60	20
3	40	60	20	50	60	10
4	50	60	10	60	60	0
5	60	60	0	60	60	0
Total loss			110			60

It will be seen that the total penalty at 40% is almost double that at 50%, a feature which can hardly be defended. The penalty to a policyholder without discount is the same as at 50%, but is made up of 30+10+10+10=60%. The penalty to a policyholder on 60% N.C.D. is only 30%, made up of 20+10=30%.

8.48 *Example B: (A scale operated by a Lloyd's syndicate)* New entrants normally start at 100% of basic premium and move up or down 20% on making one claim or no claims. The minimum premium is 40% of the basic premium. Two examples of penalties produced are given in Table 8.4, taking the *basic* premium as £100.

TABLE 8.4

Year after claim	Current premium £160			Current premium £40		
	Premium after claim (£)	Premium if no claim (£)	Loss (£)	Premium after claim (£)	Premium if no claim (£)	Loss (£)
1	180	140	40	60	40	20
2	160	120	40	40	40	0
3	140	100	40	40	40	0
4	120	80	40	40	40	0
5	100	60	40	40	40	0
6	80	40	40	40	40	0
7	60	40	20	40	40	0
8	40	40	0	40	40	0
Total loss			260			20

The tables show that this scale can produce extremely large, and very small, penalties. This is an example of a system under which premiums increase above the basic by a scale. Such a system, known as 'bonus/malus' (see para. 8.75) is not used to any great extent in the U.K. but is quite common in Europe.

Reasons for a uniform N.C.D. scale

8.49 For private cars it is easier to earn discount with non-comprehensive cover than it is with comprehensive cover since the disallowed claim frequency is perhaps only half that for comprehensive cover. It might be thought that discounts should consequently be less.

8.50 All premiums should include an element of expenses unrelated to the size of net premium, as well as expenses proportional to the size of the premium. The element of expenses unrelated to the size of net premium is more significant for non-comprehensive policies than comprehensive policies, since the average premium per policy is much less in the former. Discounts are applied to the total premium, not to the premium net of 'per policy' expenses; this is another reason for expecting somewhat lower discounts to apply to non-comprehensive policies.

8.51 It is not always the case that the higher the claim frequency the higher the rates of discount which are appropriate. For instance, young policyholders have a much higher disallowed claim frequency than older policyholders, but it would certainly not be valid to claim that the discounts to be allowed for young policyholders should be higher than those allowed for others. Rather the reverse is the case. There is evidence (using the method of paragraph 8.28 and following paragraphs) that young policyholders under a uniform N.C.D. scale will receive *more* discount than their likely future experience would justify.

8.52 Many companies, whilst apparently allowing normal rates of N.C.D., do in effect give higher rates of N.C.D. for young policyholders by imposing lower age loadings for those who have attained the higher rates of N.C.D. This effect is the opposite to that which statistics suggest the companies should be aiming at. The methods by which insurers deal with young drivers are numerous, comprising various combinations of, for example, additional premiums, compulsory excesses, adjustments to the normal N.C.D. scale and rules for changing N.C.D. following a claim.

8.53 There are several reasons, some set out below, why the same basic N.C.D. scale normally applies to all types of cover and also to the high risk as well as the low risk cases.

1 Having two or more scales would introduce more complexities both in administration and in communication with the public. It would be very difficult to explain in simple terms to a young policyholder why he was entitled to less discount than his older counterpart.

2 A sharp jump in premium might occur when a policyholder was transferred from one N.C.D. scale to another, unless special transitional arrangements were devised.

3 It would be difficult to construct two or more different scales each giving sensible penalties, in relation to those of the other scales, for those who make claims.

4 Most non-comprehensive policyholders are entitled to low discount only. This may seem surprising in view of the lower claim frequency. The reason is that once a policyholder achieves three or more claim-free years he is very likely to convert to full comprehensive cover.

5   There is a shortage of reliable information on the variation of claims experience by N.C.D. category for non-comprehensive cover. The number of claims for older, non-comprehensive insured policyholders with low rates of N.C.D., even for the whole U.K. insurance market, is less than the number needed for proper statistical analysis.

Effect on premium income of a change in N.C.D. rules

8.54 Before introducing a new N.C.D. scale, whether by changing the rules for moving up and down or by changing the rates of N.C.D. or both, it is important to estimate both the short-term and the long-term effects that the change will have on the premium income for the portfolio.

8.55 In order to see what this entails we can begin by assuming a certain frequency of claims for which N.C.D. is disallowed, and corresponding to this we can assume probabilities of having 0, 1, 2, ..., such claims in a year. For this purpose it seems reasonable to assume a Poisson distribution. For any given N.C.D. scale, it is then a simple exercise to start with a group of new entrants and work out, from the rules for moving up and down and assuming that there are no exits, what proportion of them will be in each N.C.D. category in each subsequent year, and hence what the average rate of N.C.D. will be in each year. The ultimate position can be calculated directly by solving the equations which express the conditions that the group is in a stationary state.

8.56 The process can be illustrated by a numerical example, using the scale described in Example A of paragraph 8.47. It is convenient to set out in matrix form the probabilities of moving from one category to another:

Moving *from* N.C.D. category

Moving *to* N.C.D category

	0	1	2	3	4
0	$1-p_0$	p_0	0	0	0
1	$1-p_0$	0	p_0	0	0
2	$1-p_0$	0	0	p_0	0
3	$1-p_0-p_1$	p_1	0	0	p_0
4	$1-p_0-p_1$	0	p_1	0	p_0

[where p_i is the probability of i claims $i = 0, 1$]

EXPERIENCE RATING

For those unfamiliar with matrix representation it should be explained that any particular cell of the matrix is occupied by the probability of moving *from* the category indicated by the row *to* the category indicated by the column in the year, e.g. to move from 4 to 0 in a year the policyholder must have more than one claim, a probability of $(1-p_0-p_1)$.

8.57 We shall assume an overall disallowed claim frequency of ·1, giving $p_0 = \cdot 90476$ and $p_1 = \cdot 09048$. Applying these values to 10,000 entrants in category 0 in the first year, we obtain numbers in the five N.C.D. categories as shown in Table 8.5.

TABLE 8.5

Year	\multicolumn{5}{c}{N.C.D. category}
	0	1	2	3	4
1	10,000				
2	952	9,048			
3	952	861	8,187		
4	952	861	779	7,408	
5	281	1,532	779	705	6,703
6	281	318	1,993	705	6,703
7	281	318	895	1,803	6,703
8	182	418	895	809	7,696
9	182	238	1,075	809	7,696
10	182	238	912	972	7,696
Ultimate	165	224	915	827	7,869

8.58 It would probably have been more realistic to allow for heterogeneity in the portfolio by assuming that some policyholders had a higher claim frequency than the remainder, but applying the average frequency to the whole portfolio is satisfactory as an illustration.

8.59 With the rates of discount allowed in the scale in Example A, it follows that the average rate of N.C.D. in each year is:

Year	1	2	3	4	5	6	7	8	9	10	Ultimate
Average N.C.D.	0	27·1	35·3	42·7	51·5	52·7	53·8	55·1	55·2	55·4	55·7

8.60 The situation in practice is complicated by movements in and out of the portfolio, and by variations in the mix of business and in the frequencies of disallowed claims. The proportions in the various N.C.D. categories will not usually be those corresponding to the ultimate position: because of the flow of new entrants to insurance, the proportions on the lower rates of N.C.D. will usually be appreciably higher than those in the ultimate state. Nevertheless, calculations on these lines can give a useful guide to the effect of a change in the N.C.D. scale.

8.61 Suppose, for example, that we are contemplating merely a change in the rates of N.C.D., with no change in the rules for moving up and down. Given the proportions in the portfolio at present, we can calculate the immediate effect of the change fairly readily. It should be noted, however, that the proportions used should not be those at the next renewal for the policies falling due for renewal, since these are a select group: the new entrants, even allowing for transfers from other companies, will tend to be on lower rates of N.C.D. than the existing policies falling due for renewal. It is therefore necessary either to assume a certain volume of new business in each category, for combining with the existing business (with perhaps an adjustment for selective lapses from the renewal date) or to use the proportions in the various N.C.D. categories at the last renewal (or entry) date for all renewal months combined.

8.62 Having calculated the immediate effect of the changes in N.C.D. rates, it is still advisable to make comparisons, for subsequent years, between the old and the new scales. If, for example, the choice lay between continuing the existing scale and introducing the new scale, with the basic premiums suitably adjusted to produce the same premium income in the first year, in either case, for the portfolio as a whole, it would be worth while knowing which scale would produce the greater premium income the following year, for a similar portfolio. The point is perhaps especially relevant at a time of statutory supervision of increases in premium rates.

8.63 Similar considerations apply if a change in the N.C.D. movement rules is contemplated. Here it is necessary to calculate the effect of the new scale by using the matrix corresponding to that scale.

8.64 When any N.C.D. changes are introduced, it is of course possible that the changes will themselves affect the probabilities of claiming, and it may therefore be necessary to test the effect of varying the assumptions as to the pattern of claiming.

Other classes of business

8.65 *Motor cycles* Claim frequencies for motor cycles are generally much lower than for private cars. For example, the smaller motor cycles ridden by older men may give rise to only one claim in 100 vehicle years, and this is quite inadequate to form the basis of experience rating. As a result, some companies give no discount, or very little, to motor cyclists. However, experience shows that the motor cyclist in the 16–18 age group gives rise to a claim cost up to ten times that of the adult, experienced rider. There are two methods of allowing for this:

Method I   A very high loading (say 800%) may be charged at the lowest ages, the loading reducing rapidly, but with no discounts, as the age increases to about 25.

Method II   Alternatively, much lower age loadings (of the order of 200%) may be charged, but with discounts up to about 65% and a basic premium of around three times that in Method I.

8.66 The net result to policyholders can be made much the same using either method, but Method II would probably be more acceptable to most policyholders.

8.67 *Commercial vehicles* For commercial vehicles claim rates may be very high: up to one claim, or even more, per vehicle year, and this would appear to provide plenty of scope for experience rating. However, the bulk of this type of risk is likely to be in fleets, which are not subject to N.C.D. A fleet (of either commercial vehicles or private cars) is rated on the collective experience of that fleet, using a form of experience rating which is based on total claim cost rather than on the numbers of disallowed claims. Where commercial vehicles *are* insured by individual policies (and there may be a significant volume of such business) it is common market practice to operate an N.C.D. scale although the levels of

Other forms of discount

8.68 With any form of experience rating like N.C.D. it is necessary to decide the period of time over which the claims experience will affect the discount. Having too short a period would provide insufficient claims for a proper analysis of the experience, whereas having too long a period would give weight to claims in early policy years since when the underlying risk may well have changed. Bearing in mind the extra administrative difficulties of too long a time scale, 5 or 6 years would appear reasonable.

8.69 We next need to determine which incident should count towards an assessment of the claims experience. In some countries, notably the U.S.A., incidents other than claims may count. Such incidents may include traffic violations or the issue of tickets by the police. For convenience, we shall refer to all such incidents as 'claims'.

8.70 It may be noted here that it is practicable to base experience rating on *numbers* of claims only, not on *amounts* of claims, if only because the amount of a claim may not be known until several years after the date on which the claim arose.

8.71 Earlier in this chapter we have been concerned with N.C.D. as a form of experience rating in which the main factor is the number of years since the last claim. Other methods of experience rating are possible. For example, the system could be related to the number of claims in a given period or the number of claim-free years in a given period. In either of these examples, a single claim in the last (say) 5 years would lead to the same premium whether or not the claim occurred 1 year ago or nearly 5 years ago.

8.72 In the first example (using the number of claims in a given period), if it were desired to give more weight to the most recent claims, a different number of 'claim points' could be allotted for claims in each of the 5 years, the most recent claims having the most claim points. Let the number of claims in year $n+i$ be c_i, $i=0$ to 4, and let each claim in year $n+i$

be allotted p_i points. Then, in policy year $n+5$, the total number of claim points would be given by

$$\sum_{i=0}^{4} c_i\, p_i$$

and the premium would be determined by reference to this total. The formula could be modified to include (say) $p_i/2$ claim points for each claim currently classified as 'allowed'. New entrants could be dealt with by including notional claim points dependent on their previous insurance history (if any).

8.73 With a little imagination it is possible to devise other elaborate experience rating systems. How such systems, assuming they could be implemented, would work out in practice is difficult to predict. This is where we must remind ourselves that general insurance is not just mathematics. We are operating in a market against the restraint of a price mechanism. There is always the problem that those policyholders who could obtain cheaper rates elsewhere may lapse their policies. In the U.K. there is a very strong incentive for companies to maintain an N.C.D. system on conventional lines, in order to keep in line with the rest of the market.

8.74 The suitability of any system depends partly on the features of claims experience in the country in which the system is to operate; for example much higher claim frequencies are experienced in most continental countries than in the U.K., even though the cover provided under private car policies is generally less than in the U.K.

8.75 The more interested reader may like to refer to the experience rating system of Delaporte (1964 and 1965) and to the description of bonus systems in some European countries by Vepsäläinen (1972) especially bonus/malus (Gurtler 1963). The latter is a system where as well as receiving a bonus (discount) for freedom from claims a policyholder suffers a malus (penalty) for incurring a claim. It is more complicated than N.C.D. and offers no advantage in practice. Vepsäläinen gives examples of some mathematical properties of bonus systems which were described by Loimaranta (1972). There is also in at least one company in the U.K. a system of N.C.D. in which once the policyholder has reached his maximum discount, he does not lose it on a claim, the theory being that he has established that he is a good driver. However, if his subsequent claim history becomes bad, he and his insurer part company. This kind of policy carries a small compulsory excess.

A further review of criticism of experience rating

8.76 It is possible to advance a number of arguments against operating *any* form of experience rating system.

  (i) Paragraphs 8.43 and following paragraphs of this chapter examined the penalty on claiming. But why should there be *any* penalty on making the occasional claim? Any experience rating system which provides a substantial penalty as a result of making a single claim can be charged with contravening a fundamental principle of insurance: that the policyholder who nominally has full cover should be in the same financial position after the claim is settled as before the incident which gave rise to the claim. However, it can also be argued that this principle (of indemnity) relates only to the claim monies to be paid and does not extend to the level of premiums which may be required for continuation of insurance. In general insurance, adverse claims experience will frequently lead to loaded premiums for the future.

 (ii) Paragraph 8.36 has explained that an N.C.D. system is not able to charge the high risk policies enough in relation to the portfolio as a whole, and this is an unsatisfactory feature of the system. In view of the low level of claim frequencies in the U.K., other forms of experience rating are likely to be similar to N.C.D. in this respect.

(iii) An experience rating system results in actual premium payments which are subject to large and unexpected increases (other than those arising from inflation). This can cause the policyholder great budgeting problems. He cannot insure against the possibility of losing discount before the next renewal date.

(iv) Experience rating gives rise to a lot of extra administrative work for the office, and much ill-will can be created when claims are disallowed. The case for experience rating must be strong in order to justify all the expense and trouble which are caused.

8.77 If N.C.D. were ended, risks would be rated merely according to the factor used in group rating. A further group rating factor could be introduced: number of years (if any) since passing a driving test—to provide a loading for inexperienced drivers. Claim costs would then be shared among all policyholders with the same group rating classification, and no penalty would be incurred as a result of making the occasional claim.

8.78 The obvious drawback to such a scheme is that it could lead to selection against the office. In spite of the administrative costs which would be saved if N.C.D. were ended, the policyholder with a good claims experience may still be able to obtain a cheaper premium rate elsewhere, and if so there would be a tendency to transfer, the office being left with the less profitable business. Whether it *would* be possible to obtain cheaper rates elsewhere would be determined largely by whether other offices were prepared to accept a signed statement from the policyholder regarding his claims history, since the office would have ceased to print the entitlement to discount on the renewal notice. If other offices were not prepared to accept such a signed statement, this might appear substantially to limit the selection against the office. However, there would always be selection in respect of new policyholders, and this could be very serious for the office.

8.79 Only if the whole U.K. insurance market were prepared to ignore N.C.D. would such schemes be likely to be successful. Even in that unlikely event it would probably be necessary to single out a very small proportion of motorists who had demonstrated by driving convictions and repeated claims that they were bad risks; they would be charged an underwriter's loading. One could remark that applying this loading was a form of experience rating, but it is no more so than the loading necessary for high risks in general business other than motor.

8.80 There are at present available in the U.K. a number of private motor insurance schemes which are free of N.C.D. These schemes are for the 'good' motorist, and generally specify a compulsory excess in respect of damage to the policyholder's own vehicle. To join such a scheme one generally needs to have a good insurance record, be over a specified age and own a particular type of car. It is possible to lose entitlement to remain in the scheme, but only after a particularly heavy claims experience.

8.81 This type of scheme must also be subject to a certain amount of selection, although this may be limited somewhat by a policyholder's wish to remain in the scheme because of the extra security it affords in the event of a claim. However, much depends on the profitability of such schemes in relation to other motor insurance. It can never be assumed that the low risks are necessarily the most profitable risks.

8.82 Recent articles in the press have suggested that the introduction of 'no fault' insurance would mean the end of N.C.D. This is not likely to be the case.

8.83 'No fault' is a principle of legal liability not of insurance. The term 'no fault insurance' should therefore be taken to mean insurance in conditions in which the law provides that compensation is payable regardless of fault. Insurance in such conditions could perfectly well operate with an N.C.D. or other experience rating system, although—especially if fewer recoveries were made—some minor changes might be needed in the rules for allowing claims for N.C.D. purposes.

8.84 If—as in private car insurance in the U.K.—there is evidence that policyholders' future claims experience varies appreciably within the rating groups according to whether or not they have previously made claims, then in a freely competitive market insurers must take this into account in the premiums they charge. Thus, unless some further group rating factor can be found which will account for most of this variation within the existing rating groups—and this seems rather unlikely—some form of experience rating such as N.C.D. will continue.

BIBLIOGRAPHY

BEARD, R. E. Some Statistical Problems Arising from the Transaction of Motor Insurance Business. *Journal of the Institute of Actuaries Students' Society*, 1964, **17**, 279.

BEARD, R. E. Some Observations on No-claim Bonus Schemes in Motor Insurance. *Transactions of the 18th International Congress of Actuaries*, 1968, **II**, 345.

BÜHLMANN, H. *Mathematical Methods in Risk Theory*. Springer-Verlag, 1970.

CONSUMERS' ASSOCIATION. Car Insurance. *Money Which?*, December, 1969 and September, 1972.

DELAPORTE, P. J. Principes de Tarification de l'Assurance Automobile par la Prime Modelée sur le Risque. *Transactions of the 17th International Congress of Actuaries*, 1964, **III**, 560.

DELAPORTE, P. J. Tarification du Risque Individuel d'Accidents d'Automobiles par la Prime Modelée sur le Risque. *The ASTIN Bulletin*, 1965, **III**, 251.

GÜRTLER, M. Bonus ou Malus? *The ASTIN Bulletin*, 1963, **III**, 43.

JOHNSON, P. D. and HEY, G. B. Statistical Studies in Motor Insurance. *Journal of the Institute of Actuaries*, 1971, **97**, 199.

LOIMARANTA, K. Some Asymptotic Properties of Bonus Systems. *The ASTIN Bulletin*, 1972, **VI**, 233.

VEPSÄLÄINEN, S. Applications to a Theory of Bonus Systems. *The ASTIN Bulletin*, 1972, **VI**, 212.

CHAPTER 9

REINSURANCE

9.1 Insurance is a process for spreading the strain of misfortune, i.e. the loss resulting from accident, theft, fire, misdemeanour of employees etc. In return for the payment of a premium much less in amount than the possible loss of all those who consider themselves at risk of loss from such misfortune and wish to be part of this process, the insurer agrees to meet this loss if it occurs. The premiums are so arranged (by calculation and market forces) that the insurer does not in the long run operate at a loss; on the contrary he makes a profit from which to service the capital invested in his business. However, the loss is a random event and the amount of the loss arising from such an event is also a random variable. Without any further help the insurer would be himself at risk of financial strain by a heavy run of claims above expectation or by the occurrence of a very large claim at the extreme of expectation. This further help can come either from inordinately large financial reserves or from some method of smoothing out large fluctuations in the frequency or amount of claims which have to be met. Reinsurance provides this method because it leaves the *retained* claims distribution with less variance (it is in effect a substitute for additional capital). It can also be shown that the total variance of retained and reinsurance claims is less than the variance of the gross claims.

9.2 Reinsurance is the use of the market to handle that part of these fluctuations or (what amounts to the same thing) that part of very large risks, e.g. aviation, which are beyond the working resources of the individual insurer. The insurer decides on the part of the risk he wishes to bear without help (his 'retention') and arranges with a reinsurer to handle the remainder.

9.3 There are other circumstances in which reinsurance might especially be a preferable alternative to seeking additional capital (which would need to be serviced by increased profits though it does earn interest to help the servicing). If the business of the insurer is growing rapidly there is likely to be a period during which reserves are not growing as rapidly as the risk of an adverse fluctuation in claim experience. An insurer in this position might feel the need to be assisted by the market and would seek reinsurance of part of the growing portfolio. There might also be a situation in which the insurer feels he has too much in a particular sector of his portfolio; reinsurance enables his net risks to be spread more satisfactorily over different regions of the country or different categories of business.

9.4 The purposes of reinsurance may be summarised as follows.

1 To enable the direct insurer to handle larger risks than he would otherwise be able to accept. With reinsurance a larger risk can be accepted which might otherwise have to be refused. This means growth to the market as a whole and added prestige to the direct insurer.

2 To stabilise the technical results of the insurer by reducing claim fluctuation. This means that the published results show a more stable progression.

3 To reduce the risk that in the event of a catastrophe, the direct insurer will suffer a net liability in excess of its financial resources.

4 To achieve a spread of risk so that the liabilities of the insurer are not too heavily concentrated in any one department or any one geographical area, or in any other classification.

5 To avoid the financial strain resulting from a rapid growth of the portfolio. The reinsurer might be asked to accept a share of an account on special terms which would give the needed financial support. An insurance company might be attracted to a reinsurer who offers 'services' which could be of particular help to a young or rapidly growing office. 'Services' might include technical help or administration facilities such as use of a computer for special problems.

The reinsurance market

9.5 Reinsurance is an international business. The simple reason for this is that the capacity of the market in any one country is in most cases insufficient and so the large risks are spread all over the world. To enable this international co-operation to be effective it is essential that currency restrictions should be minimal and should not operate to prevent purchase and sale of currency for the operation of reinsurance business. When a large claim occurs, it must be paid promptly in the appropriate currency. The local direct insurer can and sometimes does retain control of investment of the reinsurer's portfolio reserve and allows interest.

9.6 Reinsurance is a valuable asset to insurance companies in the developing countries and when a large claim occurs, the influx of cash to such an insurance company will provide vital support. This is particularly so if a catastrophe takes place, giving rise to a large claim. It is a specially important example of the growth situation of paragraph 9.4 (5).

9.7 The City of London has enormous financial connections all over the world, and it is natural that London has developed a very large reinsurance business. The market is complex, with interlocking and overlapping components, loosely connected by tradition and practice. Consequently, it is not easy to provide a clear picture of the constitution of the reinsurance market. The following paragraphs are an attempt to provide a general picture.

Specialist reinsurance companies

9.8 Before the First World War, there was a tendency to rely on continental reinsurers, but in the period 1914–18 several new companies specialising in reinsurance were formed to supply the gap that arose through severance of communications with Germany. Most of these reinsurance companies failed but some survived and since then other specialist reinsurers have entered the London market.

Direct companies

9.9 The direct writing offices also transact a considerable volume of reinsurance but it is not possible to estimate the volume. Such offices have branches and agency networks in many countries overseas and are therefore well placed to handle foreign reinsurance. Many of these direct writing offices are large and therefore have a big underwriting capacity. In order to spread their liabilities, they frequently offer 'reciprocity' and so part of their direct business is exchanged for reinsurance business, thus effecting a geographical re-distribution of their portfolio (see paragraph 9.59).

9.10 Many syndicates transact reinsurance while a few operate as reinsurance specialists (see Chapter 1). While it is not easy to estimate the volume of reinsurance business transacted by Lloyd's, there is no doubt that the volume is very large and Lloyd's do exercise a great influence on the reinsurance market.

Other members of the market

9.11 There are many miscellaneous underwriters who transact reinsurance. These insurers tend to be of rather modest size and rely upon London acceptances to provide a portfolio of foreign business. Some may act for groups of insurers, both domestic and foreign. In their reinsurance transactions these insurers would rely upon one or two underwriters who have knowledge of reinsurance. Some brokers have acceptance powers on behalf of overseas companies that they serve and advise. In total these underwriters do significantly extend the capacity of the reinsurance market.

Brokers

9.12 A considerable volume of resinsurance business is handled by brokers and, in consequence, many brokers have separate reinsurance departments while other brokers are specialists in reinsurance. The broker must obtain full details of the business which has to be placed and may offer such business to several reinsurers to obtain the best terms. Offers (especially for Lloyd's) are made on 'slips' which are signed by the accepting reinsurer or underwriter.

9.13 It may happen that attractive business is overplaced, i.e. the total acceptance signed on the 'slip' exceed the total cover required, in which case the acceptances are reduced in proportion to provide the required total cover.

9.14 The broker may place the business, and also collect and distribute the premium, deal with the renewal and deal with claims etc.

Foreign Markets

9.15 The pattern of the reinsurance market abroad is quite different from the London market. In Europe, there are important reinsurance companies, which have operated for a very long time and have developed reinsurance techniques that have formed the basis of reinsurance over the whole world. There are also large reinsurance companies in U.S.A. In the developing countries, there is a tendency to form State reinsurance companies, with the object of conserving the export of reinsurance business and so save foreign currency which would be needed to pay the premiums for ceded risks. Even so, these State reinsurance companies need to place their own excesses overseas and therefore take advantage of the international reinsurance market. It is to be noted that in many cases currency difficulties are mitigated by the ability of the local direct insurer to retain the reinsurer's portfolio reserve subject to payment of interest. There are some 250 professional reinsurance companies operating in the world at the present time.

Reinsurance Offices Association

9.16 The reinsurance market experienced heavy losses in the period 1960–65 and it was evident that greater co-ordination between reinsurers was essential. The Reinsurance Offices Association (R.O.A.) was formed in 1969, which is now doing useful work in encouraging discussion of current problems and improving the practice and underwriting of reinsurance.

FORMS OF REINSURANCE

Facultative

9.17 When each individual risk on which reinsurance is required is separately offered to the reinsurer, it is said that the risk is offered 'facultatively'. There is no obligation for the ceding office to offer the business, neither is the reinsurer obliged to accept it. Each case is handled on its own merits. Facultative business may be placed on a proportional basis or a non-proportional basis (see para. 9.21).

Treaty

9.18 A treaty is an agreement between the ceding office and the reinsurer whereby the ceding office agrees to place certain business with the reinsurer and the reinsurer is obliged to accept it.

9.19 The treaty document sets out all the relevant details of the arrangement and would include (*inter alia*):
  (i) The retention of the ceding company
  (ii) The amount of cover granted automatically by the reinsurer
  (iii) The classes of business covered, and business that is excluded
  (iv) The territorial scope
  (v) Provision for premiums due
  (vi) Provision for commission payable
  (vii) Provision for claim payments, including special provision for large claims payable in cash rather than credited in accounts
  (viii) Provision for rendering and settlement of accounts
  (ix) Period of agreement and requirements for notice of cancellation
  (x) Arbitration clause in case of differences arising

9.20 The operation of a treaty is relatively simple and since it deals with all risks within a defined class a great saving of administration costs is secured, as compared with the facultative method in which each risk is dealt with separately.

PROPORTIONAL AND NON-PROPORTIONAL FORMS OF REINSURANCE

Proportional

9.21 When the proportional system is adopted, the reinsurer covers a proportion of the risk covered by the original policy and is therefore liable to that proportion of claims which arise under the policy. The reinsurer receives a proportion of the original premium. In theory it follows that commission should also be on a proportional basis, but the reinsurer may be expected to pay (i) an over-riding commission to assist the ceding company in its general expense, (ii) a profit commission for attractive business, and (iii) brokerage if the business is secured through a broker. The reinsurer may also be required to pay a share of certain other expenses, e.g. fire brigade levies.

9.22 The proportional form may be further subdivided into:

1 *Quota share* under which the reinsurer accepts a *fixed* proportion of the total direct business of the ceding office of the class of business being reinsured. This reinsurance is proportional both on the basis of each risk and on the basis of the whole business and therefore the reinsurer's fortunes follow exactly those of the ceding office. In practice the ceding office places a limit on the amount ceded to the reinsurer a balance being struck between giving too much away on small, usually profitable, business and retaining too much on large risks. Quota share is therefore usually combined with other forms of reinsurance, e.g. surplus or excess loss (see below).

2 *Surplus* under which the reinsurer takes a varying proportion of each risk exceeding a predetermined figure based on either the sum insured or estimated maximum loss (E.M.L.). The premium which the reinsurer receives is proportional to the ceding office's premium for each risk insured, and the liability assumed is similarly proportional to the whole risk. The reinsurance account as a whole will not now be proportional to the whole account of the ceding office, and so the experience of the reinsurer may be very different from that of the ceding office's retained account. ['Estimated maximum loss' (E.M.L.) is defined by the Reinsurance Offices Association 'for fire and explosion, material damage only as—an estimate of the monetary loss which could be sustained by insurers on a single risk as a result of a single fire or explosion considered by the underwriters to be within the realms of probability. The

estimate ignores such remote coincidences and catastrophes as may be possibilities but which still remain unlikely.' Though this is an official definition it is not satisfactory in statistical terms since it implies, without specific description, a distinction between probable and possible rather akin to the conventional adverse odds of 20:1 (or more stringently 100:1) used in tests of statistical significance. Nevertheless the intention is clear and there is no pretence that anything other than a subjective albeit experienced judgment is involved. The definition suggests that the total E.M.L. should be built up from separate assessments on buildings, machinery, stock, etc. and should be in the currency of the policy issued. A 'single risk' is defined and is in effect a definition of what constitutes a separate building, i.e. an individual building or group of buildings considered to be at risk from a single event. The definition also lists factors which should be taken into account in assessing the maximum monetary loss that could be envisaged, e.g. size, height, shape, nature of contents, etc. and the factors which should *not* be taken into account, e.g. horizontal separations, fire resisting doors, fire detecting devices or sprinklers (though these might affect retention levels).] In fire insurance it is usual for acceptance of reinsurance to be based on expected maximum loss and not to the sum directly insured.

Non-proportional

9.23 The non-proportional system relates to the whole of a certain class of business and is a system of limiting the loss made by the ceding office. The main classes of non-proportional reinsurance are as follows.

1 *Excess of loss*, under which the reinsurer will pay the amount by which any claim or accumulation of claims arising out of one event exceeds a predetermined figure. In practice the excess may be spread amongst several reinsurers but this does not affect the principle. It will be obvious that the forms of insurance for which this system

will be more suitable are those in which there is no reasonably foreseeable limit to the amount that may have to be paid on a policy although this may be very large, e.g. third party liability. The method is also used to protect the retained business where proportional reinsurance has been effected.

2 *Stop loss*, under which the reinsurer pays the amount by which the total claims payable by the ceding office over a period of time (usually 1 year) exceed a predetermined figure or ratio to premiums (after all other reinsurances have been taken into account).

9.24 It can be said that proportional reinsurance is a sharing of risk by the ceding office and the reinsurer while non-proportional methods may be likened to the ceding office insuring itself against large losses or overall abnormal experience.

9.25 The circumstances in which a particular method is to be preferred can only be expressed in the most general terms, but with this reservation it can be said that proportional methods are usually found in fire and marine hull insurance as a first cover. Excess of loss is used mainly in casualty and catastrophe insurance and to protect a net account. In countries where all classes of business are reinsured under an 'omnibus' reinsurance arrangement because of the prevalence of casualty and casualty type business, excess of loss would be used as the main basis for the arrangement. A practical point is that in some countries an insurer may be required to give a quota share to the local government reinsurance body.

9.26 Proportional reinsurance arrangements lend themselves easily to the wide dissemination of the ceded business and create an easily ascertainable means for reciprocal exchange. A possible criticism of surplus arrangements is that the risks on which reinsurance is required need to be identified and properly accounted for in the ceding office's records whereas other methods involve minimum administration. Computer accounting has removed some of the force of this objection.

SOME EXAMPLES

(i) Excess of loss

9.27 The reinsurer is liable to pay the excess over the retention of the company in respect of any one claim. The reinsurer pays that excess up to a maximum figure, which is the amount of cover granted by the excess of loss treaty.

Suppose the retention of the ceding office is £5,000
Suppose the cover granted by the reinsurer is limited to £20,000
Then the scheme works as follows:

Claim	Ceding office	Reinsurer
£4,000	£4,000	Nil
£10,000	£5,000	£5,000
£50,000	£30,000	£20,000

9.28 Thus, if the claim exceeds the sum of the retention of the ceding office and the reinsurance cover, the balance falls back on the ceding office and to provide for this another 'layer' may be placed to cover claims exceeding the total of ceding office and (first) reinsurer.

9.29 So there may be covers for:
1st layer   the excess above £5,000   (£20,000)
2nd layer   the excess above £25,000   (say £20,000)
3rd layer   the excess above £45,000   (say £20,000)
which would take care of claims up to £65,000.

9.30 Or if a policy contains a heavy potential liability a facultative cover might be obtained to cover the higher layer.

9.31 It may be the view of the reinsurer that the ceding office should participate in the heavy claims, and the cover may be restricted to (say) 90% of the claim arising.

9.32 Excess of loss business has been greatly affected by inflation and a fixed retention means that the reinsurer covers the whole of the increase of a claim resulting from inflation. To meet this situation, it is considered fair that the ceding office should bear a share of the cost of inflation, corresponding to its retention. The 'stability clause' which is usually carried by excess of loss treaties provides that the ceding office shall increase its retention, according to an agreed index. When a claim is paid, the retention of the ceding office is adjusted by the index value as at the date of payment of the claim. There is a practical complication as some claims are paid in stages, a partial payment being paid and the balance paid later. In this case, the partial payment must be indexed at the date of such payment and the relevant index for the final payment applied at the date of final payment (see para. 9.47).

9.33 The premium paid for excess of loss cover is usually expressed as a percentage of the premium income of the ceding office for the class of business covered. The calculation of the premium for an excess of loss cover involves some difficulty, as the experience (statistics) of past years which may be produced to enable the reinsurer to assess the risk will relate to an earlier period when inflation may have been at a lower rate than for the period covered by the new contract. The statistics for past years will need to be adjusted for I.B.N.R. (claims incurred but not reported) and for future inflation.

(ii) Stop loss (or excess of loss ratio)

9.34 The retention of the ceding office may be expressed as a loss ratio of a certain percentage, and the reinsurer covers an additional percentage. For example, the reinsurer may cover the claims exceeding 90% of the earned premiums, up to a limit of 120%, so that the reinsurer's liability is limited to 30% of the premiums. The cover may not be for 100% of this figure, and there may be a specified maximum cash figure. A specimen clause might be:

> 'To cover 80% of all losses in excess of a loss ratio of 90% up to and including a loss ratio of 120% with a maximum loss to the reinsurer of £60,000.'

(iii) Quota share or surplus

9.35 A quota share treaty for a given class of business is an automatic reinsurance whereby the ceding office is bound to cede, and the reinsurer is bound to accept, an agreed percentage of every risk written in the class. The reinsurer receives an agreed percentage of all premiums and pays that percentage of all claims. The reinsurer may insist on a maximum liability for any one claim so that in conjunction with application of the percentages, the portfolio of the ceding office must be reinsured to reduce the maximum risk to a certain level. (Thus, a surplus cover is required before the quota share treaty operates.) The commission payable for a quota share treaty should relate to the commission and expenses incurred by the ceding office. If the commission paid by the reinsurer is too high, the ceding office could be in a position of making a profit, while the reinsurer makes a loss in a particular year (though the latter might be content because there are interest earnings and his business is gaining greater spread). The terms need to be assessed carefully to ensure that the aim of break-even, which many reinsurers regard as a minimum target, is in the long run achieved. A surplus treaty grants cover in excess of an agreed retention by the ceding office. If the retention is a fixed figure then the liability of the reinsurer will be for the excess over that fixed figure. As this is a proportionate system, the reinsurer receives the same rate of premium as the ceding office.

9.36 We might consider an example which brings together all three types of reinsurance. Suppose the arrangements are:
(a) Quota share 5%
(b) Basic retention £50,000
(c) Surplus treaty, 5 lines with a stop of £250,000 (As is explained in para. 9.45 a 'line' is the amount retained by the ceding office, in this case £50,000, and a surplus treaty would have an upper limit or 'stop' in this case of £250,000.)
(d) Excess of loss on the net amount retained in excess of £75,000

The reinsurance would then operate as follows:

	Gross Risk (E.M.L.)	Quota	Surplus	Net Retained
1.	50,000	2,500	NIL	47,500
2.	100,000	5,000	45,000	50,000
3.	200,000	10,000	140,000	50,000
4.	400,000	20,000	330,000*	50,000

* This risk would need facultative reinsurance as well because the treaty is limited to £250,000.

Suppose on risk No. 3 a claim arises of £350,000 so that the E.M.L. is exceeded. The division of the claim would be:

Quota 5% of £350,000	17,500
Surplus 350,000 × (140,000)/(200,000)	245,000
Net	75,000
Excess treaty	12,500
	350,000

Rating of excess of loss

9.37 A common method for calculating a premium to cover losses under an excess of loss treaty is to use the so called 'burning cost' method. The burning cost of a treaty is the amount required to cover only the claims cost arising during a treaty year. This rating method means calculating burning costs over a number of past years of experience assuming that the cover being rated had been in force throughout. For example, the losses which on this assumption have affected the treaty over the last five years might be £20,000, £25,000, £35,000, £35,000, £145,000 with written premiums of the ceding company in these years being £1,750,000, £2,000,000, £2,250,000, £2,500,000, £3,000,000. The burning cost rate for the whole period would be:

$$\frac{[20,000+25,000+35,000+35,000+145,000]}{[1,750,000+2,000,000+2,250,000+2,500,000+3,000,000]} = \cdot 0226 \text{ or } 2 \cdot 26\%$$

Alternatively, since this rate is heavily weighted by the growth in business towards the end of the period, it might be preferable to calculate burning costs for each year independently and to average the rates; this gives 2·04%.

9.38 There would then have to be adjustments to make allowance for I.B.N.R. and inflation over the run off of the claims. A common practice is to quote the premium as 100/75 times the actual burning costs subject to a minimum and a maximum rate per cent. The loading is intended to allow for inflation, I.B.N.R., expenses, etc.

9.39 A more actuarial approach is to use the methods discussed in Chapter 5. From an examination of the claim rate and the claim amount distribution, as described in that chapter, it would be possible to calculate $H(x)=$ the expected number of claims that will exceed the retention x and $M(x)=$ the average excess claim over retention, giving a net premium $P(x)=H(x).M(x)$.

9.40 A difficulty to which Guaschi (1969) draws attention is that the reinsurer requires, for the reliable calculation of the premium, data covering either the whole of the market or at least a number of large ceding offices who would have to be prepared to arrange their records to assist the reinsurer. Another difficulty is that in order to estimate $H(x)$ and $M(x)$ we need to consider a claim amount distribution which starts at x and is thus truncated. The curve fitting method has been explored by Harding (1965).

9.41 The representation of claim distributions in excess of loss reinsurance has been studied extensively by Benktander and Segerdahl (1960). They concentrate upon ensuring that the tail of the distribution is adequate since 'practical experience shows that in the branches of insurance where reinsurance is motivated by the risk, the essential features of the claim distribution are supplied by a fairly small number of large claims'. Referring to the formula in paragraph 9.39 *viz.* $P(x)=H(x).M(x)$, they examine $M(x)$ when the underlying distribution of the probability $p(x)$ of the total loss amount per year takes different forms—one-side Normal, exponential, Gamma, Pareto, etc., i.e. curves with increasing degrees of skewness. They introduce the concept of the 'dangerous' distribution as an extreme of skewness embracing the most likely experience of large claims. The Pareto distribution is found to be essentially the most 'dangerous' analytical expression that can be used to describe a claim distribution but it is considered by the authors that in some circumstances the Pareto distribution converges too slowly. The log-Normal is also sometimes found to be appropriate. [See also paragraphs 5.42–5.46 for a discussion of typical curves.] In a later paper Benktander (1975) considers a distribution which converges more quickly. This is the distribution $M(x)=x^{1-b}/a$. When $b=1$, then $M(x)=1/a$ and we have the exponential distribution, whereas if $b=0$ then $M(x)=x/a$

which is a Pareto distribution, so that $0 < b < 1$ gives a distribution with a rate of convergence between the two. It has been found in practice that satisfactory results can be obtained by taking $b = 0.5$. It can be shown that if $b = 0.5$ so that $M(x) = (x)^{\frac{1}{2}}/a$ the following relationships hold.

$H(x)$ = number of claims in excess of $x = c \cdot a \cdot x^{-\frac{1}{2}} \exp(-2a\sqrt{x})$

$P(x)$ = expected amount of claims in excess of $x = c \cdot \exp(-2a\sqrt{x})$

Furthermore if the number of claims is Poisson distributed,

$V(x)$ = variance of amount of claims in excess of $x = c \cdot a \cdot^{-2} (1 + 2a\sqrt{x}) \exp(-2a\sqrt{x})$

9.42 As an example of the way in which the Benktander (1975) distribution described in 9.41 could be applied in practice, the data in Table 9.1a have been extracted from an actual reinsurance experience which combines all classes of risk.

TABLE 9.1a

Excess point x	Total of claim greater than x $P(x)$	Number of claims $H(x)$	Mean claim $M(x)$
0.50	95.5	48	1.99
0.75	88.5	36	2.46
1.00	80.6	26	3.10
2.50	52.6	8	6.58
5.00	35.5	3	11.83
7.50	25.4	2	12.70

Using the relationship shown in Table 9.1a for $M(x)$ and $E(x)$ we get the values of a and c in Table 9.1b.

TABLE 9.1b

x	a	c
0.50	0.355	157.8
0.75	0.352	162.8
1.00	0.323	153.8
2.50	0.240	112.4
5.00	0.189	82.6
7.50	0.216	82.9

It will be seen that this is not a particularly good fit, but if we take $a = 0.32$ and $c = 155$ as an approximation the results are as in Table 9.1c.

REINSURANCE

TABLE 9.1C

x	M(x) Expected	M(x) Actual	H(x) Expected	H(x) Actual	P(x) Expected	P(x) Actual
0·50	2·21	1·99	44·6	48	98·6	95·5
0·75	2·71	2·46	32·9	36	89·1	88·5
1·00	3·13	3·10	26·1	26	81·7	80·6
2·50	4·94	6·58	11·4	8	56·4	52·6
5·00	6·99	11·83	5·3	3	37·1	35·5
7·50	8·56	12·70	3·1	2	26·9	25·4

The expected values are all calculated from the formulae of para. 9.41. It is clear that at the higher excess points the expected values of $M(x)$ and $H(x)$ are not close to the actual values but in practice it is the premium $P(x)$ which is usually required and here the fit is good throughout. The use of the formulae for a limited layer is obviously appropriate.

9.43 Having arrived at a net premium for the risk it is necessary to load for contingencies. As is discussed elsewhere this loading can be a function of the variance or standard deviation of the expected total claim, i.e. $P(x)$ in the notation of the previous paragraph, Benktander (1975/2) discusses a rule of thumb calculating the standard deviation σ.

For a layer (m, km) $k > 1$ the 'rule' is

$$\sigma = \frac{P(m,km)}{[H(m)]^{\frac{1}{2}}} \cdot \frac{2}{1 + 1/k}$$

Benktander shows how the formula is derived and in particular demonstrates that the formula is exact for a Pareto distribution with parameter $\alpha = 3$. Using the data of paragraph 9.42 the results for the infinite layer are (P and H being expected values) set out in Table 9.2.

TABLE 9.2

x	V(x)	σ	Rule
0·50	1398	37·4	29·5
0·75	1352	36·8	31·1
1·00	1309	36·2	32·0
2·50	1107	33·3	33·4
5·00	880	29·7	32·2
7·50	722	26·9	30·6

The distribution in this example is not a Pareto and as would be expected the approximation is not very close at higher excess points. In other situations, for example, in motor insurance the estimate is usually very close.

Retentions

9.44 In general business, the ceding office does not usually fix its retention at a constant figure. It varies according to the quality of the risk according to the policy laid down by the underwriter. For example, for fire business, the retention may vary according to the type of building and its construction. A table of limits is prepared by the underwriter and if any risk exceeds the figure for its class in the table, it must be reinsured.

9.45 The retention is called 'a line' and so the actual figure depends on the actual risk. The surplus treaty covers 'x lines' and so the money value of the cover varies according to the risk. If for a particular class the 'line' is £5,000, a 10-line treaty would give £50,000 cover for a particular class of risk.

9.46 This system has been called the 'Fixed Line Limit'. There is another system called 'The Variable Line Limit' which depends upon the Expected Maximum Loss (E.M.L.). If a building is insured for £500,000 and it is estimated that it is unlikely to produce (in the event of fire) a loss exceeding £100,000 (i.e. 20% E.M.L.), then if the retention is £10,000, the treaty represents 10 lines.

9.47 Mention has been made, in para. 9.32, of the stability clause (sometimes known as the equalisation clause). This is the clause in an excess of loss treaty which seeks to share between cedant and reinsurer, the effect of inflation over the period from the inception of the contract to the date of the settlement of the claim. The effect of the clause (which defines the dates referred to) is to maintain the monetary relativity between cedant's and reinsurer's liabilities, increasing both by the rate of inflation (defined in the clause by reference to some established measure, e.g. index of hourly wage rates for all workers in manufacturing industries as published in the *Monthly Digest of Statistics* by H.M.S.O.). This affects the premium calculation since, clearly if the cedant is to share a liability which the reinsurer would otherwise be incurring, the reinsurance premium must be reduced. Benktander, in a private communication, has suggested the following approximate formula to relate the rates for business with the stability clause to those for business without the clause:

$$\frac{\text{Net premium with clause}}{\text{Net premium without clause}} = R = \left[1 + \left(\frac{i.t.x}{M(x)}\right)\right]^{-1}$$

where x is the excess point
  $M(x)$ is the average excess claim
  i is the average annual rate of wage increase
  t is the average delay in settlement, i.e. the interval between incurrence and payment of the claim

R is then a fraction (the premium is reduced) which in practice varies very little with the excess point. The fraction in brackets in the formula represents the proportion $x/M(x)$ of the total inflation $(i.t)$ which the cedant takes to restore the liability relativity as at the beginning of the delay period.

Retention policy

9.48 Beard et al. (1969) have described the insurance operation in the form

$$u_t = u_o + P_t(1+\lambda) - C_t$$

where u_t refers to the free resources which can be called upon at time t, P_t are the premiums required to time t (the expectation of claims), λ is a loading required to cover the service of the capital invested, C_t are the actual claims to time t. It is assumed that the expense loadings in the premiums exactly match the actual expenses. If u_t becomes negative, we have a ruin situation. *The ruin probability* is the probability that u_t is negative and it can be shown to be approximately $e^{-k\lambda u_o}/1+\lambda$ where k is a scale factor depending on the claims distribution and varying therefore from class to class of insurance. If this probability is too high it can be reduced by (1) increasing u_o (see para. 9.1) though this has also the effect of increasing λ, (2) reducing k, i.e. reducing C_t by reinsurance (though this may mean increasing P_t). Since the factor k is approximately 2 (average claim)/variance, it is clear that the required reinsurance as a simple proportional reduction in k is not the same simple proportional reduction in claims because the variance of the claim distribution is involved, but it could be calculated if the various parameters were known.

9.49 If M is the retention limit (as an amount) a very approximate but practical rule is to assume that $u_t = 2\sqrt{P_t . M} - \lambda P_t$. Two obvious but interesting conclusions follow. (1) If premiums increase without any increase in reserves then the retention limit must fall, (2) if the reserves *and* premiums are *correspondingly* increased (in the same ratio) the retention limit can rise. Thus in the merger of two companies, the combined companies can write to a retention higher than either of the individual companies. A company can write to a higher retention by merging all its business for the purposes of reinsurance.

9.50 This reasoning leaves the loading λ out of account. If we write the equation as $u_t + \lambda P_t = 2\sqrt{P_t . M}$ then it is clear that as an addition to resources an addition to λ permits M to be increased. It can be shown mathematically that for maximum profitability the retention for various classes or lines of business should not be the same but should be proportionate to the various contingency loadings in the premiums.

9.51 It would clearly be expected that the greater the expected profit of a class the greater the amount which should be retained but Taylor (1975) has given the following formal explanation:

Let a reinsurance arrangement be described by a function $g(.)$ where $g(X(t))$ is the amount of claims *retained* by the direct insurer when *incurred* claims are $X(t)$. Let there be N classes of business. The main types of reinsurance he considers are:

1 Proportional reinsurance on the ith class
 $g_i(X_i(t)) = a_i . X_i(t)$ where $X_i(t)$ denotes the aggregate claims in the ith class and a_i is a constant.
2 Excess of loss reinsurance on the ith class, i.e.
 $g_i(X_i(t)) = \min(X_i(t) M_i)$, where M_i is a constant called the *excess point* or *retention*

3 Stop-loss reinsurance on the whole portfolio, i.e. $g(X(t)) = \min(X(t), M)$ where

$$X(t) = \sum_{i=1}^{N} X_i(t)$$

and the constant M is again the excess point or retention.

[Note that in (1) the class could be a class of a single policy whereas (2) is a single claim.]

9.52 Taylor then refers to Bühlmann (1970) who considered relationships between retentions of different classes of business in the context of proportional and excess of loss reinsurance. For the former we write

$$a_i = C\gamma_i$$

where the γ_i's are to be optimised and C is a constant of proportionality to be determined by a more general consideration of management objectives. If the γ_i's are determined but C remains arbitrary, then, though the a_i's are not fully determined, the ratios a_i/a_j ($=\gamma_i/\gamma_j$) are. Bühlmann shows

$$\gamma_i = \frac{P_i(t) - E[X_i(t)]}{\text{Var}\,[X_i(t)]}$$

where $P_i(t)$ is the premium which the reinsurer would charge to reinsure the whole of the ith class (it being assumed that the reinsurance premium is proportional to the amount of business ceded). This equation can be rewritten as

$$\gamma_i = \frac{\eta_i\, E[X_i(t)]}{\text{Var}\,[X_i(t)]}$$

where

$$\eta_i = \frac{P_i(t) - E[X_i(t)]}{E[X_i(t)]}$$

is the risk loading charged by the reinsurer in respect of the ith class of business. This formula can be reinterpreted as showing that the greater the reinsurer's risk loading η_i the greater the retention, the greater the volume of business and therefore the greater the effect on profitability, the greater the retention; the greater the uncertainty of the class as measured by the variance, the less the retention.

9.53 For excess of loss reinsurance we write $M_i = k\sigma_i$ where the σ_i's are to be determined and k depends on management objectives. It is assumed that the premiums for given $g_i(.)$ take the form

$$(1+\beta_i)\, E[X_i(t) - g_i(X_i(t))]$$

The result is not as simple as for proportional reinsurance but M_i can be deduced from the implicit equation

$$M_i = k\beta_i - \varepsilon_i \int_0^M [1 - \beta_i(X)]\mathrm{d}x$$

where β_i is the distribution function of $X_i(t)$ and

$$\varepsilon_i = \frac{\mathrm{Var}\,[N_i(t)] - E[N_i(t)]}{E[N_i(t)]}$$

$N_i(t)$ being the random variable represented by the number of claims in the ith class during $[0, t]$. If $N_i(t)$ is Poisson distributed, ε_i reduces to zero and the implicit equation reduces to $M_i = k.\beta_i$. Again the greater the reinsurer's risk loading the greater the retention.

9.54 There may well therefore be different retentions in different classes of business. There may also be particular differences. An underwriter may for good practical reasons (e.g. an isolated risk in respect of which there is little or no experience) decide to vary his retention (and particularly the amount placed on treaty reinsurance) according to the degree of hazard which he attaches to the risk.

9.55 Retention policy is not determined entirely by theory though as we have said already on many occasions theoretical considerations cannot be ignored and do increasingly illuminate the decision taking of the cedant and the reinsurer. The practical view of the cedant office is indeed consistent with the theory already set out in paragraphs 9.50 to 9.54, i.e. it would wish to retain business that is expected to be more profitable. The reinsurer would wish to inspect the distribution of risks in the direct insurer's portfolio so as to examine the effect of different degrees of retention on that office's solvency margin. In general, given sound rating and reserving practice, the higher the premium income, the higher the retention of the direct insurer because the relative variance of the larger claims experience will be less and the need for reinsurance will be less. Indeed an arrangement of offices by retention and premium income shows a marked positive linear relationship.

Portfolio premium: portfolio withdrawal premium

9.56 A reinsurance treaty may relate to a portfolio of existing business and the portfolio may be taken over, say, on 1 January. As at the previous 31 December, there would be a 'premium reserve' and to assume the risk on 1 January, the reinsurer must receive a sum in respect of the premium reserve. If the portfolio is cancelled as at 31 December, a sum in respect of the premium reserve must be returned to the ceding office.

9.57 Although the premium reserve may be fixed at 40% of the current premium income, the reinsurance treaty will specify the amount of reserve to be received (or returned) and this is called 'portfolio premium' or 'portfolio withdrawal premium'. The basis varies but it is usually of the order of 35% of the premium, rather than 40% of the premium which may be the figure shown in the ceding office's balance sheet.

Motor quota share treaty

9.58 This is an excellent example of a quota share treaty. If motor business is expanding rapidly, there may be the need to help in the financial strain of setting up reserves. However, the experience of motor business varies from year to year and an astute underwriter may foresee that competition will not enable rates to be maintained or increased to a satisfactory level while inflation may increase claims, so producing a probable loss for the year. If high commissions can be obtained for a substantial quota share treaty, the ceding office may benefit considerably from such a reinsurance treaty. Clearly, the reinsurer needs to view such offers with care.

Reciprocity

9.59 A direct writing office may wish to re-distribute its business and so widen the territorial spread. In such circumstances it may be willing to exchange some home business for an equivalent volume of foreign business. This amounts to 100% reciprocity.

9.60 A professional reinsurance company on the other hand has no direct business to exchange and it will be clear that it would be impossible for a professional reinsurer to grant 100% reciprocity for all of its business. In the absence of such a bargaining counter the professional reinsurer must obtain its business by fair trading, by granting 'services' and by showing a very high standard of technical efficiency.

9.61 There is an important financial advantage flowing from reciprocity. If two companies each retain their proportion of the total business of the two and reinsure the balance with the other they will each finish up with the same premium. For example, Company 1 whose premiums are P_1,

will retain $\quad\quad\quad\quad \dfrac{P_1}{P_1+P_2} \times P_1$

and will receive $\quad\quad \dfrac{P_1}{P_1+P_2} \times P_2$

giving a total of $\quad\quad \dfrac{P_1(P_1+P_2)}{P_1+P_2} = P_1.$

The claims position is however changed in that instead of there being two independent sets of claims the companies will each participate in the claims of the combined business. Taking the two companies together the result is the same as if they had merged and as we saw in paragraph 9.39 this has the effect of strengthening their financial backing. Reciprocity enables the two companies together to write to a higher combined capacity. The extension to more than two companies is obvious.

The optimum form of reinsurance

9.62 Attempts have been made to ascertain theoretically whether any one method of reinsurance has advantages over others. It is axiomatic that what is best for the ceding office may be the worst for the reinsurer, and yet reinsurers, to perform their function, must be adequately rewarded. There may also be practical considerations, for example it was stated in paragraph 9.23 that where there is no upper limit on the claim, e.g. in liability classes, excess reinsurance will be the only practical answer. Nevertheless, it is useful to examine the theoretical answer.

9.63 In the case of fire insurance, where acceptance is related to an expected maximum loss and not the sum insured, the claim amount on the net retained account can exceed the retention limit. Also because of random fluctuations below this limit the total paid in claims in a year will fluctuate. If the object is to reduce to a minimum the amount of this fluctuation and it is decided to spend only a fixed amount of net risk premium for protection, then it can be shown that the best protection is obtained by a stop loss arrangement. This definition means that, conversely, the fluctuations of the reinsurer's account will be maximised. In consequence, a stop loss underwriter will require substantial contingency loadings and the gross premium payable for protection is therefore relatively high. Under present conditions the market for this type of cover is virtually non-existent in the general insurance field.

9.64 An alternative approach to avoid this difficulty is to examine which form of reinsurance will give the lowest reinsurance cost by minimising the reinsurer's fluctuations whilst accepting a pre-determined fluctuation in the net retained account. A useful theoretical note has been given by Benktander (1975) in which he studies the simplest possible market situation of an insurance company and one reinsurer and tries to optimise simultaneously the situations of both. This paper introduces utility theory to consider the cedant's and the reinsurer's risk aversions, and determine the maximum price that is acceptable to each. Of all possible treaties the choice is directed to that for which the maximum price which the cedant is prepared to pay is not less than the minimum price which is acceptable to the reinsurer and, within this constraint, to an arrangement which gives a fair division of claim variance between the two parties. A substantial part of the variance disappears if there is high correlation between the results for the cedant and the reinsurer and this points to the quota share treaty as most advantageous. However, if in practice the cedant office wishes to limit its total expenditure for reinsurance this excludes the quota share treaty. Benktander then considers excess of loss reinsurance, and the relative risk reduction for each party. He is able to show, not unexpectedly, that the reinsurer should ask the cedant office to adopt a higher retention the more 'dangerous', i.e. skew, the claims distribution. However, the more dangerous the claims distribution the more efficient is the excess of loss reinsurance from the cedant's point of view. The reinsurer has to take over a high amount of risk—in spite of the fact that the cedant has to hold a comparatively large amount for its own account. The total risk reduction is not impressive in this demonstration and leads Benktander to question excess of loss protection for 'dangerous' portfolios and to ask whether a proportional arrangement would not be better.

Practical considerations

9.65 In the application of risk theory the most important element is the claims distribution, by which is meant the proportions of claims falling within certain bands of amounts of claim. As indicated in paragraph 9.41 there are practical problems of estimating the parameters of this distribution due to the relative infrequency of claims for large amounts but considerable development of the statistical methodology has now been made. Each line of business will have a different distribution and care must be taken to ensure that over the period of any investigation there has been no substantial change in underwriting practice. It follows that it is unlikely that a reinsurer can obtain the basic distribution of all the classes of all the ceding offices which pass business to him. To this extent the ceding office has an advantage but, as will be seen, it would be unwise for a ceding office to exploit this situation.

9.66 In the case of quota share reinsurance the fortunes of the reinsurer follow exactly those of the ceding office, and if the underwriting standards of the ceding office are not satisfactory the reinsurer can take action by refusing to participate, or, as a first step, by reducing commission thus, in effect, increasing the cost of the reinsurance. Without reinsurance the direct writer *must* limit his business to the retentions his own resources will support. In practice this will rapidly mean loss of lead on important business, loss of prestige and generally what could escalate to a reduction in business and profit.

9.67 The excess of loss reinsurer, to some extent, is in a worse position because by the nature of his business his results must fluctuate with respect to each ceding office. In the absence of claims distribution data his only course is to assess his premium on the actual experience of the ceding office. For example, his net premium may be calculated by taking the average over the last 3 years of the actual amounts which would have been payable if the reinsurance had been in force. This net premium will be loaded for fluctuations, but even so, it is obvious that a bad year will be reflected in the excess premium for the next 3 years. All that the reinsurance has achieved is to spread excess losses in a bad year over the next three years. While this gives a smoothing effect which is one of the reasons for reinsurance, it does little to prevent a potential ruin situation for either the reinsurer or the ceding office if several bad years follow in succession.

9.68 It is therefore almost a truism to state that the direct writer must underwrite to produce a profit on a gross basis, using reinsurance for the purposes set out in paragraph 9.4. This is so important that it needs to be stressed and it can be summarised by reminding direct underwriters that they are also underwriting the reinsurer's account and if they want to maintain status in the market or even to stay in business, they must see that the reinsurer makes a profit. In those markets where there is a strong tariff discipline, the reinsurer will have more confidence in the likely outcome of his results if the ceding office is a tariff office.

Catastrophe

9.69 It used to be thought that a catastrophe was such a rare event that insurance or reinsurance of catastrophes was impracticable. Today, floods, tornadoes, multiple air disasters, etc. have become more frequent. The liabilities that are involved are enormous and it may be felt that only a government could handle such situations. However, the problems are receiving increasing attention from the reinsurance market and they are not now considered to be as intractable as was once thought. Almost by definition catastrophes are sudden, without the history of periodicity normally required for the estimation of risk premium and involve amounts of claim, insurance against which would, with normal backing resources, represent a very high ruin probability. The capacity of the whole market must necessarily be recruited through reinsurance. On some kinds of catastrophe, e.g. floods, earthquakes and windstorms, information on frequency in specific geographical regions is beginning to accumulate and attempts have been made to construct empirical probability models and to use simulation methods as a means of calculating the necessary reserves. An important consideration for the market is how to make adequate provision during the years of quiescence between disasters. A very full account of developments in this field, especially of the application of simulation methods has been given by Friedman (1972).

BIBLIOGRAPHY

BEARD, R. E., PENTIKÄINEN, T. & PESONEN, E. *Risk Theory*. 1969, Chapman & Hall, London.
BENKTANDER, G. & SEGERDAHL, C. O. On the Analytical Representation of Claim Distributions with Special Reference to Excess Loss Reinsurance. *Transaction of the 16th International Congress of Actuaries*, **I**, 626.
BENKTANDER, G. A Note on Optimal Reinsurance. *The ASTIN Bulletin*, 1975, **VIII**, 154.
BENKTANDER, G. The Calculation of a Fluctuating Loading for an Excess of Loss Cover. *The ASTIN Bulletin*, 1975/2, **VIII**, 272.
BÜHLMANN, H. *Mathematical Method in Risk Theory*, 1970, Springer-Verlag.

FRIEDMAN, D. G. Insurance and the Natural Hazards. *The ASTIN Bulletin*, 1972, **VII,** 4.

GUASCHI, F. E. *Accident Excess of Loss*, 1969, The Mercantile & General Reinsurance Co.

HARDING, V. Non-life Insurance and the Statistician. *Journal of the Institute of Actuaries Students' Society*, 1965, **17,** 452.

NEAVE, J. A. S. Reinsurance in the Seventies. *Journal of the Insurance Institute of London*, 1969, **58,** 66.

TAYLOR, G. A Survey of the Principal Results of Risk Theory. A note deposited with the Institute of Actuaries Library.

FURTHER READING

GOLDING, C. E. *The Law and Practice of Reinsurance.* 1965, Buckley Press.

CHAPTER 10

TECHNICAL RESERVES IN GENERAL INSURANCE

10.1 It will be helpful in discussing the provision of reserves to recapitulate the basic conditions of general insurance. In return for the payment of a premium, an insurance company accepts the liability to make a monetary payment to the insured on the occurrence of a specified event within a specified period of time. This principle forms the basis of both life and general insurance. The expectation under a policy is a compound process comprising the probability that the event will occur and the likely amount payable when that event occurs. The risk structure of general insurance is, as we have already seen, more complicated than that underlying life assurance policies. Whilst in both branches of insurance the probability of claim (in a defined risk group) is a random variable which may be regarded as having a fixed estimable expectation, in general insurance the amount payable is also random and is related to the damage suffered during the event which gave rise to the claim. Claims payments may be bounded by a sum insured which establishes the maximum liability of the insurer, or they may be unbounded, the insurer then being on risk to the full extent of any legal liability incurred by the insured. Reinsurance facilities are available to limit the payments on any one claim or over any portfolio, although someone must, as 'insurer in the last resort', accept the risk of an unlimited liability, however small the probability of its occurrence. This person may, of course, be the insured himself.

10.2 Since the risk of claim may change with time, particularly at the option of the insured, general policies are usually short term contracts and can be revised at each renewal in the light of changed circumstances, thus remaining fair to both the insurer and the insured. The insurer's liability, however, does not necessarily cease at the expiry of the risk period.

Firstly, the settlement of claims is subject to delay, quite considerable in some classes where several years may elapse before the final payment is made. The delay to settlement frequently depends on the determination of legal liability but the timing may also be affected by administrative procedures within the company. Whilst partial payments may be made during the delay period, the actual ultimate liability is unknown and must be estimated and provided for by way of reserves. The central point is that each time a company's accounts are drawn up, the 'profit' declared is only an estimate (until all claims have been settled) and the valuation process should ensure that any apparent surplus is not released prematurely.

10.3 Secondly, claims may arise which are not reported during the period of exposure. The liability for these incurred but not reported claims (I.B.N.R.) should be provided for from the premiums earned (i.e. exposed) during the risk period, but it is only in recent years that such special reserves have been set up. The problem of I.B.N.R. claims is more acute in the liability classes where several months, even years in some cases, may elapse before a claim is reported. Reinsurers suffer particularly from delays in reporting claims since they are not usually notified until the ultimate liability appears to be likely to exceed the ceding company's retention limit.

10.4 A claim is generated by a compound process comprising two random variables, the probability of claim and the amount payable. This process is often further complicated by delays in settlement. Investigations, whether into claims frequency, expected numbers of I.B.N.R. claims or the estimation of outstanding liability, must encompass the possible effects of random variations. These random variations assume great importance when we consider the large number of factors associated with the risks insured under a particular portfolio. If, for example, an experience analysis is carried out for rating purposes with the object of fixing differentials between types of risk, then some partition of the portfolio is essential. Account then has to be taken of the correlations which exist between many of the risk factors and also of the statistical instability of relatively small samples. In other investigations a collective approach can provide reasonable results. Changes in the relative mix of the underlying risk factors will give rise to disturbances in the trend of claim frequency and claim amounts, and care is needed when interpreting results and particularly when extrapolating from historic data. In most insurance portfolios, heterogeneity occurs both in respect of claim frequency and claim size.

10.5 With this reminder of intrinsic variability and heterogeneity we now consider some of the methods used to estimate technical reserves on a collective basis.

Technical reserves

10.6 Sound insurance management implies, *inter alia*, the control of expenses, an appropriate investment policy and the provision of reserves sufficient to meet any liabilities which remain outstanding at any point in time. In view of government concern about the operations of general insurance companies, reserves must not only be adequate but must also be seen to be adequate.

10.7 Technical reserves can be divided into six categories.

(i) *Unexpired premium reserve* The reserve for that portion of the premium received which is attributable to a period of risk falling beyond the valuation date. This reserve is to take account of liabilities for continued cover until the next renewal or, if the insurer goes into liquidation, up to the date of liquidation. In the latter event there will be a liability for a return of premiums for the period from liquidation to next renewal.

(ii) *Unexpired risk reserve* An estimate of the total liability (i.e. including expenses) in respect of the exposed to risk after the valuation date of policies written prior to that date could show that the reserve required was greater or smaller than the unexpired premium reserve (U.P.R.). If the required reserve is greater then an additional reserve is needed and this additional reserve has come to be known as the 'unexpired risk reserve' (see para. 10.14) although it might be more logical to refer to the total amount of the estimate of the reserve by this name.

TECHNICAL RESERVES

(iii) *Outstanding claims reserves*   The outstanding liability for claims which have already been reported and not settled.

(iv) *I.B.N.R. reserve*   Prior to the date at which the reserves are being established, a number of incidents will have occurred but will not then have been reported to the company. A reserve is required to cover the future liability for claims arising from these incidents. Not infrequently, payments have to be made on claims thought to have been finally settled and a reserve for these re-opened claims needs to be established. Statistically, they can be dealt with on similar lines to the I.B.N.R. claims or included with them.

(v) *Catastrophe reserve*   Occasionally a single event or a combination of events (e.g. earthquake, a drug disaster of the thalidomide scale) may give rise to multiple claims of huge total dimensions far beyond what would be regarded as adequate provision for claims to be expected within normal experience. By the same token a catastrophe if an insured risk could put a severe strain on or even extinguish the assets of a company. Some prior strengthening of assets on this account is only prudent especially if the company is operating on a world wide basis.

(vi) *Claims equalisation reserve*   This is in addition to the specific provisions already detailed and its purpose is to cushion any large year to year fluctuations in the actual claims experience. By definition the large claim at the tail of the frequency distribution is a rare event but must happen *some* time. One year may well have more than another and without a cushion the company's accounts would progress irregularly. The reserves (v) and (vi) may not be held explicitly but may in practice be represented by the shareholders' equity or in the case of a mutual company, excess assets.

Unexpired premium reserve

10.8   The exposed to risk under general insurance policies usually falls into more than one accounting period. A proportion of the premiums written in a given financial year are therefore reserved to meet the liability arising from the exposure contracted and paid for by the premium falling after the end of that accounting period. It is common practice to assume that the risk is uniform over the duration of the policy so that, after deducting initial expenses, the liability may be met by reserving a *pro rata* proportion of the balance of the premium. If it is further assumed that the risk under an annual policy written in month m of the accounting period commences in the middle of that month, then the U.P.R. is:

$$\frac{(2m-1)}{24} . P' . (1-E/100) \quad m = 1, 2, \ldots, 12$$

where P' is the annual premium of which $E\%$ covers initial expenses—including commission. Thus profit margins, claim handling costs and expenses of servicing the business are also attributed to the correct year of exposure. This method can be improved by using a more accurate measure of the time on risk. One could for example subdivide the period into shorter periods than a month: even down to days. Given a computerised data system it would not be difficult to make an aggregation of fairly precisely calculated unexpired proportions of premiums.

10.9 For a long time there was a convention that the unexpired premium reserve should be 40% of the premiums received in the accounting period. This fraction was arrived at by assuming that 20% of the premium was absorbed by initial expenses and commission, within the accounting period, that on average, assuming a uniform distribution of business over the year, half the period of risk was unexpired, so that half of 80% should be reserved. The more exact method now used does not require an assumption of uniform distribution of premiums over longer periods than the interval employed as a unit for calculation, e.g. a month for the 24ths rule shown above; it also allows for a more exact estimate of E based on experience rather than an arbitrary fraction of 20%.

10.10 *Allowance for inflation.* In times of high inflation, particularly, U.P.R. on the above basis may prove to be insufficient. If we assume that premium rates are revised annually and come into force at the beginning of a financial year (for simplicity), then policies written at these rates will be exposed during a period of up to 2 years following their introduction. (It should be noted that inflation is not the only

TECHNICAL RESERVES

reason; changes in experience may also cause the U.P.R. to be insufficient. The effective lag in the introduction of new rates is a general point.)

10.11 Let $C(t)$ be the expected cost per claim at time t after the beginning of the year of account and r the expected rate of claim (assumed constant). If the underwriter estimates a value $C(0)=C$, assumes a rate of inflation of claims cost i, and assumes that $N(m)$ policies will be written in month m, then $C(t)=C(1+i)^t$ and the average risk premium required for the portfolio is given by

$$P = \frac{\sum_{m=1}^{12} N(m) \int_{(2m-1)/24}^{(2m+23)/24} rC(t)\,dt}{\sum_{m=1}^{12} N(m)}$$

$$= \frac{\sum_{m=1}^{12} N(m)(1+i)^{(2m-1)/24} \int_0^1 Cr(1+i)^t\,dt}{\sum_{m=1}^{12} N(m)}$$

$$= \frac{Cr\left\{\dfrac{i}{\ell n(1+i)}\right\} \cdot \sum_{m=1}^{12} N(m)(1+i)^{(2m-1)/24}}{\sum_{m=1}^{12} N(m)}$$

The effects of inflation are thus averaged over policies taken out at different times. Assuming a constant flow of business in each month, say $N(m)=N$, we have

$$P = \frac{i \sum_{m=1}^{12} (1+i)^{2m-1/24}}{\ell n(1+i)} \cdot \frac{Cr}{12}$$

and if we remember that $\dfrac{i}{\ell n(1+i)} = \dfrac{i}{\delta} \doteq (1+i)^{\frac{1}{2}}$

and that also $\sum_{m=1}^{12} \dfrac{1}{12}(1+i)^{2m-1/24} \doteq (1+i)^{\frac{1}{2}}$

we can write $P \doteq r.C.(1+i)$.

10.12 At the end of the year of account, a policy taken out during the year at time $t = T$ ($0 < T < 1$) will require a U.P.R. of

$$R(T) = \int_1^{1+T} rC(t)dt = \frac{rC[(1+i)^T - 1](1+i)}{\ell n(1+i)},$$

which expressed in terms of the written risk premium is

$$R(T) = \frac{12(1+i)}{i\sum_{m=1}^{12}(1+i)^{(2m-1)/24}} \cdot \left\{(1+i)^T - 1\right\} \cdot P$$

and this also can be expressed in approximate terms as

$$\frac{1}{i}(1+i)^{\frac{1}{2}} \cdot [(1+i)^T - 1]P \text{ or } (1+i)^{\frac{1}{2}} P \cdot s_{\overline{T}|} \text{ or } P \cdot \bar{s}_{\overline{T}|}.$$

10.13 For a uniform flow of business, and claims inflation of 20% p.a. the reserves set up on the above basis exceed those of the standard 24ths basis by about 5% of the risk premiums. This is not large in terms of total reserves but is often significant when compared with the underwriting 'profit' declared for the year.

10.14 As the year unfolds, several of the assumptions made in the foregoing paragraphs may prove to be erroneous. The number of policies written may follow a different pattern from that assumed, with the result that the premiums may prove insufficient when the portfolio as a whole is considered. Rates of inflation are unpredictable and the claims ratio often suffers wide fluctuations. In these circumstances, the expected claims liability under the unexpired risks can differ significantly from the U.P.R. provision. Should the U.P.R. be regarded as inadequate, an additional reserve is necessary. This extra reserve can be approached by estimating the *total* liability in respect of unexpired risks and deducting any amounts already set aside by way of the U.P.R. (see para. 10.7 (ii)). We consider this *total* liability of unexpired risks in the following paragraphs.

Unexpired risk reserve

10.15 As we have already seen in previous chapters, a major problem in general insurance, which applies to both rate-making and setting up reserves, is the choice of a unit of exposure.

For many portfolios, the main practical unit is the premium, although vehicle years provide an acceptable alternative in the case of the motor portfolio. Premiums are, however, relative to a particular rating structure within a portfolio and changes in the mix of business and in the experience of each risk group can result in an apparent failure to reproduce the experience basis unless reasonably homogeneous sub-groups are considered. A further point to bear in mind is that since commission and expense loadings vary between portfolios and also between risks groups within a portfolio, the use of the net risk premium is essential in order to reduce distortions.

10.16 The reserve required to meet future claims on the balance of the unexpired risk may be estimated as

unearned risk premiums × expected earned claims ratio,

where the expected earned claims ratio is derived by examining the ratio in past experience of

$$\frac{\text{total incurred claims liability in respect of earned risk premiums}}{\text{earned risk premiums}}$$

and allowing for such effects as inflation and changes in the experience in the various risk sub-groups and their relative proportion of the total premium. This method suffers from the lack of knowledge of the total incurred claims liability for the most recent, and therefore most relevant, claim years which will not yet have been fully developed.

10.17 Settlement delays result in a large part of the total liability remaining outstanding for lengths of time which are often considerable though unavoidable. These outstanding liabilities can only be estimated so that the above reserve is only a second degree estimate of the actual liability in respect of unexpired risks. We consider the reserves for outstanding claims in paragraphs 10.18–10.46. Certain claims settlement expenses may be included in the estimates of total incurred claims liability. The balance of the claims handling expenses, together with other expenses of servicing the policies during the unexpired risk period, must then be estimated, with suitable allowance for inflation, and added to the reserve for future claims. Finally a prudent fluctuation margin is added which represents the degree of uncertainty in the elements of the estimation procedure. It will be noted that where an unexpired risk reserve is held it will alter the emergence of surplus between accounting periods as compared with the reserves held for U.P.R. only. To hold an unexpired risk reserve will defer the emergence of any profit and will anticipate a loss when business has been put on the books at unprofitable rates of premium.

Outstanding claims reserve

10.18 In the past, and to a large extent now, the commonly used method of estimating outstanding claims reserves consisted in obtaining individual estimates in respect of all outstanding claims at an accounting date. These individual estimates have been made by the claims staff handling the claims. In making these estimates they have been expected to make a number of assumptions covering (a) the seriousness of the claim, (b) the time likely to be taken to complete settlement, (c) the rate of inflation on claim costs between the accounting date and settlement, and (d) judicial trends in claims settlements. Some of these matters are discussed more fully below but it should be stressed that these assumptions are difficult for claims staff to make. The seriousness of claims especially in liability insurance may not emerge until two years or more after incurrence. Some experience is accumulated in the normal process of monitoring large claims though this may be limited to indicating a general upward fluctuation in claim size. The estimation of the time taken to settlement could have a large margin of error (as indeed does the estimation of the likely rate of inflation although the latter is likely to be laid down by the general management).

10.19 Steps have been taken to reduce the errors in this approach to the estimation of outstanding claims reserves. The claims staff have been required to separate individual years of claim so as to allow for year to year changes in underlying experience; and, of course, the different classes of business have been separated.

10.20 Apart from errors intrinsic to the individual case estimate method which may in some classes (e.g. liability) be considerable, there is the problem that in some classes of business where there are large numbers of claims or where the time lag to settlement is significant causing the accumulation of a large number of outstanding cases, the method may be impracticable owing to the sheer volume of estimation involved. Other methods with a statistical basis have therefore been sought and three of these are described in the following paragraphs. The first two methods are based on analyses of the run-off pattern of claim payment whilst the third derives the reserves from the progression in the average cost of a reported claim.

Run-off analyses

10.21 The basic data comprise the distributions over time of the amounts paid in the settlement of various claims cohorts, i.e. claims incurred in a particular year of origin. This distribution has a long tail, especially for some classes of business, e.g. employers' liability, and this is the essential problem. See Appendix A(ii). Several factors distort the distribution of payments over time and these should ideally be separated in order to determine the true underlying trends in settlement. The main factors are as follows.

(a) *Inflation* Unless bounded by a sum insured, claims are usually settled in terms of value of the currency at the time of settlement, rather than at the value at the date of incurrence. If the rate of inflation is changing, different cohorts will exhibit apparently differing payment distributions.

(b) *Speed of settlement* Changes in company policy may result in changes in the rate of claims settlement from year to year, i.e. the underlying trend is itself changed.

(c) *Type of portfolio* This distribution of claims payments will differ both between different classes of business and between risk groups within the same class of business. A change in the underwriting policy and thus in the mix of risk factors within a portfolio will alter the time taken to settle claims and the amounts paid at different durations.

(d) *Size of portfolio* The smaller the portfolio, the more pronounced will be the statistical fluctuations inherent in the observed data. Reinsurance arrangements will restrict the magnitude of these variations but changes in the level of retention limits introduce further differences between cohorts. Furthermore, if a portfolio is rapidly changing in size the run-off pattern may be severely distorted. This can be demonstrated by considering the run-off pattern for a given year of origin as the superposition of individual run-off patterns for each month of claim comprising that year of origin.

(e) *Court settlements* This applies particularly to liability claims where the extent of compensation may vary from time to time over and above the effects of changes in the value of the currency.

10.22 Of the above factors, direct allowance can be made for the effects of inflation whilst statistical fluctuations may be reduced by a suitable graduation of the results. The treatment of other factors depends on adequate disaggregation of the calculations.

10.23 The basic data may be represented in the form shown in Table 10.1.

TABLE 10.1 The Run-off triangle (chain ladder)

Year of Origin	Development year					
	0	1	2	.	.	K
0	C_{00}	C_{01}	C_{02}	.	.	C_{0k}
1	C_{10}	C_{11}	C_{12}	.	.	
2	C_{20}	C_{21}	C_{22}	.		
.	.	.	.			
.	.	.				
K	C_{k0}					

where C_{ij} is the *cumulative* amount paid by the end of year j in respect of claims incurred in year i. The elements C_{ij} will be random variables. We require to estimate the value of C_{ik}, for $i = 0, 1, \ldots, k$ from the payment data, contained in the run-off triangle shown in Table 10.1.

Chain ladder method

10.24 In the absence of exogeneous factors such as inflation, changing mix of risks, changing size of portfolio etc., it has been found that the distribution of delays between the incident giving rise to a claim and the payments made in respect of that claim remain relatively stable over time. If it is assumed that the exogeneous influences are small, then we may regard $E[C_{i,j}/C_{i,j+1}]$ as an estimation of the progression from $C_{i,j}$ to $C_{i,j+1}$ for incomplete rows i.e. for values of i for which $C_{i,j}$ is known but $C_{i,j+1}$ is not.

10.25 If b_j represents the ratio of the expected value of the cumulative payments made by the end of year j to the expected value of the cumulative payments made by the end of year $j-1$, then b_j may be estimated by

$$b_j = \frac{\sum_{i=0}^{k-j} C_{ij}}{\sum_{i=0}^{k-j} C_{i,j-1}}, j = 1, 2, \ldots, k.$$

It will be seen that this is an average ratio for all years of origin by taking the ratio of sums of adjacent columns in Figure 10.1.

10.26 An estimate $\hat{B}_j$ of the ratio, $\hat{b}_j$, of the expected value of the total payments eventually to be made for a given year of origin to the expected value of the cumulative payments at the end of year j, is then given by

$$\hat{B}_j = \hat{b}_{k+} \cdot \prod_{\alpha = j+1}^{k} \hat{b}_\alpha, \quad j = 0, 1, \ldots, k-1$$

$$\hat{B}_k = \hat{b}_{k+}.$$

$\hat{b}_{k+}$ is obtained from an *estimate* of the outstanding liability as at the end of development year k (for year of origin 0).

10.27 The outstanding liability in respect of year of origin i is then

$$C_{i,k-i}(\hat{B}_{k-i} - 1).$$

It must be stressed that this is the ultimate amount that the company expects to pay, *not* the present value.

10.28 This method can also be used to provide an estimate of the payments cash flow arising from a given year of claim.

10.29 The rather sweeping assumptions required by this method are its essential weakness. However, it is possible to make some allowance for the distortion in the run-off triangle due to inflation, by assuming, *a priori*, appropriate rates of inflation (based on past experience) for each year since the year of origin 0 (base year) and disinflating the actual annual payments to monetary values in force during that year. The above method is then applied to the run-off triangle formed by accumulating the deflated annual payments and the cash flow for each year of origin is calculated in terms of base year monetary values. With appropriate assumptions about future rates of inflation, the cash flows can be reflated into monetary values appropriate to the year of payment and hence the value of the outstanding liability is obtained. Note that the inflation rate brought out by comparison of average claims of year x with those of year $x-1$ is a function of the duration of settlement, i.e.

$$\frac{\text{Mean claim settled at duration } t, \text{ year } x}{\text{Mean claim settled at duration } t, \text{ year } x-1}$$

is greater than the ratio for the duration $t-1$. The generally accepted explanation is that the longer the claim takes to settle the more the liability content and the less the property damage content.

10.30 Finally, we note that whilst it would be possible to introduce further factors to represent other exogenous influences, it would be extremely difficult, in the presence of random fluctuations, adequately to estimate the past values of these factors from observed data and probably even more difficult to project them into the future.

10.31 The following is an example of the methods described in the foregoing paragraphs. We begin with the data in Table 10.2a where $E_{71}, E_{72}, E_{73}, E_{74}$ are the reserves to be estimated.

TABLE 10.2a

| Year of origin | Earned premium | No. of claims | Cumulative payments to development year ||||| Outstanding reserve | Liability |
			1	2	3	4	5		
1970	2304000	62725	753535	1402469	1714158	1887666	1958980	219464	2178444
1971	2274000	56403	642252	1290684	1540330	1746833		E_{71}	
1972	2735000	53837	715761	1376898	1686306			E_{72}	
1973	2642000	54122	841599	1704180				E_{73}	
1974	4129000	50994	968835					E_{74}	

TECHNICAL RESERVES 247

The assumed past inflation rates are:

1971/70	11·3%
1972/71	12·4%
1973/72	14·0%
1974/73	17·3%

The assumed future inflation rate will be a constant 20% p.a.

1 *Chain ladder without inflation adjustment*

$E_{71} = 1746833 \times (M_1 - 1)$

$$\text{where } M_1 = \frac{2178444}{1887666} = 1\cdot154$$

$E_{72} = 1686306 \times (M_1 \times M_2 - 1)$

$$\text{where } M_2 = \frac{1887666 + 1746833}{1714158 + 1540330} = 1\cdot117$$

$E_{73} = 1704180 \times (M_1 \times M_2 \times M_3 - 1)$

$$\text{where } M_3 = \frac{1714158 + 1540330 + 1686306}{1402469 + 1290684 + 1376898} = 1\cdot214$$

$E_{74} = 968835 \times (M_1 \times M_2 \times M_3 \times M_4 - 1)$

$$\text{where } M_4 = \frac{1402469 + 1290684 + 1376848 + 1704180}{753535 + 642252 + 715761 + 841599} = 1\cdot955$$

Therefore the outstanding claims reserve is:

1971	269,000
1972	487,000
1973	962,000
1974	1,995,000
Total	3,713,000

2 *Chain ladder with inflation adjustment*

The values of the claims payments deflated to 1970 values are given in Table 10.2b where 1971 development year 3:

$$1270421 = \frac{1540330 - 1290684}{1\cdot113 \times 1\cdot124 \times 1\cdot14} + 1095373.$$

TABLE 10.2b

Year	Development year					Outstanding reserve	Total liability
	1	2	3	4	5		
1970	753535	1336584	1585733	1707395	1750025	109325	1859350
1971	577046	1095373	1270421	1393863			
1972	572146	1035726	1220681				
1973	590118	1105745					
1974	579143						

The values of M_i calculated by similar methods to example (1) are:

$$M_1 = 1\cdot 089$$
$$M_2 = 1\cdot 086$$
$$M_3 = 1\cdot 176$$
$$M_4 = 1\cdot 835$$

The expected outstanding reserves allowing for 20% future inflation will be:

1971	285,000
1972	535,000
1973	1,074,000
1974	2,209,000
Total	4,103,000

Separation method

10.32 As an alternative to allowing for each of the exogeneous factors individually, it is possible to separate out the basic (assumed stationary) settlement delay distribution and express the total effects of exogenous influences in terms of a portmanteau factor.

10.33 Thus, we assume that if the factors which affect the stability of the claim size distribution are constant, then the ratio, r_j, of the claim payments made in the development year j to the total of the payments made to the end of development year k, is independent of the year of claim origin. It is further assumed that the size of the payments in a particular development year for a given year of origin is proportional to the product of two factors, one an index relating solely to the year of origin and the other, an index relating solely to the year

TECHNICAL RESERVES 249

of payment as measured from some base year. The first factor represents a standardisation measure which relates the experience for each year of claim to a given base year. Under the above assumptions, the expected claims payments arising in development year j, for year of claim i, may be represented by $n_i r_j \lambda_{i+j}$. By way of example, n_i may be representative of the size of the effects on claim payments due to the size of portfolio and the mix of risk factors for year of origin i, whilst λ_{i+j} may represent the effects of inflation.

10.34 We require to separate the elements $\{n_\alpha\}, \{r_\alpha\}, \{\lambda_\alpha\}$ in the expected run-off triangle of Table 10.3.

TABLE 10.3 Run-off triangle (separation method)

Year of origin	Development year				
	0	1	2	.	k
0	$n_0 r_0 \lambda_0$	$n_0 r_1 \lambda_1$	$n_0 r_2 \lambda_2$	.	$n_0 r_k \lambda_k$
1	$n_1 r_0 \lambda_1$	$n_1 r_1 \lambda_2$	$n_1 r_2 \lambda_3$	.	
2	$n_2 r_0 \lambda_2$	$n_2 r_1 \lambda_3$	$n_2 r_2 \lambda_4$	.	
.	.	.			
.	.	.			
k	$n_k r_0 \lambda_k$				

using the corresponding triangle of observed annual payments $P_{ij} = C_{ij} - C_{i,j-1}$. The r_j are again considered to be random variables with $E\{P_{ij}\} = n_i r_j \lambda_{i+j}$.

10.35 At the present time, the use of this model has mainly been restricted to a motor portfolio under the assumption that the standardisation measure n may be taken as the number of claims—including the number of I.B.N.R. claims. The problem then reduces to that of separating the elements $\{r_i\}$, $\{\lambda_{i+j}\}$ from the run-off triangle comprising elements of the form $r_i \lambda_{i+j}$, using the triangle of observed values

$$\frac{P_{ij}}{n_i}$$

10.36 By definition,

$$\sum_{i=0}^{k} r_i = 1,$$

so that the diagonal sum involving λ_k gives

$$d_k \equiv \lambda_k \{r_0 + r_1 + \ldots + r_k\} = \lambda_k.$$

λ_k can therefore be estimated as $\hat{\lambda}_k = \hat{d}_k = \sum_{i=0}^{k} \frac{P_{i,k-i}}{n_i}$

Similarly, $d_{k-1} \equiv \lambda_{k-1}\{r_0 + r_1 + \ldots + r_{k-1}\} = \lambda_{k-1}(1 - r_k)$,

so that,
$$\hat{\lambda}_{k-1} = \frac{\hat{d}_{k-1}}{1 - \hat{r}_k} = \sum_{i=0}^{k-1} \frac{P_{i,k-i-1}}{n_i(1 - \hat{r}_k)}$$

$$= \frac{1}{1 - \hat{r}_k} \sum_{i=0}^{k-1} \frac{P_{i,k-i-1}}{n_i}$$

where $\hat{r}_k$ is an estimate of r_k. Now the kth value of row 0 gives $r_k \lambda_k$, so that r_k may be estimated as

$$\hat{r}_k = \frac{r_k \lambda_k}{\hat{\lambda}_k} \equiv \frac{1}{\hat{\lambda}_k} \left\{ \frac{P_{0k}}{n_0} \right\}.$$

10.37 In general, we have

$$\hat{\lambda}_j = \frac{\sum_{i=0}^{j} \frac{P_{i,j-i}}{n_i}}{1 - \sum_{i=0}^{k-j-1} \hat{r}_{k-i}} \quad j = 0, 1, \ldots, k-1$$

$$\hat{r}_j = \frac{\sum_{i=0}^{k} \frac{P_{k-i,j}}{n_i}}{\sum_{i=j}^{n} \hat{\lambda}_i} \quad j = 0, 1, \ldots, k-i.$$

10.38 With suitable assumptions as to the changes in the values of λ_j for $j > k$, i.e. as to future inflation, the outstanding claims payments in each year up to development year k can be estimated for each year of origin. There still remains the problem of the outstanding liability, P_{ik+}, at the end of development year k. Provided that P_{ik+} is only a small proportion of the total liability, it is sufficiently accurate, in view of the uncertainty surrounding the future values of λ, to take as estimates of the oustanding liability

$$\hat{P}_{ik+} = \frac{n_i}{n_o} \cdot \hat{P}_{ok+} \cdot \frac{\lambda_{k+i+1}}{\lambda_{k+1}},$$

where $\hat{P}_{ok+}$ is an estimate of P_{ok+}, which we may take as the oustanding liability derived from the individual estimates of the claims staff in respect of the base year of claim. Implicit in this method of calculating the outstanding liability is the assumption that the tail of the delay distribution does not extend much beyond development year k. Furthermore, it is essential that the assumption of a stable set of values of r underlies the payments deriving from each claim year. If the delay distribution is lengthening, the oustanding liability beyond development year k is likely to be under-estimated by this method.

10.39 For some portfolios, it is possible that the factors $\{n_i\}$ relating to the year of origin are dominant, with values of λ_j being relatively stable from year to year (or least predictable). In this case it would be possible to separate the elements $\{n_i\}$, $\{r_j\}$ by solving equations involving rows and columns of the observed data triangle.

10.40 It should be noted, when the payments data are recorded by year of accident, that both the chain-ladder and separation methods automatically include provision for reserves in respect of I.B.N.R. claims.

10.41 The separation method produces results similar to those of the adjusted chain ladder method except where the average cost per claim is changing due to changes in the mix of business. In the latter case it can produce less reliable results.

Average cost per claim method

10.42 Both the number and size of claims in general insurance are random variables. When a suitable measure of exposure exists, a claim frequency distribution can be calculated and the mean value can be estimated. Similarly, the mean of the claims size distribution can be estimated and, with suitable allowance for the effects of inflation upon claims size and the distortion due to the delay period, the product of

mean frequency × exposure × average cost per claim

provides an estimate of the total liability during the period of exposure.

10.43 When reserves for outstanding claims are required, the number of claims is known (we assume that I.B.N.R. reserves are calculated separately) so that the variance in the total liability is restricted to deviations in the mean claims cost. The liability for outstanding claims can be obtained from extrapolating the mean cost per claim.

10.44 Using the notation of paragraph 10.33, the average cost per claim for year of origin i is

$$C_i = \frac{1}{n_i}\left\{\sum_{j=0}^{k} P_{ij} + P_{ik+}\right\}$$

whence it follows that

$$E\{C_i\} = \sum_{j=0}^{k} r_j \lambda_{i+j} + r_k \lambda_{k+}^i$$

$$= \sum_{i=0}^{\infty} r_j \lambda_{i+j}, \text{ where } r_{k+}\lambda_{k+}^i = \sum_{i=k+1}^{\infty} r_j \lambda_{i+j}$$

This may be expressed as

$$E\{C_i\}\sum_{j=0}^{\infty}\left\{\left(\frac{r_j}{E\{C_i\}}\right)\lambda_{i+j}\right\} = E\{C_i\}\sum_{i=0}^{\infty} R_j^i \lambda_{i+j}, \text{ say,}$$

where $\sum_{0}^{\infty} R_j^i \lambda_{i+j} = 1$

10.45 λ_k is an index of claims inflation and can be expressed as

$$\lambda_k = \lambda_0 \prod_{j=1}^{k}(1+f_j).$$

TECHNICAL RESERVES

Thus, $E\{C_{i+1}\} = \sum_{j=0}^{\infty} r_j \lambda_{i+j+1}$

$$= E\{C_i\} \left\{ \sum_{j=0}^{\infty} \left(\frac{r_j}{E\{C_i\}} \right) \lambda_0 \prod_{\alpha=1}^{i+j+1} (1+f_\alpha) \right\}$$

$$= E\{C_i\} \left\{ \sum_{j=0}^{\infty} R^i_j \lambda_0 \prod_{\alpha=1}^{i+j} (1+f_\alpha)(1+f_{i+j+1}) \right\}$$

$$= E\{C_i\} \left\{ \sum_{j=0}^{\infty} R^i_j \lambda_{i+j} + \sum_{j=0}^{\infty} R^i_j \lambda_{i+j} f_{i+j+1} \right\}$$

$$= E\{C_i\} \left\{ 1 + \sum_{j=0}^{\infty} (R^i_j \lambda_{i+j}) f_{i+j+1} \right\}$$

i.e. the expected cost per claim from year of origin $(i+1)$ = the average expected cost per claim from year of origin $i \times$ a weighted average of future claims inflation.

10.46 The weight $\{R^i_j \lambda_{i+j}\}$ is simply the expectation of the proportion of the expected cost per claim for the year of origin i, payable in development year j. The expected total liability is then obtained by multiplying $E\{C_{i+1}\}$ by the number of claims. Subtraction of the payments to date then leaves an estimate of the reserve for outstanding claims.

10.47 In practice, the weights are obtained from an average of the most recent years' claims' payments run-off (of the chain ladder method) or by using a standard run-off. Both these methods suffer from the disadvantage that inflation rates are not constant from year to year and in theory, the weights used to project from year of origin i to year of origin $i+1$ should be based on the actual experience of the claim payment cohort originating in year i. Furthermore, in the case of a long run-off pattern, C will not be known, with any accuracy, for many years since the average claim cost largely depends on the (individual) estimate for the outstanding liability. It is therefore necessary to project forward the results from a cohort originating several years in the past. Investigations should be carried out to ensure that the average cost per claim for that year is suitably representative to form the base for the projection.

10.48 As a further development, a particular class of business may be divided into its constituent risk groups and the results for each group projected individually. This allows for year to year changes in the mix of risk, especially advisable where one or more risk groups are expanding much more rapidly than the rest of the portfolio.

I.B.N.R. claims incurred but not reported

10.49 Since reserve calculations often take place at some time after the valuation date, claims which were incurred prior to the valuation date are continually being reported up to, and beyond, the date at which the calculations are completed. Since a large proportion of I.B.N.R. claims are reported after only a short delay, a substantial number of the total I.B.N.R. claims for a given year of claim may in fact be known before the reserve calculations are made. In these circumstances, part of the provision for an unknown number of claims of unknown amounts is converted to a reserve for a known number of claims, but still of unknown amounts. The uncertainty underlying the exact liability for I.B.N.R. claims is to that extent reduced.

10.50 I.B.N.R. reserves may be calculated as

Expected number of late reported claims × Average cost per claim.

Under the assumption that the distribution of delayed claims by month of delay is reasonably stable from year to year, for a particular risk group, a table of factors can be constructed giving the cumulative proportion of the total number of incurred claims which have been reported by the end of the delay time d.

10.51 We may now consider the valuation of I.B.N.R. claims. Dealing first with numbers of claims and taking a unit interval of time as one month we may denote the number of claims which are incurred in calendar month i and reported in calendar month r by

TECHNICAL RESERVES

n_r^i. It follows that the total number of claims incurred in month i is

$$\sum_{r=i}^{i+t} n_r^i$$

where $t + 1$ is the total number of months over which the delay distribution is spread, i.e. all claims incurred in month i will have been reported by month $(i + t)$.

10.52 Generally the value of t will vary but if for the purpose of illustration we assume t to be constant the situation may be portrayed by the following scheme of arrays:

Month of incurment	\multicolumn{8}{c}{Month of notification}	Total number incurred
	1	2	3	4	...	$t+1$	$t+2$	$t+3$	$t+4$	
1	n_1^1	n_2^1	n_3^1	n_4^1		n_{t+1}^1				$\sum_{r=1}^{t+1} n_r^1$
2		n_2^2	n_3^2	n_4^2		n_{t+1}^2	n_{t+2}^2			$\sum_{r=2}^{t+2} n_r^2$
3			n_3^3	n_4^3		n_{t+1}^3	n_{t+2}^3	n_{t+3}^3		$\sum_{r=3}^{t+3} n_r^3$
4				n_4^4		n_{t+1}^4	n_{t+2}^4	n_{t+3}^4	n_{t+4}^4	$\sum_{r=4}^{t+4} n_r^4$
+										

10.53 Alternatively we may represent the above situation in terms of the proportions of the total number incurred which have been notified at the end of various delay periods. Thus we define

$$U_d^i = 100 \times \frac{\sum_{k=i}^{i+d} n_k^i}{\sum_{k=i}^{i+t} n_k^i}$$

where d is the delay, in months, varying between 0 and t.

This leads to the following scheme:

Month of incurment	\multicolumn{6}{c}{Months of delay}					
	0	1	2	3	—	$t-1$	t
1	U_0^1	U_1^1	U_2^1	U_3^1		U_{t-1}^1	100
2	U_0^2	U_1^2	U_2^2	U_3^2		U_{t-1}^2	100
3	U_0^3	U_1^3	U_2^3	U_3^3		U_{t-1}^3	100
4	U_0^4	U_1^4	U_2^4	U_3^4		U_{t-1}^4	100

10.54 The development of practical estimating methods rests on the hypothesis that the observed delay distributions conform to a stable pattern; and that the underlying 'population' distribution can be estimated from the observed values. It is assumed that it is possible to construct a smooth experience table of factors $\bar{U}_d$ ($d = 0$ to t) from the observed data.

$\bar{U}_d$ represents the cumulative proportion of the total number of claims incurred which have been notified to the end of delay month d.

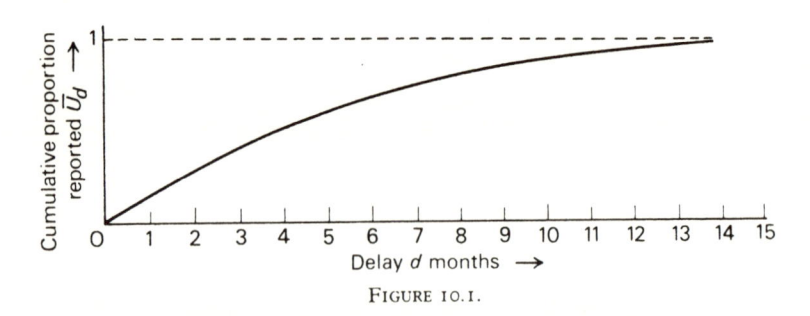

FIGURE 10.1.

Typically $\bar{U}_d$ has the graphical form shown in Figure 10.1.

10.55 Reverting to the type of tabulation of paragraph 10.52 in which numbers of incurred claims are analysed into the months of notification the closing-date of an accounting period may be represented by a vertical line dividing the scheme of arrays into two portions. The area to the left of the line is the notified or 'known' segment; i.e. it represents the actual record of notified claims as known at the closing-date. To the right of the line is the 'unknown' triangle of I.B.N.R. claims.

The basic problem is to estimate the I.B.N.R. triangle.

10.56 We assume that the closing-date occurs at the end of month c. For month of incurment i the available data are the number of claims notified n_r^i for values of $r = i$ to c. The I.B.N.R. component is estimated as

$$\sum_{r=i}^{c} n_r^i \left(\frac{100}{\bar{U}_d} - 1\right) \text{ where } d = c - i$$

Hence, the complete I.B.N.R. triangle is given by summing the above expression over all the relevant values of i; thus

$$\sum_{i=c-t+1}^{c} \sum_{r=i}^{c} n_r^i \left(\frac{100}{\bar{U}_d} - 1\right) \text{ where } d = c - i$$

10.57 The above analysis of the underlying structure of numbers of I.B.N.R. claims forms the foundation of most of the practical methods of estimation currently in use.

The particular choice of method will depend *inter alia* upon the degree of detail in which the statistical information is available, and the size of the portfolio in question.

10.58 The analysis of numbers of claims could be paralleled by a similar portrayal of claim costs.

In practice it may be difficult to construct the necessary scheme of costs; and these are further problems connected with the estimation of the cost of known claims which are outstanding. For these reasons the methods used in practice usually involve a different approach.

10.59 Theoretically it is possible to envisage a matrix scheme similar to that in paragraph 10.52 in which claim amounts S_r^i are substituted for numbers of claims. Given such a scheme, the development of an experience table of factors corresponding to $\bar{U}_d$ and the consequent formulae for projecting future reserves would be a straightforward matter.

10.60 However, there are practical difficulties in constructing the necessary matrix.

(a) General insurance claims may take a considerable time to settle (sometimes many years). Only when the claim is finally settled is its cost known for certain; until then it can only be estimated. Thus, in constructing the matrix of costs the choice is between using up-to-date data involving estimated costs which may contain a significant error element, or using mature settled data which may be several years out-of-date and therefore inappropriate for current conditions.

(b) The patterns exhibited by the factors U_d^i relating to numbers of claims are usually sufficiently stable to enable the smooth experience factors $\bar{U}_d$ to be determined with some confidence. However, the random incidence of large claims may produce very wide statistical fluctuations in amounts so that the patterns of costs in the matrix of claim amounts are less readily identifiable and the derivation of a reliable experience table of costs is conjectural.

(c) The arrays of historical costs will reflect the varying incidence of past inflation or assumed future inflation implicit in estimates of outstanding claims; strictly speaking an attempt should therefore be made to 'disinflate' the amounts to a common price level before developing the experience table. In using the experience table to estimate the costs of I.B.N.R. claims it would be necessary to build in adjustments for anticipated future inflation.

10.61 For purposes of the present discussion we will assume that an average cost of an I.B.N.R. claim can be used in association with the valuation expression of paragraph 10.56. The average cost of an I.B.N.R. claim often differs from that of currently reported claims so that it is advisable to develop a ratio

$$\frac{\text{average cost of I.B.N.R. claims}}{\text{average cost of reported claims}}$$

and adjust this to allow for the changing mix of risk within a class and underwriting conditions. The projected average cost must also allow for inflation. As with the method of reserving for unexpired risks, this method suffers from the element of estimation in the average cost of a claim which necessarily

TECHNICAL RESERVES 259

appears in the data if fairly recent results are to be used. There may well be differences in amount as between early reported and later reported claims. Furthermore, the random incidence of large claims manifests itself in fluctuating values for the past average claim cost, so that some smoothing may be necessary.

10.62 It should be noted that we are emphasising the need for a scientific approach to the calculation of I.B.N.R. reserves because in the U.K. the Inland Revenue will only allow the provision to be charged before tax if there is statistical evidence to support it. A U.K. company must show in its consolidated accounts one overall outstanding claim reserve which is sufficient to cover all claims including I.B.N.R. for the world wide business of the company and its subsidiaries. A separate I.B.N.R. reserve is not shown. This means that the company must ensure that I.B.N.R. and outstanding reported claims reserves *together* must be adequate for any class of business. It follows also that despite what we have said about the need for a scientific approach, it is pointless to strive for greater precision in the estimation of I.B.N.R. reserves than can be achieved for the reserves for reported claims. We need to keep a sense of proportion in our statistical work. In addition to the statistics we have to be ready to make special allowances for example if a catastrophe or near-catastrophe occurs just in the closing days of the accounting period. Lastly in these general considerations for I.B.N.R. we need to bear in mind the special position of the reinsurance companies where the delay between incurrence and reporting will depend upon how soon a particular layer of reinsurance is reached and may therefore be lengthy; indeed for a reinsurer the bulk of the outstanding claim reserve may be I.B.N.R.

Catastrophe reserves

10.63 There is no specific basis for the estimation of a catastrophe reserve (if there were it would mean that catastrophes had ceased to be unusual). They must be related to world wide situations and, beyond that, are a matter of prudence. But they have to be set up out of taxed income so that a company has also to consider its operating position and the effect of provision upon the presentation of its results. Theoretically, the reserve would in the long run be expected to equate to the accumulated catastrophe loadings in premiums less any claims and expenses.

Claims equalisation reserve

10.64 This reserve is to smooth out the effects of year to year fluctuations in the incidence of larger claims. In U.K. practice there are not any specific bases for estimating claims equalisation reserves. If it were necessary it would be possible to make a theoretical provision on the basis of past experience of the frequency of claims above a specified amount, deriving the probability density function of this risk and using it in combination with a mean size of 'large' claim amount to assess the range of fluctuation. While such an investigation might be worthwhile as a guide it should be borne in mind that we are seeking no more than a cushion against year to year fluctuations and not a reserve which has to meet an inevitable liability. It is not so much solvency that is in question as the orderly development of the company's accounts.

Practical considerations

10.65 How do these various methods fit together? It is the general view of those with experience in the industry that it is not appropriate to rely solely upon statistical methods; that there is at present no substitute for the experience and judgment of a skilled claims manager. It could and would immediately be argued by those with statistical training that statistical methods are used as an objective way of codifying experience. The classical stance of the statistician is that such analysis of experience is safer than the subjective unformalised evaluation, i.e. intuition. The argument will go on for some time; indeed until statistical methods prove to be reliable and managements feel confident about their use. Meantime it is likely that case-estimates will remain the basic method; statistical methods will be used to check the reasonableness of case-estimates and perhaps to replace them when the first estimate is less than some small amount which has been decided in advance and which will include a high proportion of the total number of claims. For example, a typical fire insurance portfolio (domestic and industrial) in 1974 would have shown that 95% to 97% of claims by number would be less than £1,000 although they represented only 20% by value. To use statistical methods on small claims would therefore be fully justifiable. It *is* accepted that it is prudent to employ more than one method to estimate outstanding claims. It is worthwhile to remind ourselves that some difficulties affect statistical and non-statistical methods alike. Small groups make variances large. In personal injury it is not possible to assess the claim until the claimant has either recovered or the doctors say his position is stationary.

10.66 Let us remind ourselves of the role of information in decision taking either in insurance or in any other enterprise. In business management situations the use of accounting methods and statistical techniques only illuminate the decision making; they help management to understand their problems; but they do not offer automatic decisions. These various methods do not, and ought not to, pre-empt the responsibilities of management which, after due appreciation of the implication of the statistics, must decide what is best for the healthy future trading of the company *and* be accountable (as the statistician is *not*) for the consequences if these are eventually unfavourable. Statistics illuminate by indicating the limits within which management can safely move and beyond which they may get into difficulties; and the word 'may' can be qualified with a probability statement.

10.67 Management is operating in a market in conditions of uncertainty. The statistics and accounts take an important amount of the uncertainty out of the situation. They help to narrow a little the widening funnel of future uncertainty but they leave management with an element of unpredictability which may be large or small in differing circumstances. This is the beginning and the end of the information contribution.

10.68 Prediction, moreover, is not the end of the story; it has to be accompanied by the monitoring of the out turn of events so that estimates can be improved as the erstwhile distant future becomes less distant and comes, as it were, closer into focus. Just as in life and pensions assurance, periodical valuations enable the actuary to 'home' on to the ultimate liability target, so the prediction and subsequent monitoring offers a similar process in general insurance. Monitoring with statistical analysis too offers the opportunity to identify the source of past errors in estimation. Methods of estimation whether traditional or mathematical can be subject to the learning discipline of checking them against the actual outcome.

10.69 We have also to remember that information in terms of data collection and analysis costs money; this cost can be balanced against the amount of uncertainty which can be regarded as being taken out of the decision-taking process. If the trade-off is not favourable, management may justifiably dispense with statistics. In this sense, statistical methods are on trial.

10.70 It does seem likely that as more knowledge is gained of the value of statistical methods in conditions of changing mix of risks, changing size of portfolio, different rates of expansion of business and very skew claim amount distributions, confidence in their use will grow.

10.71 So far we have considered only the element of uncertainty. There is the other important consideration referred to in paragraph 10.65 namely that management is operating in a market; a market in which competitors are also operating. Management's consideration of statistical information must embrace the likely action of competitors. In addition to the statistical options presented there may be other options determined by the market. This is generally true of all enterprises. More specifically in relation to general insurance the aim is that technical reserves (and free capital reserves) shall be invested to the best advantage and shall be so used as to produce a return that will contribute to the business. It is the overall return on the capital employed over a period of time that is important. Within this overall aim gains in some branches of the business may be balanced against losses in others; and generally short term losses may be necessary to achieve long term gains. The premiums actually charged may be decided by reference to what will lead, overall, to a strong market position as well as to the expected claims cost and expenses. If the market premium should be less than the true risk premium then the assessment of reserves will be affected since taking all branches of business together it will be necessary to avoid overstating profit. It also follows, from a total view of the enterprise, that solvency, which we consider in the following chapter, and technical reserves must be considered together and not separately.

Practical illustrations

10.72 Appendices 10.1 and 10.2 provide illustrations of reserve provision and of the analysis of accounts. The basic data are set out in Appendix 10.1. The accounts are shown in aggregate form for each year of account but the claims payments are also shown by year of origin and year of payment.

10.73 In Appendix 10.2 (i) the underwriting accounts have been subdivided by claim year of origin and Appendix 10.2 (ii) and (iii) indicate the movements in the company's estimates for outstanding liabilities. It will be noted that, as is the usual practice, no interest has been credited to the underwriting accounts; examination of profitability would however need to bring interest into account. In addition it would be necessary to allocate expenses to the appropriate claim year of origin and proper reserves for future expenses would have to be set up at the valuation date. It will also be borne in mind that revenue accounts are produced net of reinsurance. Finally it will be noted that traditionally reserves for outstanding liability and expected future claim payments are *not* discounted to their present value at the accounting date (see Chapter 12).

10.74 The tables in Appendix 10.2 show that, for example, the overall underwriting loss of £57,000 for 1973 (Table A) can be analysed by year of origin of claim as

1970 and earlier	loss	£19,300
1971	profit	£11,000
1972	loss	£87,400
1973	profit	£38,700
	loss	£57,000

10.75 These figures however depend on the movement in the reserves for outstanding liability from one year to another for any particular year of origin. That these reserves sometimes increase from one year of account to another, despite the payment of substantial claim amounts, indicates a revision of the case-estimates. Such an upward revision can hold back the release of what would otherwise appear as underwriting profit. Conversely a downward revision could advance the release of profit; the scope for such an enhancement of the appearance of the accounts would obviously be greater if the company (as in the example) has a rapidly expanding premium income.

10.76 Appendix 10.2 (ii) and (iii) suggest the likelihood of the need for upward movement in the reserves for outstanding liability for the most recent claim years. Assuming an ultimate claims ratio of 95% for the years of origin 1972–74, there will be ultimate claims of £4,555,000 arising from premiums of £4,794,000 and since, at the end of 1974, £1,286,000 has been paid on claims, there is an outstanding liability of £3,269,000. This compares with a reserve of £2,816,000—an under provision of £453,000.

Three year accounting

10.77 Mention was made in Chapter 1 of the 3-year accounting system commonly used for marine, aviation and transport and we recall it here since it is a method of reserving (Benjamin 1976). In a 3-year account, the premiums for a 'year of account' say 1975 are those relating to policies commencing their year of risk in 1975. An income and outgo revenue account (excluding interest earnings) is followed through on that year's business for 3 development years, at the end of which any profit is assessed. At any point of time, 3 years of account will be open, e.g. (i) 1975, (ii) 1974 and (iii) 1973 and earlier. At the end of 1974 the '1972 and earlier' account would have been closed by carrying a reserve, assessed in the light of outstanding liabilities, into 1973 as a reinsurance transfer premium and allowing the 1973 (and earlier) account to absorb the corresponding claims until it, too, became rolled into 1974 (and earlier) at the end of 1975. If at any time before an underwriting year is 'closed' it is felt that the fund in hand may prove insufficient to meet future claims then a transfer is made from profit and loss account. There is no attempt to set up a deliberately cautious basis from the start. The method 'charges' the actual claim payments to the reserve (which is taken as equal to the fund) as opposed to those 'expected' on the risk premium basis. If at any time the fund to meet future payment on claims is strengthened by a transfer from profit and loss account this can be regarded as a change of reserving basis thus capitalising future losses. Equally, if there is no such transfer, the method can be regarded as capitalising the future profits inherent in the premium basis; all profit is held up until the account is closed at the end of 3 years. Since interest earnings are not added to the fund but are carried to profit and loss account the method does provide an annual release of interest 'surplus' if we regard the risk premium as based on a 0% rate of interest. In the discussion on Benjamin's paper Hey (*loc. cit.*) pointed out that the major difference in practice between a 1-year account and a 3-year account were first, that with a 1-year account it was necessary at the end of the year to make provision for unearned premiums; second, that it was customary in many 1-year accounts to make a realistic estimate of the cost of claim payments and expenses outstanding at the end of the year of account and again at the end of the following year without any reference to the premiums written or earned; and third, that it was customary to make transfers to or from profit and loss account in both those years whereas this did not normally happen in 3-year accounts. In other words in a 3-year account the outstanding liabilities for the first 2 years were generally assumed to be exactly equal to the receipts less payments to date whereas in 1-year accounts considerable trouble was taken to estimate and verify the liabilities each year.

Changes in reinsurance arrangements

10.78 In the discussion of statistical methods in this chapter, the factor of reinsurance has been ignored since we have been working in terms of retained business. However, it should be borne in mind that changes in reinsurance arrangements can cause difficulty. This may not be important in motor insurance where the reinsurance will be excess of loss at some fairly high value. It is important in fire business if proportionate reinsurance is involved. If the retentions or stop limits on a surplus treaty have changed it is not possible to work on actual payment except on a gross basis. Then the difficulty is to project on to a net basis. Underwriters in practice do not retain the authorised maximum on all risks, and where because of their judgment of the risk they retain less than the maximum they will usually make a corresponding reduction in the amount placed to treaty. This results in the business put to treaty tending to be a fixed proportion of the retained. If the maximum retention is increased by $r\%$, the proportion retained over a portfolio will also tend to be increased by $r\%$. This facilitates the estimate of the net reserve from the calculated gross figures. Discussion with underwriters is essential to determine a value for r. Alternatively a similar method could be used to adjust the historical figures before the change in treaty arrangements to get notional net figures for these years, to use in the methods described earlier.

BIBLIOGRAPHY

ABBOTT, W. M., CLARKE, T. G., REYNOLDS, D. I. W. & TREEN, W. R. Some Thoughts on Technical Reserves and Statutory Returns in General Insurance. *Journal of the Institute of Actuaries*, 1974, **101**, Part 2, No. 417, 217.

BEARD, R. E. Claims Provisions for Non-life Insurance Business—Some Historical, Theoretical and Practical Aspects. *Institute of Mathematics and its Applications*, 1974 *Symposium Proceedings No. 3*, 15.

BEARD, R. E. Technical Reserves in Non-life Insurance with Particular References to Motor Insurance. *The ASTIN Bulletin*, 1969, **V**, Part II, 26.

CLARKE, T. G. & HARLAND, N. A Practical Statistical Method of Estimating Claims Liability and Claims Cash Flow. *The ASTIN Bulletin*, 1974, **VIII**, Part 1, 26.

CLARKE, T. G. An Actuary Looks at Claims Provisions in General Insurance. *The Institute of Mathematics and its Applications*, 1974. *Symposium Proceedings No. 3*, 84.

GUASCHI, F. E. Delay Problems in Reinsurance. *Institute of Mathematics and its Applications*, 1974. *Symposium Proceedings No. 3*, 124.

INSTITUTE OF ACTUARIES' GENERAL INSURANCE STUDIES GROUP I.B.N.R. Reserves. A paper prepared for seminar, November 1975, deposited in the Institute of Actuaries' Library.

SAWKINS, R. W. Some Problems of Long Term Claims in General Insurance. *Transactions of the Institute of Actuaries of Australia and New Zealand*, 1975, 336.

SKURNICK, D. A Survey of Loss Reserving Methods. *Proceedings of the Casualty Actuarial Society*, 1974, **LX,** 1973, 16.

APPENDIX 10.1

(i) Underwriting accounts for years ended 31st December 1971 to 1974 inclusive

(Figures in £000's)

	1971	1972	1973	1974
Written premiums	668·8	1048·8	1802·9	2982·5
U.P.R. brought forward	+180·5	+301·0	+472·0	+811·3
U.P.R. carried forward	−301·0	−472·0	−811·3	−1342·1
Earned premiums	548·3	877·8	1463·6	2451·7
Claims paid	219·2	376·3	558·3	852·0
Outstanding liability brought forward	−245·0	−470·0	−857·9	−1565·3
Outstanding liability carried forward	+470·0	+857·9	+1565·3	+2876·5
Incurred claims	444·2	764·2	1265·7	2163·2
Expenses	97·6	149·1	254·9	430·7
Underwriting profit	6·5	(35·5)	(57·0)	(142·2)

(ii) Claims payment data (£000's)

No. of claims incurred	Year of origin	1970	1971	1972	1973	1974	Outstanding as at 31.12.74
1,179	1970	78·9	86·8	60·2	48·2	35·2	49·3
1,435	1971	—	92·7	127·7	93·8	99·4	131·7
1,981	1972	—	—	169·8	184·6	151·5	321·9
2,165	1973	—	—	—	221·4	281·7	753·7
2,530	1974	—	—	—	—	276·1	1608·0

APPENDIX 10.2

(i) Underwriting accounts for years ended 31st December 1971 to 1974 inclusive subdivided by year of claim origin

	1970 and earlier	Year of claim origin			
		1971	1972	1973	1974
(a) Year ended 31.12.71					
Earned premiums	—	548·3			
Claims paid	126·5	92·7			
Outstanding liability brought forward	−245·0	—			
Outstanding liability carried forward	+188·0	+282·0			
Incurred claims	69·5	374·7			
Expenses	—	97·6			
Underwriting profit	(69·5)	76·0			
(b) Year ended 31.12.72					
Earned premiums	—	—	877·8		
Claims paid	78·8	127·7	169·8		
Outstanding liability brought forward	−188·0	−282·0	—		
Outstanding liability carried forward	+149·8	+314·4	+393·7*		
Incurred claims	40·6	160·1	563·5		
Expenses	—	—	149·1		
Underwriting profit	(40·6)	(160·1)	165·2		
(c) Year ended 31.12.73					
Earned premiums	—	—	—	1463·6	
Claims paid	58·5	93·8	184·6	221·4	
Outstanding liability brought forward	−149·8	−314·4	−393·7	—	
Outstanding liability carried forward	+110·6	+209·6	+296·5	+948·6*	
Incurred claims	19·3	(11·0)	87·4	1170·0	
Expenses	—	—	—	254·9	
Underwriting profit	(19·3)	11·0	(87·4)	38·7	

continued over.

APPENDIX 10.2 (continued)

(i) Underwriting accounts for years ended 31st December 1971 to 1974 inclusive subdivided by year of claim origin

	1970 and earlier	\multicolumn{4}{c}{Year of claim origin}
		1971	1972	1973	1974
(d) Year ended 31.12.74					
Earned premiums	—	—	—	—	2451·7
Claims paid	43·3	99·4	151·5	281·7	276·1
Outstanding liability brought forward	−110·6	−209·6	−296·5	−948·6	—
Outstanding liability carried forward	+61·2	+131·7	+321·9	+753·7	+1608·0*
Incurred claims	(6·1)	21·5	176·9	86·8	1884·1
Expenses	—	—	—	—	430·7
Underwriting profit	6·1	(21·5)	(176·9)	(86·8)	136·9

* Is the reserve for outstanding claims as at the end of the year of claim including a reserve for I.B.N.R. claims.

(ii) Claims ratios

Year	Earned premium	Incurred claims as at end of claim year	Claims ratio	Total liability as at 31.12.74	Claims ratio
1970	332·4	273·9	82·4	358·6	107·9
1971	548·3	374·7	68·3	545·3	99·5
1972	877·8	563·5	64·2	827·8	94·3
1973	1463·6	1170·0	79·9	1256·8	85·9
1974	2451·7	1884·1	76·8	1884·1	76·8

(iii) Movement in estimates for outstanding claims reserves

Year	Reserve for outstanding claims as at end of claim year	Corresponding value as at 31.12.74	% movement after year 1	2	3	4
1970	194·7	279·7	26	38	44	44
1971	282·0	452·6	57	53	60	
1972	393·7	658·0	22	67		
1973	948·6	1035·4	9			
1974	1608·0	1608·0	—			

CHAPTER 11

SOLVENCY

11.1 Insurance exists to turn uncertainty into certainty and so provide a sense of security to the policyholder. As Mayerson (1967) describes the situation, the insurance mechanism cannot provide certainty to others unless it is itself secure. An institution that attempts to provide a sense of security for the public must itself be secure. The security of insurance companies is therefore a matter of public interest and one of the principal reasons for the existence of insurance regulations dealing with 'solvency'. The first part of this chapter is concerned with the problems of defining solvency and the application of such definitions in practice to the accounts of a company. The second part of the chapter covers the role of the regulatory authorities in ensuring that companies are in a position to keep their promises to policyholders.

Defining solvency

11.2 The *Oxford English Dictionary* defines solvency as 'having money enough to meet all pecuniary liabilities'. This definition in an insurance context gives rise to two concepts of solvency which can be regarded as representing the extremes of a range of possibilities.

11.3 At one extreme the liabilities are those paid on the immediate liquidation of the insurance enterprise and the money is that received on the sale of the assets available to meet such liabilities. The value of the liabilities and assets is the value actually paid or received by the liquidator. It is a value only quantified after a liquidation has been completed. In other words if the liquidation makes a payout to the shareholders on liquidation, the company is solvent.

11.4 At the other extreme, a company could be regarded as solvent if it pays all its debts as they mature. It could achieve this state of affairs by paying claims out of new premium income, even though its assets are insufficient to pay its outstanding liabilities. This state of affairs, if persistent, is a condition for future disaster, especially on a rapidly growing account. However, there are, in all probability, many companies, spread throughout the world, that have temporarily been in such a position but have subsequently recovered and are now solvent by any standard.

11.5 The first of these concepts of solvency is the one which can be extended to some practical meaning. The value of the assets and liabilities can be estimated at any point of time. If on these estimates the shareholders would receive a payout on liquidation, then the insurance concern would be considered solvent in the dictionary sense. The first problem here is to establish what the liabilities and assets to be estimated represent. The liabilities of a company are normally greater if a liquidation is enforced on an immediate basis than if it is allowed to proceed in a more orderly fashion by allowing existing debts to mature. Similarly the value of assets is often less on an enforced sale than on normal valuation principles. Thus the value of the excess of assets over liabilities is greater when the insurance enterprise is regarded as a going concern than in a break up situation. The Vehicle and General Tribunal Report came close to considering that the values should be those which could be obtained at liquidation. This is contrary to the normal accounting practice of valuing a company as a 'going concern', a viewpoint explained by Allen (1974) in his summary of how an accountant looks at insurance reserves and provisions. It must be borne in mind however that the accountant looks at a company's accounts in a different way from that of the Department of Trade.

11.6 Once the valuation principles have been established, an expected value can be put on the assets and liabilities. However, as insurance is a random process, there is a measure of probability underlying the value of the assets and liabilities and of course also underlying the difference between the two. This means that it is possible, in theory, to say that a company is solvent if its assets exceed its liabilities with a certain probability. This has sometimes been expressed as assets exceeding liabilities with a given safety margin, or contingency reserve. This definition of solvency is more informative than that described in the previous paragraph though it is not strictly in line with the dictionary definition. It is more informative because it goes beyond a single deterministic statement—only *one* possible outcome even if the most likely—to a range of possibilities and adds together the chances of all favourable outcomes. It takes more uncertainty out of the situation.

11.7 So far we have considered only the problem of deciding whether a company is solvent according to the liabilities already accepted at a particular point in time. However, a policyholder desires to know not only that an insurer is currently 'solvent', but also that the insurer will remain 'solvent' as long as the insured's policy is on the insurer's books. Effectively this concept can be incorporated into the solvency definition of the previous paragraph by requiring a greater safety margin, i.e. a greater probability that assets exceed liabilities, *if* it is a fair assumption that by demanding a larger margin of assets over liabilities *now* the margin will be large enough to meet all future contingencies. We shall have to look at this assumption again presently since it clearly begs the question as to what 'greater safety margin' really means.

11.8 No consideration has yet been given in this chapter as to the discretion an insurer has in choosing the basic assumptions for valuing assets, liabilities and the resultant safety margin. Each country in which an insurance company transacts business restricts the freedom of choice to a greater or lesser extent, sometimes explicitly and sometimes implicitly. There is always a level below which the government will not permit a company to trade further. This leads to the highly practical definition of solvency, namely a company is solvent whilst it is allowed to continue trading. For the rest of this chapter, however, we will assume that we are concerned not with merely keeping within the law, but with keeping an adequate surplus of assets over liabilities for sound business reasons. If it is possible to define and understand what is meant by 'adequate' in this sense, then a practical legal definition can naturally follow. Whatever the legal definition, there will be a possibility that a company can be declared insolvent according to the law of the land whilst being solvent in the sense that on the actual liquidation, assets would be found to exceed liabilities. It is quite possible in fact for a company legally insolvent to be able to repay all debts to policyholders and also to return all money subscribed by shareholders. On the other hand it is possible for a company to be considered solvent by the authorities though it could not at a given moment pay all its debts. The problem legislators face is that they have to make a statistical test of whether an insurance company is insolvent, and as with all such tests there is the possibility that a company is allowed to continue trading though it is actually insolvent and that a solvent company can be prevented from trading.

11.9 In the published literature the word 'solvency' has been used in all the senses described above. Occasionally alternative words have been used, for example 'soundness'. The Americans use the term 'solidity' as a broad description of ability of insurers to keep their promises. There can never be absolute certainty that an insurer can always meet its obligations. There will always be the chance, however remote, of the occurrence of a catastrophe that will ruin the 'soundest' of insurers.

11.10 Let us consider how far statistical theory can take us. The problem of ruin to which reference has just been made will be studied within the collective theory of risk (see for example Beard, Pentikäinen and Pesonen, 1969). Briefly the approach is as follows. The insurance operation, stripped to its bare essentials, is written as:

$$u_t = u_o + P_t(1+\lambda) - C_t$$

where u refers to the free resources, i.e. resources which can be called upon at time o, t respectively.

P_t represents the premiums received to time t, assumed to be equal to the expectation of claims.

λ is a loading to cover the service of the capital invested in the operation.

C_t represents the actual claims to time t

If u_i becomes negative, then we have an excess of liabilities over free reserves—a ruin situation.

11.11 The quantities in this insurance process are random variables and the overall process is stochastic. Theory enables a calculation to be made of the probability that u_t may become negative, i.e. the ruin probability. It is approximately $e^{-k\lambda u_0}/(1+\lambda)$ where k is scale factor depending on the claims distribution. It might perhaps be considered that an insurer is solvent if the ruin probability over a specified period is less than some value which could be accepted conventionally as extremely unlikely (just as in statistical significance tests we use a probability value of ·001 as a conventional level of extreme unlikelihood). Most people would accept odds against an event of 999 to 1 as being so long that the contingency could be ignored.

11.12 However, as Mayerson (1967) has stressed, there are economic and financial factors some random and some non-random other than those of premium income and claim outgo that need to be brought into account. Failures in general underwriting policy, poor investment performance and the general fluctuations in the economy of the country and the world, all play a part in determining the real solvency position. The mathematics of risk theory and of model building do not at present cover these kinds of business risks other than by incorporating past investment experience. It is doubtful whether the necessary information input would ever be available in time and at tolerable cost to so extend the insurance model in any practically valuable way. It would be very difficult to establish a set of comparable situations from which to derive probability distributions. We are left with a large element of uncertainty and we have to fall back upon judgment. Past experience must form a basis for judgment in predicting obligations and in assessing the safety margin needed to guard against adverse fluctuations. As we have already remarked in Chapter 10, statistical theory can help to improve this judgment by providing insight into the meaning of past experience and in narrowing the uncertainty surrounding the judgment; doubtless this contribution will increase as methodology develops. At the end of the day, however, it must be a matter of judgment, albeit informed and rational.

Retrospective and prospective views

11.13 We have so far considered solvency in a retrospective way, that is, looking at the assets and liabilities situation after the business has been written. Long-term solvency demands that the premiums being charged are sufficient to meet all net outgo in addition to ensuring that the assets exceed current liabilities with an appropriate safety margin. A prospective view of solvency could be obtained by looking at the adequacy of premiums at all times, although in practice a supervisory authority would find this task impossible. Nevertheless the prospective view is different from the retrospective view in an important respect. A premium rate which is adequate in a no-growth situation is inadequate when a portfolio is growing because additional profit margins are needed to finance the growth in the free reserves which back the operation. The full prospective view must include projections of revenue accounts (which would properly include investment return) and of the statutory solvency position to ensure that the premium rates are consistent with the continued solvency of an insurer.

Establishing the value of assets and liabilities for solvency purposes

11.14 As already we have seen, solvency can only be established when values have been put on both assets and liabilities. The process of valuation must therefore be discussed. In the following paragraphs this is dealt with only in broad principle. It will be seen that there is a continuous conflict between treating the company as a going concern and treating it as in liquidation.

Liabilities

11.15 The pecuniary liabilities consist of:
1 Liabilities to third parties arising ahead of, or *pari passu* with, the policyholders' liabilities, subject to normal company law.
2 Unsettled liabilities from claims already incurred including those not yet reported (i.e. outstanding claims including I.B.N.R.).

SOLVENCY

3 Liabilities from claims (or, arguably, return of premiums) yet to arise from cover purchased but not expired (i.e. unearned premiums and unexpired risks, sometimes called the provision for 'future' claims).

11.16 The estimates of outstanding and 'future' claims taken together are the technical reserves which form the subject of the preceding chapter. The E.E.C. directive on freedom of establishment for general insurers stipulates in Article 15 that 'sufficient technical reserves' be established, although the amount of such reserves is not laid down and can be determined by fixed rules or by 'established practice' depending on the custom of the individual States. These technical reserves must be covered by equivalent and matching assets localised in each country where business is carried on, although a member State can permit relaxation of this rule. It may indeed be impossible to ascertain in which country a liability will arise, for instance in marine business where the currency liability will depend on where a ship puts in for repair. No specific rules have been formulated in the U.K. for the calculation of technical reserves at the time of writing (1976), although such rules are expected. The existing procedure is that the Department of Trade have the facility to study the adequacy of reserves by examining statistical returns made to them annually.

11.17 The directive allows member States to decide for themselves whether claims against reinsurers are allowable as cover for the gross technical reserves or not. Each State may also fix the percentage so allowed. The choice of each authority will depend on the rights of an insurer in liquidation to make recoveries from its reinsurers, and the rights of an insurer to recover from a reinsurer in liquidation. Different attitudes have developed as between the U.K., where reinsurance is covered by insurance legislation, and the rest of Europe where reinsurance is considered a commercial transaction outside the insurance legislation.

11.18 In their most generalised form, the liabilities form a stream of outgo of various future dates, so this immediately raises the questions of whether this outgo should be discounted and what rates of inflation and interest should be assumed. Similar considerations arise in valuing the assets as a stream of income.

11.19 There are two ways of looking at the provision for future claims. On a prospective view, the amount set up is determined as the estimated sum required to discharge the liabilities. The other view is retrospective, in which an amount is set up to balance the original premiums after deducting the outgo incurred up to the close of the account. The prospective view is more appropriate for solvency as it anticipates expected losses on premiums.

11.20 On a going concern basis, the liabilities arising on unearned premiums consist of claims and running expenses. On the other hand, a break-up basis would value an immediate return of the gross unearned premium to the policyholder. U.K. practice has been to deduct a somewhat arbitrary percentage, normally 20% for 'pre-paid' expenses from the value of the provision for unearned premiums. The pre-paid expenses are sometimes called 'deferred' acquisition costs and are valued separately. For solvency purposes on break-up principles, it can be argued, as it is in the U.S.A., that no such deduction from unearned premiums should be made.

11.21 The logic of this argument could be extended to saying that, although no deduction is made for commission, etc. on the gross premium because commission might not be recovered, commission should be deducted from the unearned reinsurance premiums recoverable. This arises from the fact that it is the ceding companies themselves rather than intermediaries who receive the commission. This effectively means reserving more than 100% of net unearned premiums.

11.22 On a going concern basis the 'future claim reserve' should include provision for handling expenses on these future claims. An alternative method of dealing with 'future claims' is to pass the liability for such payments onto a reinsurer. The payment made to a reinsurer transferring this liability is known as a 'portfolio premium' and is normally valued at 30%–40% of the premium written in the preceding 12 months.

11.23 The valuation of outstanding claims is central to the assessment of solvency. The technical problems of the valua-

SOLVENCY 279

tion have already been dealt with in Chapter 10, but these reserves and the provision for 'future' claims could have a valuation formula stipulated by law. However, whilst a formula for attaching a minimum value to outstanding claims is being sought, the difficulty of doing so is becoming increasingly obvious. Alternative approaches which could be suggested are that there are no such formulae but:
(i) Reserves and provisions could be certified by a professional, either an independent or an employee in a position equivalent to a company's Actuary (this is the view expressed by the Institute of Actuaries); *or*
(ii) Reserves and provisions could be 'verified' by the supervisory authority.

11.24 The size of the total technical reserves for solvency purposes depends on how the two basic parts, i.e. outstanding claim and unearned premium, are treated. An actuary might consider there to be sufficient technical reserves if the *total* reserves were sufficient, allowing a shortfall in, say, the outstanding claims to be compensated by over-provision in the unearned premium. The Vehicle and General Tribunal (1972) did not accept this view, considering that the outstanding claim reserve should be sufficient in itself.

11.25 One possible way of setting up an implicit minimum formula for technical reserves is to restrict the declaration of profit for each year's business for a number of years. Lloyd's accounts do this for a 3-year period. Proportional treaty reinsurance business commonly has a 2-year period. The Institute of Actuaries (1974) has suggested a 1-year delay for short-tail business and a 3-year delay for long-tail business. Bailey (1969) has advocated a 2-year period. Holding up profits is one thing. Meeting losses is another. There must be provision for meeting losses once it is thought that they are likely.

11.26 Beard (1969) has discussed methods for calculating and monitoring of technical reserves largely based on the provision of statistics of claim frequency and claim amount distribution. He discussed the problems of estimating fluctuation reserves and the particular problems of inflation and of rapid business growth. Many of the statistics which he suggested should be examined were subsequently specified in the

Department of Trade Returns designed to enable the adequacy of the technical reserves to be verified. In 1973 the Institute of Actuaries set up a working party which considered the returns. The working party was asked to review the data available in Department of Trade Returns, to consider methods of analysis of such data with reference to uniformity and verification of general reserves. A description of the preparation and use of the returns appears in the report of the working party. They found considerable inconsistency between companies in their interpretation of the requirements of the returns, the elimination of which would enhance the value of the returns as a body of data relating to the insurance industry. The report examined factors peculiar to different classes of business which might affect reserve levels. It was considered that the returns might serve a number of supervisory purposes: to assess the returns of smaller companies in the light of the returns of larger companies; to review the size of technical reserves for all companies; to obtain a measure of the variability of liabilities and hence an indication of the level of solvency margin required to embrace it. The working party drew attention to an important difference in the focus of interest as between technical reserves where the focus is upon expected values of total claims and the solvency margin where the interest is in the variance (and extreme values) of claim amounts rather than the expected values. The Department of Trade Returns cover the former but not the latter aspect of claim experience.

Assets

11.27 The basic consideration in assessing the adequacy of the assets is, as for the liabilities, whether they are to be valued on a going concern basis or on a liquidation basis. The latter assumption can be harsh and in fact can never be reasonably adopted for calculation—even the market price of quoted stocks is a 'marginal' value reflecting only current interest in a proportion of the stock. The Department of Trade has nevertheless approached the valuation of both liabilities and assets on a winding-up basis. Sidney Benjamin (1976) has pointed out some important consequences. First the approach, as we have already stated, requires the use of market values both for equities and for fixed interest assets with no allowance for close matching of assets and liabilities, which is normally regarded as immunising against market value variation. Second, matching is difficult in general insurance because the liabilities are not fixed but rise with inflation during delayed settlements and it is also impossible if equities or properties are purchased; it thus becomes necessary to compare market values of securities against the discounted value of the liabilities. The market values can fluctuate to an extent that can seriously damage a solvency margin in a short time. Third, if, because of a fall in market values, a company accepts a loss and switches to matching investments, e.g. deposits with first class banks, there would be a deficiency. The possibility of such a deficiency (mismatching reserve) ought to be allowed for in the solvency margin.

11.28 It may be assumed that an insurance concern would, in the investment of its assets, have followed sound investment principles with risks well spread. A supervisory authority can however impose contraints. Even if an authority does not stipulate explicitly the manner of conduct of investments, it can introduce rules for the valuation of assets which effectively limits the choice of investments. Such rules would probably restrict the extent to which such items as large individual properties and balances outstanding with agents could count in the asset valuation.

11.29 The E.E.C. directive deferred questions relating to the determination of categories of investments and valuation of assets. It did stipulate that assets matching the technical reserves should be kept in the countries in which the liabilities lay.

11.30 A company must have sufficient liquid resources to pay its claims. On an expanding account, there is enough cash flow coming in to meet the outgo, on even a deteriorating account. Overtrading by a company may therefore conceal a worsening situation and this is one of the most likely insolvency situations.

11.31 Some classes of insurance have liabilities stretching as long as 20 years into the future. The problems are therefore comparable to those of life assurance in many respects. The essential problem is the projection of a series of income and outgo and their commutation to present values. Discounting of future payments is at the time of writing a rare practice in general insurance, since the present high rate of inflation of claims counteracts any reduction in values by discounting.

Establishing the safety margin needed

11.32 The difference between the assets held and the technical liabilities is often described as the free reserves. The size of these free reserves is entirely dependent on the strength of the valuation of both the assets and the liabilities. If the technical reserves have been calculated to exactly cover the payments to current policyholders, then the free reserves are equivalent to the residual assets of the company belonging to the shareholders. An alternative way of looking at the free reserves is to express it as the sum of share capital, general reserves and insurance funds less technical reserves, plus possibly hidden reserves such as the excess over book values of market values of investments.

11.33 Pentikäinen (1969) has set out four objectives of the free reserves:
 (i) Smoothing random fluctuation of claims (in addition to any provision made in the technical reserves)
 (ii) Acting as a cushion against adverse fluctuations or trends in the basic probabilities of claims, such as the effect of weather conditions on fire claims or legislative changes on liability claims
 (iii) Acting as a cushion against losses on investments
 (iv) Covering miscellaneous risks such as:
    —natural catastrophe, cyclones, earthquakes, etc.
    —failure of reinsurance
    —embezzlement or other misappropriation

11.34 Sawkins (1973) has added a fifth objective:
 (v) Providing a cushion for potential losses arising from bad management, e.g. inability to reasonably control expenses, reserve adequately or control expansion properly

11.35 In Finland, the function of equalising the claims experience has been excluded from the free reserve. Instead a 'fluctuation reserve' has been prescribed by law. This fluctuation reserve is grouped in the technical reserves and the Finns are able to obtain tax relief on it. Instructions have been issued by the Finnish authorities setting out precise rules for calculating an upper limit and a lower limit to the fluctuation reserve. The lower limit is the minimum requirement for the safety of the company. The upper limit corresponds to far wider margins, and aims to guarantee the continuation of the existence of the company. The reserve operates so that when a claim ratio is favourable, the resultant surplus is deposited in the fluctuation reserve, provided the upper limit is not exceeded. *Vice versa*, losses can be covered by a transfer from the reserve provided that the lower limit still holds. One consequence of this reserve is to reduce the need for reinsurance to stabilise results.

11.36 The probability of ruin was described in paragraph 11.11 in terms of pure insurance risk. Stewart (1974) has extended the concept to include the investment risk. In theory, given the right model to describe the insurance operation, a regulatory authority could specify a minimum value to the ruin probability which would then be translated into a minimum value to the free reserves. As stressed in paragraph 11.12, no such model is yet available, so the converse applies, i.e. the authorities set a minimum level to the free reserves, normally called the solvency margin. As the same formula is applied consistently to all companies, the result is an implicit and unspecified ruin probability which will vary from one company to another dependent on the mix of business of each company and on the investment portfolio and general management policy of the company.

11.37 Some national authorities' rulings have not gone beyond stipulating that the minimum solvency 'margin' is a constant amount. Other authorities have produced an approximation to a risk theory basis, i.e. that under certain conditions the minimum solvency margin should be proportional to the square root of premium income. Sawkins (1973) has shown graphically the extent to which the margins of the U.K., Australia and Finland approximate to this rule.

11.38 The U.K. regulations determine the solvency margin by the following formula:

Premium income	Solvency margin
Less than £250,000	£50,000
Between £250,000 & £2,500,000	20% of premium income
Over £2,500,000	10% of premium income plus £250,000

11.39 The E.E.C. directive sets out the margin as the higher of the following two calculations (see Chapter 2, paras 2.56 and 2.57). (The monetary units (E.M.A.) are based on a weighted average of European Economic Community currencies. For 1977 the unit of account is approximately 70p.)

1 18% of the first 10m E.M.A. units of premiums;
   16% of the excess premiums over 10m E.M.A. units.
   The premiums are gross of reinsurance but can be reduced by up to 50% to allow for reinsurance. The netting down factor is based on net claims paid in the previous year.
2 26% of the first 7m E.M.A. units of the average annual claims over the last 3 years;
   23% on the excess claims over 7m.
   The percentages are based on gross claims which can be netted down by up to 50% to allow for reinsurance.

11.40 In the United States there is no statutory margin as such. However there are different requirements from one State to another for the starting capital for a company. Most authorities require a minimum capital and minimum 'paid in surplus' to be put up. The amounts vary from State to State and also vary according to the class or classes of business transacted. Capital is intended to constitute a cushion of protection for policyholders, not to be drawn upon except in case of insolvency. An insurer whose capital is impaired may not continue to operate; either more capital must be contributed or the company is placed in receivership. Paid in surplus, on the other hand, is intended as an initial working fund to pay expenses until the company obtains a sufficient volume of business to meet its overheads and to cover losses due to fluctuations in claims experience. Surplus may, in the course of business, drop well below its initial level without causing any real concern to the authorities. Some States, however, require the paid in surplus to be maintained. In some States the formation of mutual insurers are permitted when only paid in surplus is put up. It is usually required that a certain proportion of this surplus be maintained.

11.41 Although there is no margin enshrined in law, the New York insurance department, at the time of writing, uses a 2 : 1 rule as a rule of thumb to determine whether an insurer's financial condition requires further scrutiny. This means that a $100 surplus would justify the writing of $200 of premiums (i.e. a margin of 50%).

Lloyd's

11.42 The E.E.C. directive makes a special exception of Lloyd's. Since Lloyd's is an association of underwriters, supervision can be applied to the underwriting members collectively, and as such can be similar to company legislation.

11.43 The following conditions apply:
1 Corporate control is exercised by the Committee of Lloyd's, elected by underwriting members, the constitution of which is governed by Lloyd's Act 1871–1951. Each member belongs to one of about 600 underwriting syndicates but carries unlimited liability for his own account and risks.
2 A member must have adequate financial resources which can be proved before election. At the time of writing he must show at least £75,000 of readily accessible personal wealth.
3 On election a member must deposit cash and/or approved government securities worth £15,000.
4 Net premiums for each class of business written by a member are limited by the level of deposits. On a deposit of £15,000, the upper limit of net premium is £100,000. This implies a 15% of premium solvency margin on deposits and 75% on personal wealth. Further premium can be written only if guaranteed by another Lloyd's underwriter.
5 Premium income is paid into a Premium Trust Fund which constitutes a permanent reserve fund. Further reserves are usually held by Trustees. There are minimum

technical reserves prescribed in advance for syndicates by the Committee of Lloyd's.
6   There is restricted freedom of investment.
7   Annual contributions are made to the Lloyd's Central Fund, which provides ultimate protection for policyholders should the Premium Trust Fund, underwriting reserves, personal wealth and Lloyd's deposit of a member be insufficient to discharge his liabilities.

Managing solvency reserves

11.44   All commercial enterprises wish to grow both by the expansion of the overall market and by an increase in their share of the market. An insurance company has also to accommodate enforced growth resulting from inflation which makes it necessary for insured values to be continually adjusted upwards so that they will represent true values should property be destroyed. The process of law in liability actions will also reflect changes in the value of money so that insurance against liability will also increase in times of inflation. Though inflation has its effect also upon assets, overall the likelihood is that it will strain the adequacy of the solvency margin. New business will bring the need for additional solvency reserves before resulting profits accrue to the company's resources.

11.45   Because the claims distribution varies from one class of business to another, the relationship of future inflow to future outflows of money also vary. The ratio of the true solvency margin to premiums (solvency ratio) is therefore higher in some classes of business than in others. Less additional resources will be needed to back expansion in a class of business with a low solvency ratio. A company can therefore exercise some control over the solvency situation by changes in the mix of business. This is, however, easier in theory than in practice. It is very difficult to increase, say, motor business from 35% to 40% without *reducing* other lines substantially. To put it another way the reduction of a line unless it is a large one has only a marginal effect on mix (though not necessarily on profit) and hence on the solvency margin.

11.46   A company can also improve its solvency by increasing its free resources. To the extent that trading profits are made and not distributed to policyholders or shareholders, these resources are increased. It is, therefore, in the long-term interests of the insured public that insurers should make profits to enable them to increase resources and thereby improve solvency. Solvency reserves can also be increased by the return from the investment of any money not required for immediate payments to the extent that this return is not distributed; this applies to all technical and solvency reserves and any assets surplus to these reserves. It is therefore important that a maximum investment return consistent with safety should be obtained. It is possible that in the future, regulatory authorities will insist upon investment return being reflected in premium rates; this too emphasises the importance of investment return. It is worth stressing here that part of any surplus of assets over liabilities must be regarded as investment reserve.

11.47 Another way of increasing resources is to increase the capital base of the company. This would only be appropriate if the company had expanded to the point that solvency reserves had become closer than desirable to the essential minimum, and if the expansion could be held to justify the servicing of additional share capital. Normally a proprietary company would in these circumstances proceed by making a rights issue to existing shareholders. It would not be expedient to do this at a time when confidence in the insurance and in the stock markets happened to be at a low ebb, since the market value of existing shares would be below a realistic figure. The terms of the issue would then have to be overgenerous so that even if in the prevailing climate the issue were to succeed (which is doubtful) the company would be paying too high a price. As the new money is intended to be invested, an alternative is to acquire the investments directly, for scrip, by a take over of an established investment or property company.

11.48 A company can improve its solvency margin by merging with a company writing similar business and in a similar solvency position. This is because the relative variability (variance in relation to mean) of size of claim is the most important factor in determining ruin probability, and, given a claim distribution of a particular shape, the relative variability is reduced by increasing the total number of claims in the distribution. If the two companies have such similar business mixes that claim distributions are similar, a merger would increase the total claims without altering the shape of the distribution. Thus for a given low ruin probability the solvency reserve for the combined companies will be less than the sum of the reserves for the companies operating separately. The merger will therefore result in an improved solvency margin.

11.49 It is essential to the good management of the company that the level of solvency reserves should be closely monitored. While a company will, hopefully, continue to expand, it can also encounter an adverse environment. High rates of inflation or market pressures which push premiums below optimum levels or even below adequacy or a period of bad underwriting experience can put strains on reserves and corrective action will need to be taken while there is still time for this action to be such that it does not jeopardise the longer term trading ability of the company or disturb the accounts in such a way as to weaken confidence in the company (and, perforce, in the market generally).

11.50 It will be borne in mind that a decision to strengthen the basis of technical reserves and additional solvency reserves is also a decision to require more capital to support a given volume of business. Conversely it is a decision to service a larger amount of capital from the same volume of business, so that unless profitability can be increased, shareholders may be getting a smaller return by way of dividends. This may therefore have implications for increasing profit loadings in office premiums in order that the larger capital can be serviced. Increased interest income on the invested reserves may provide some offset.

Premium loadings and growth

11.51 The following example shows the relationship between growth and premium loadings. It is assumed that the business must produce sufficient profit to meet the increase in the solvency margin required by the insurer having regard to the increase in business and the cost of the shareholders'

SOLVENCY

dividend. It is further assumed that technical reserves are 100% of premiums.

Let d = gross dividend expressed as a factor of written premiums
S = solvency reserve expressed as a factor of written premiums
i = gross interest earned (allowing for a proportion of assets uninvested)
t_1 = tax rate applicable to profit including interest
t_2 = tax rate applicable to dividends
k = rate of expansion of premium, i.e. $100k\%$
λ = contingency loading in the premium, i.e. $100\lambda\%$

The operation of tax is such that increases in solvency reserves must come from taxed profits.

Let P_r be the premium income for the year just ended, and consider the position as between year r and year $r+1$.

Increase in solvency reserves required $= S(P_{r+1} - P_r) = S \Delta P_r = SkP_r$

Dividend to be paid in respect of year $P_{r+1} = d \cdot P_{r+1} \cdot (1 - t_2)$
Total provision to be made $S \cdot kP_r + d \cdot P_{r+1} \cdot (1 - t_2)$

Investment income (assuming ½ year delay and including income from solvency reserve)

$$i \cdot \tfrac{1}{2} \cdot (P_r + P_{r+1})(1 - t_1)(1 + S)$$

Loading $\qquad \lambda P_{r+1}(1 - t_1)$

For equality $S(P_{r+1} - P_r) + dP_{r+1}(1 - t_2)$
$$= \tfrac{1}{2}i(P_r + P_{r+1})(1 - t_1)(1 + S) + \lambda P_{r+1}(1 - t_1)$$

As $P_r(1+k) = P_{r+1}$ writing all in terms of P_r and eliminating

$S(1 + k - 1) + d(1 + k)(1 - t_2)$
$$= \tfrac{1}{2}i(1 + 1 + k)(1 - t_1)(1 + S) + \lambda(1 + k)(1 - t_1)$$

or

$S \cdot k + d(1+k)(1-t_2)$
$$= i(1 + \tfrac{1}{2}k)(1 - t_1)(1 + S) + \lambda(1 + k)(1 - t_1)$$

Hence the contingency loading for break-even

$$\lambda = \frac{Sk + d(1+k)(1-t_2) - i(1+\tfrac{1}{2}k)(1-t_1)(1+S)}{(1+k)(1-t_1)}$$

Example 1 Let $k=0.15$ $S=0.16$ $t_1=0.50$ $t_2=0.35$ $d=0.04$ $i=0.09$

$$\lambda = \frac{1}{(1.15)0.5}\{(0.16)\cdot 15 + (0.04)(1.15)0.65 - (0.09)(1.075)(0.50)1.16\} = 0.0039,$$

i.e. nil loading.

This is a low contingency loading arising out of the relatively low solvency margin of 15% as recommended by E.E.C. A more realistic basis would be to allow for some investment reserve and take a 3 to 1 premium ratio, i.e. $S=0.333$. Nevertheless Example 1 does show that when solvency requirements are low and investment yields high, it is possible to comply with the initial conditions of this paragraph with virtually no underwriting profit.

Example 2 Effect of a higher solvency requirement
As in Example 1 but $S=0.333$

$$\lambda = \frac{1}{(1.15)0.5}\{(0.333)0.15 + (0.04)(1.15)0.65 - (0.09)(1.075)(0.50)1.333\} = 0.027,$$

i.e. $2\tfrac{3}{4}\%$ loading.

This is essentially a practical example at the present time. The loading is not uncompetitive, 15% expansion is reasonable and 9% gross yield (allowing for uninvested assets) which is equivalent to $11\tfrac{1}{4}\%$ is certainly attainable.

Example 3 Effect of rapid expansion
In this case we take the same parameters as Example 2 but expand at 25% instead of 15%, i.e. $k=0.25$

$$\lambda = \frac{1}{(1.25)0.5}\{(0.333)0.25 + (0.04)(1.25)0.65 - (0.09)(1.125)(0.50)(1.333)\} = 0.077,$$

i.e. $7\tfrac{3}{4}\%$ loading.

This is close to an uncompetitive situation which would make 25% expansion possible only with extensive promotion (*not* taken into the equation).

11.52 Solvency management, as we have stressed elsewhere in this chapter, is a matter of embracing a number of interests which may be in conflict; it is a really difficult problem of business strategy.

The role of supervisory authorities

11.53 The supervisory authorities can only operate within the framework of the law, although they often are instrumental in framing the laws. A balance must be struck between not having the power to take action about a company which it knows to be unsound and having the power to stop a company trading which must be enforced even though the company is considered to be sound. In framing the legislation, and the rules concerning solvency margins and asset and liability valuations in particular, the authority must take regard of whether it is effectively:

1 Merely dealing with problems which arise when a company has stopped trading
2 Preventing an insolvent company from trading
3 Ensuring that remedial action be taken before a company is forced to stop trading

11.54 The first two attitudes mean that the authority is failing in its job of ensuring that an insurance concern can meet its promise to policyholders. In each case the 'solvency margin' is the indication which decides that the authority must take action. To take remedial action requires a higher solvency margin than to prevent trading. If there is to be a choice between remedial action and winding up there must be, as stipulated in the E.E.C. directive, a two-tier system, with remedial action taken at the higher level and winding up at the lower. Thus the specified solvency margin should be a function of the action to be taken by the insurers and the underlying philosophy of the legislation.

11.55 The regulations must also pay due regard to cost and confidence. Cost includes not only the expense paid out of the national purse in running a supervisory authority, but the cost to the policyholders in the increased expense element of premiums to cover the cost of collecting information and to finance imposed safety margins. The insurance industry needs an environment of confidence. If confidence in a sound firm is lost, then that in itself can bring about the failure of the concern. Loss of confidence will bring a loss of business. With high fixed expenses and redundancy payments no concern can contract quickly. The solvency margin will soon be breached and shareholders if not the policyholders will lose. Solvency supervision must ensure that no unwarranted adverse publicity is given to a sound firm. This is particularly important in relation to international business which as a rich source of foreign currency earnings must not be needlessly harmed.

11.56 Homewood (1974) writing from the viewpoint of a supervisory authority has produced a list of desirable features to be satisfied by a method of valuing liabilities. They are of interest more generally in a solvency context as illustrative of the problems to be faced. The method of estimation should:

(a) Be objective
(b) Be prospective
(c) Reflect adequately the conditions of the individual company's business and its actual experience
(d) Provide for adjustments to estimates projected from past experience to take account of changes in:
    (i) external factors, i.e. general market trends and economic conditions likely to affect claims incidence or costs of settlement
    (ii) internal factors, such as policy conditions, e.g. no claims discounts, selection of risks, arrangements for administration of claim settlement
(e) Not involve the maintenance by companies of elaborate records, particularly of data of no value for their commercial purposes or assume the ability of companies to process data electronically
(f) Not require unduly complex calculation

These points have already been discussed in Chapter 10 and

are repeated here as indicative of the attitude of the U.K. supervisory authority.

11.57 Kimball (1960) stresses the wider issues of solvency and the conflicts of interest which supervisory authorities and the government face. Ensuring more stringent solvency requirements may have side effects in other areas. The objective of the supervisory authority should cover not only the 'solidity' of the insurance concern, but 'fairness, equity and reasonableness'. An example given for the latter concept is rating, where solidity demands higher rates while consumer interests demand lower rates.

11.58 There are also wider objectives. Political objectives could include 'liberalism', 'local protectionism' and 'federationism'. Liberalism objectives means fulfilling political beliefs on personal liberty (e.g. fingerprinting of insurance company chief executives in line with New York procedures would be regarded unfavourably in the U.K.) and on freedom from government restriction (what is acceptable in many other E.E.C. countries would be viewed with concern in the U.K.). Local protectionism is designed to protect the insurers of a particular country. Federationism is the desire for each member state of a community to make its own laws and keep decision making within that state. Social-cum-political objectives could lead to a desire to provide insurance to certain sectors of the population at prices they can afford rather than at the right price; so selection against a company in such areas might abrogate one of the first principles of solvency, namely that a company should charge a premium adequate to cover the risk. There might be social reasons such as the need to finance housing or to finance government debts leading to demands on companies to carry out an investment policy which might run counter to sound investment principles, based on matching theory. Other objectives could be to ensure that new entrants could always come into the market or that the taxation income to the fiscal authorities should not be reduced.

11.59 An insurance concern can transact business in many different territories and have to satisfy the different requirements as to solvency laid down in the various territories in which it operates. Each supervisory authority must be satisfied that a company is solvent on a worldwide basis and not just in the authority's own territory. Unless there is some measure of agreement between the various supervisory authorities, the result could be a multiplicity of forms and restrictions with an insurer trying to satisfy each authority in all the territories in which it operates within its worldwide activities. There is therefore a need for a solvency standard which is internationally acceptable.

Authorising a new company

11.60 Before an authority can give a new company authorisation to begin trading, the authority ought to seek satisfaction in four areas.

(i) *Integrity of those in control of the company:* regulations could be framed to prevent a company being controlled by undesirable operators.

(ii) *Initial solvency margin:* a new company ought to put up an initial deposit to provide a solvency margin. This deposit could be invested in specified assets and possibly put into trust.

(iii) *New business plan:* a plan of the company's proposed method of operations, together with expected premium volumes and the rates to be charged, allows for a sounder understanding of a company. Such a plan is of limited value unless it imposes restrictive conditions upon a company.

(iv) *Reinsurance:* properly used, reinsurance treaties help to preserve an insurer's free reserves from adverse claim fluctuations and catastrophic risks. Misused, reinsurance can either hide insolvency by deferring losses, or give rise to bad debts by reinsuring with a company unable to meet the apparent obligations of the reinsurance contract, or be a means of transferring assets from one country to another. For these reasons, supervisory authorities ought to have a working knowledge of both the reinsurance arrangements and also the reinsurers of each company. The complexity of reinsurance treaties and the multiplicity of reinsurers throughout the world makes this task somewhat daunting. Limitation of reinsurance to reinsurers given specific authorisation by the insurer's supervisory authority implies some standard for giving authorisation. Finding standards of authorisation has its own particular problems, including the 'international' problems of paragraph 11.57. U.S.A. Commissioners have a test for *end of year* temporary reinsurance where a *full* year's reinsurance commission is brought into the accounts.

Allowing an existing company to continue operating

11.61 Having established conditions for an insurer to begin operating, an authority ought to ensure that these conditions continue to hold whilst the insurer remains in business. The application of this principle means that any change in control or significant change in reinsurance arrangements ought to be notified to, and possibly authorised by, the authorities. Rather than to have to keep asking for business plans, an authority could be content with receiving data showing that premiums are sufficient. In practice this often conflicts with one of the political objectives of governments, namely, to satisfy consumer demands by keeping premium rates as low as possible. Tolerance of a tariff system which effectively keeps rates at a sensible level is one indirect method by which an authority could achieve some degree of rate regulation. Most rate regulation is designed however to regulate the maximum rate which can be charged. The powers granted to the Department of Trade under the Counter Inflation Act 1973 are an example of this. The question of the initial deposit for a solvency margin evolves into the issues of solvency margins and asset and liability valuations described elsewhere in this chapter.

How can a supervisory authority monitor?

11.62 Whatever the regulations that have been enacted in law, a supervisory authority must have some means of ascertaining the facts about each concern under its jurisdiction. It can try to ascertain the facts directly from information provided by the insurance concern, or indirectly by relying on the opinion of a qualified professional such as an accountant or actuary. Reliance on these professionals allows for some measure of self-regulation. Standardisation of a basic form of account, such as that prescribed by the American 'Generally Accepted Accounting Principles' would help, however far from ideal such a standardisation may be (see para. 11.64). To ascertain the facts directly, the authority could rely on standardised returns which insurance companies could send in every quarter or year. The Institute of Actuaries' General Insurance Studies Group (1974) did comment on one such set of annual returns. The main problem arising from the Department of Trade returns, even after considerable effort to standardise the interpretation of the requirements, is the very heterogeneity of insurance business, which means that returns tell an incomplete story. The situations which give rise to insolvency are the situations most likely to be masked by standardised returns. However, returns as such are vital to the supervision of solvency. Collectively these form a standard for the interpretation of an individual company's returns. Seeking satisfactory solutions to the questions arising from the returns should help both the supervisory authorities and the insurers themselves in their quest for soundness. Publication of returns increases common knowledge of the profitability of insurance and reduce the chances of insolvency through the lack of awareness of company management.

11.63 An alternative to producing standard returns is to keep internal records in a standard form. This reduces the need for costly publication of statistics, many of which are of little importance. The authorities would have access to such records, which would contain detail more appropriate to an individual company. This method is well adapted to the normal periodical visits to companies by a supervisory authority. On these visits the supervisory authorities can familiarise themselves with the particular features of a company which might affect solvency.

11.64 The problems affecting the major composites with their portfolios spread widely over both classes of business and countries of operation are very different than those of a

SOLVENCY 297

small insurer conducting only private car business in the U.K. It can be argued that the two enterprises should be treated at different levels of intensity of supervision.

11.65 In order that promises to policyholders may be met even though an insurance concern has failed, it could be possible to pay off the outstanding liabilities from a solvency guarantee fund. This is a centralised fund beyond the control of the insurance companies, run by the State or some other collective body. It can be funded by regular payments or it can charge the contributory companies on a pay as you go basis. Such funds have existed in some American States, at Lloyd's and for the compulsory motor insurances issued in the U.K. Occasionally the fund has been an *ad hoc* one to cover the failure of a single company organised on a voluntary basis by companies anxious to preserve confidence in the industry. The danger in such funds is that, unless there are stringent safeguards, it allows unscrupulous operators to enter the market and follow unsound if temporarily profitable practices in the knowledge that the policyholders will always be bailed out by the other companies. Nevertheless, the U.K. Government have now made general arrangements under the Policyholders' Protection Act 1975 for assisting policyholders affected by the failure of insurance companies, out of money obtained by levy from the insurance industry (see Chapter 2, paras 2.44–2.51).

G.A.A.P.

11.66 Reference was made in paragraph 11.60 to the method of accounting promulgated in the U.S.A. by the Certified Public Accountants under 'Generally Accepted Accounting Principles (G.A.A.P.)' and accepted by actuaries practising in the U.S.A. The method arose from a desire to show a 'true and fair position' from the point of view of shareholders, but largely for the benefit of investment analysts. In brief the method aims to show the difference between the office premium basis and the emerging experience. If this emerging experience follows the underlying premium assumptions then profit is released according to the profit margins in the office premiums. The method prevents any temporary diversion of profits to new business strain, i.e. to the provision of additional capital to back the solvency of growing business. Sidney Benjamin (1976) has criticised the method on two grounds: that it is arbitrary to stipulate that profit should emerge as a constant proportion of office premiums; a company simply could not release surplus in that way, i.e. it could not reserve only on the basis of future claims less future net premiums (net of profit margin) but would have to hold more orthodox reserves. Benjamin focuses attention on the value of the company at a point of time as represented by the present value of all future profits which may be earned. The difference between the value at the beginning and end of a year represent earnings for the year. He re-expresses his criticism as follows: 'given two companies which are identical as regards premium rates, quality of business, experience, etc., the only difference being that the first reserves on a stronger basis than the second, then the former is worth less to its shareholders in terms of the return per £1 invested which they are receiving. The actual reserving basis is ignored under G.A.A.P. and hence that real difference is ignored.'

National Association of Insurance Commissioners' early warning system

11.67 The reader's attention is drawn to a monitoring system or 'early warning system' as it is called which has been developed in the U.S.A. by the National Association of Insurance Commissioners for property and liability companies. The purpose of the system is to help State insurance department personnel quickly to identify companies requiring close surveillance and to determine the form which that surveillance should take. The system operates by selecting 'priority companies' that require closer than usual monitoring by the insurance department. The selection is effected by comparing certain test results against the yardstick of the results of the same tests for companies which have become insolvent in the previous five years. Companies that fail on four or more out of eleven tests are treated as priority companies. The tests are:

1 The premium to surplus ratio, i.e. net premium written plus portfolio reinsurance ceded premium as a percent-

SOLVENCY 299

age of surplus after adjustment for estimated reserve deficiency or redundancy and for the excess of statutory cover over case basis reserves. ('Surplus' may be taken as approximately equal to the company's free reserves although the precise method of calculation for the purpose of the tests is prescribed.)

2 Change in writings, i.e. the increase or decrease in net premiums written as a percentage of net premiums written in the previous year.

3 Surplus aid to surplus. Surplus aid consists of commissions on ceded reinsurance unearned premium. It is estimated by multiplying the ratio between ceded commissions and ceded premium for all reinsurance ceded by the amount of unearned premium on reinsurance ceded to non affiliated companies. This estimated surplus aid is taken as a percentage of stated surplus.

4 The operating ratio (profitability). This ratio is the net result of three component ratios:
Loss ratio: the total of losses, loss adjustment expenses and policyholders dividends taken as a percentage of net premium earned. (Policyholders dividends are rebates allowed on account of favourable experience.)
Expense ratio: the underwriting expenses (net of other income) divided by net premium written.
Investment income ratio: net investment income earned on funds contributed by policyholders taken as a percentage of net premium earned.
The investment income ratio is subtracted from the sum of the loss and expense ratios. The operating ratio is calculated on both a 5-year and 1-year basis.

5 Investment yield. This is net investment income as a percentage of the average invested assets during the year.

6 Change in surplus. This is the difference between surplus at the end of the current year and surplus at the end of the previous year, as a percentage of the earlier surplus.

7 Liabilities to liquid assets. This ratio is the adjusted liabilities taken as a percentage of liquid assets. Adjusted liabilities are equal to stated liabilities less the excess of statutory over case basis reserves and plus or minus the

current reserve deficiency or redundancy (estimated as the average of the numerators of the three reserve tests—Tests 9, 10 and 11).
8 Agents' balances to surplus. Agents' balances as a percentage of stated surplus.
9 One year reserve development to surplus. This is the difference between the current estimate of losses that were outstanding a year ago and the reserves that were established at the end of the previous year.
10 Two year reserve development. As (9) but operating over a two year span.
11 Estimated current reserve deficiency or redundancy as a percentage of the surplus. A ratio fails if it falls outside a permitted range. It is stressed that the system is not foolproof nor is it exhaustive but only a warning that more intensive examination is necessary.

Conclusion

11.68 Solvency issues go a long way beyond the mathematical formulation of the probability of ruin. Even if a company is regarded as solvent as long as the supervisory authorities say it is, the wider issues cannot be neglected. A supervisory authority cannot guarantee, beyond all measure of doubt, that an insurer will not fail to meet its obligations under any circumstances. Any judgment it makes as to the level at which it decides to prevent an insurer from continuing to trade ought to be tempered by the knowledge of the effects of this action in the rest of the market.

BIBLIOGRAPHY

ABBOTT, W. M., CLARKE, T. G., HEY, G. B., REYNOLDS, D. I. W. & TREEN, W. R. 'Some Thoughts on Technical Reserves and Statutory Returns in General Insurance' *Journal of the Institute of Actuaries*, 1974, **101**, Part 2, No. 417, 217.

ALLEN, T. W. 'An Accountant's Viewpoint'. *Institute of Mathematics and its Applications*, 1974, *Symposium on Claim Provisions for Non-life Insurance*.

BAILEY, R. A. Insurance Investment Regulations. *Proceedings of the Casualty Actuarial Society*, 1969.

SOLVENCY

BEARD, R. E. Technical Reserves in Non-life Insurance with Particular Reference to Motor Insurance. *The ASTIN Bulletin*, 1969, **5**, 177–98.
BEARD, R. E., PENTIKÄINEN, T., PESONEN, E. *Risk Theory*, Chapman & Hall, 1969
BENJAMIN, S. Profit and Other Financial Concepts in Insurance. *Journal of the Institute of Actuaries*, 1976, **103**.
DEPARTMENT OF TRADE, Insurance Companies (Accounts and Forms) Regulations 1968. *S.I. 1408*, H.M.S.O., 1968.
DEPARTMENT OF TRADE, Report of tribunal Appointed to Enquire into Certain Issues in Relation to the Circumstances Leading up to the Cessation of Trading by the Vehicle and General Insurance Co. Ltd. H.M.S.O., 1976.
EUROPEAN ECONOMIC COMMUNITY, The Co-ordination of Laws, Regulations and Administrative Provisions Relating to the Taking-up and Pursuit of the Business of Direct Insurance Other than Life Insurance, *Directive 73/229/EEC*, 24th July 1973.
HOMEWOOD, C. J. An Administrator's Definition of the Problem. *Institute of Mathematics and its Applications*, 1974, *Symposium on Claim Provisions for Non-life Insurance*.
INSTITUTE OF ACTUARIES' GENERAL INSURANCE STUDIES GROUP, Memorandum on the Application of Actuarial Principles to the Determination of Non-life Insurance Technical Reserves, 1974. Deposited in the Institute of Actuaries' Library.
KIMBALL, S. L. *Insurance and Public Policy*, The University of Wisconsin Press, Madison, U.S.A., 1960.
MAYERSON, A. L. Ensuring the Solvency of Property and Liability Companies. *Insurance—Government and Social Policy*, Editors: Kimball, S. L., Danenberg, H. S. and Huebner, S. S., Foundation for Insurance Education, 1967, University of Pennsylvania, Philadelphia, U.S.A.
PENTIKÄINEN, T. On the Solvency of Insurance Companies. *The ASTIN Bulletin*, 1969, **4**, 236–47.
SAWKINS, R. W. Solvency in Non-life Insurance. *Transactions of the Institute of Actuaries of Australia and New Zealand*, 1973.
STEWART, C. M. Report of the discussion. *Institute of Mathematics and its Applications*, 1974. *Symposium on Claim Provisions for Non-life Insurance*.

CHAPTER 12

ANALYSIS OF PROFIT

12.1 In Chapter 10, in which we discussed technical reserves, reference was made to the emergence of profit and an example was given to show that the method of provision of reserves, especially in the allocation of reserves to the years of origin of the unexpired risks and unsettled or unreported claims, could affect the time scale for the emergence of profit. In the present chapter we shall look more closely at the way in which profit arises in general insurance.

12.2 In the actuarial management of a life office a full analysis of surplus is essential for proper control and the equitable distribution of surplus. Similarly in general insurance an analysis of the sources of profit is essential to proper management. In particular it is required to know to what extent underwriting profits or losses in any year are due to the experience of business currently on the books or to differences between amounts paid and reserved in respect of claims arising in previous years. An assessment is also needed of the profitability of the business being written at current rates of premium.

12.3 In general insurance, as in life assurance, there may be margins, implicit or explicit, in the reserves which are held, as explained in paragraph 12.21. Also it is not generally accepted practice to discount outstanding claims reserves for interest even though it is appreciated that settlement will not occur immediately. For a full examination of profit it would be helpful to consider the results both on the basis of the published reserves and also on a basis where those reserves are stripped of any margins. The latter would give a better understanding of the underlying profitability of the business.

12.4 The actual revenue items received and paid by a general insurance company during the year are premiums (P), investment income (I), claims (C), expenses (E) and tax (T). However, as in the same way as for a life assurance company,

ANALYSIS OF PROFIT

a general insurance company has liabilities at the beginning and end of the year to be taken into account, so that the excess of income over expenditure is not the profit for the year.

12.5 Table 12.1 is a representation in symbolic form of the revenue account. For ease of illustration separate reserves have been shown for outstanding claims and for I.B.N.R.

TABLE 12.1 Revenue account

Capital and reserves	R_0	Claims	C
U.P.R.	V_0	Expenses + Commission	E
Outstanding claims reserves	L_0	Capital and reserves	R_1
I.B.N.R.	D_0	U.P.R.	V_1
		Outstanding claims reserves	L_1
Total reserve 1st Jan.	F_0	I.B.N.R.	D_1
Premiums	P		
Gross investment income	I	Total reserve 31st Dec.	F_1
		Tax	T
		Profit	G

12.6 Initially we shall take a simplistic view and ignore both the possible need to provide any additional reserve such as the unexpired risk reserve (see Chapter 10) and the need to subdivide the amounts by type of risk.

Reserves

12.7 (a) *Unexpired premium reserve (U.P.R.)* As we have already seen in Chapter 10 most policies effected during the year will be in force for part of the following year and it is necessary to reserve part of the premium to cover this risk. It is normal to deduct a percentage (x) of the premium to cover expenses and so if a policy is effected after a proportion r of the year:

expenses deduction	$= x \cdot P$
premium earned during year	$= (1-r)(1-x) \cdot P$
U.P.R.	$= r \cdot (1-x) P$

We saw in Chapter 10 that this is summed for all values of r. We also saw that if x is ·20 and r is one half on average, the U.P.R. is ·40P a proportion which has been commonly used.
(b) *Outstanding claims and I.B.N.R.* The liability for outstanding claims is in respect of claims notified but not settled.

The I.B.N.R. (incurred but not reported) reserve is in respect of claims which have occurred but have not been reported to the company. The method of derivation of both these reserves has been set out in Chapter 10.

Let $L_t^i =$ amount (inc. expenses of payment) in respect of claims arising in year $(t-i)$ still unpaid at end of year t.

D_t^i amount (inc. expenses of payment) in respect of claims arising in year $(t-i)$ not notified to the company by the end of year t.

Therefore $$L_t = \sum_{i=0}^{\infty} L_t^i \text{ and } D_t = \sum_{i=0}^{\infty} D_t^i$$

The above amounts will have to be estimated as at the end of year t. It will be noted that outstanding claims reserves will normally include direct expenses related to claims but not expenses only indirectly related to the claims themselves. However, it should also be noted that in future it is likely that the Department of Trade will require that both direct and indirect expenses are included in the outstanding claims reserves for Department of Trade Returns purposes. In this respect, as in others, Department of Trade Returns and Companies Act Accounts are likely increasingly to diverge in the future.

Claims paid and expenses

12.8 Expenses can be split into claim expenses (E_c) and others.

$$E = E' + E_c$$

The claims paid during the year are the sum of:
1. C_t^o which arose during the current year t,
2. C_t^i which arose in year $(t-i)$ and were notified before the beginning of year t, and
3. $'C_t^i$ which arose in $(t-i)$ but were notified during the current year.

C^o, C^i and $'C^i$ are assumed to be calculated including the expenses of payment; thus

$$E_c + C = C_t^o + \sum_{i=1}^{\infty} C_t^i + \sum_{i=1}^{\infty} {}'C_t^i$$

Analysis of profit

12.9 As a first approach we shall assume that:
(a) The reserves make no allowance for future interest and inflation
(b) The data are sufficiently subdivided as to be homogeneous
(c) Premium rates have remained unchanged during the year of account
(d) The risks have remained unchanged during the year so that no additional reserves are required to allow for inadequacy of premium bases (see Chapter 10)

Then, the *underwriting profit* for the year = earned premiums—incurred claims

$$= [V_0 + (1-x)P - V_1] - [C_1^o + L_1^o + D_1^o]$$

This is the provisional underwriting profit for the current year but the true profit will not be known until all outstanding claims, including those not yet reported, have been settled. Consequently the current year contains amounts which are, strictly, attributable to the underwriting profits of previous years as the outstanding claims are settled and may be termed claims adjustments to those profits.

12.10 These adjustments may be calculated as follows.

Claims adjustments

$$= \sum_{i=0}^{\infty} (L_0^i + D_0^i - C_1^{i+1} - {}^1C_1^{i+1} - L_1^{i+1} - D_1^{i+1})$$

i.e. (reserves at the beginning of the year less claims paid during the year less reserves held at the end) for each past year. This is the excess of the reserves released over the paid claims which release them.

12.11 *Expense profit* will be $(x)P - E^1$.

Investment income

12.12 As no allowance has been made in the reserves for investment income the whole of that income is profit. If assumption (a) is modified and L and D made functions of an assumed rate of interest j, the claims adjustment becomes:

$$\sum_{i=0}^{\infty}[(L_0^i+D_0^i)(1+j)-(C_1^{i+1}+{}^1C_1^{i+1})(1+j/2)-(L_1^{i+1}+D_1^{i+1})]$$

The interest profit is now investment income less the expected interest at rate j, i.e.

$$I-j\sum_{i=0}^{\infty}[L_0^i+D_0^i-\tfrac{1}{2}(C_1^{i+1}+{}^1C_1^{i+1})]$$

Inflation and claims escalation

12.13 If estimates of outstanding claims at each year end were made on the assumption that the claims would be paid immediately, i.e. at the then present level of claims costs, there would be a loss incurred owing to inflation (or other reason for claims escalation) between the date of estimate and date of payment (see Chapter 10). In that case there would be a loss, in the year, of

$$\sum_{i=0}^{\infty}(L_0^i-C_1^{i+1}-{}^1L_1^{i+1}),$$

where ${}^1L_1^{i+1}$ is that part of L_1^{i+1} which relates to claims included in L_0^i. As investment income and inflation in respect of outstanding claims influences profit in opposite directions, it may be possible to estimate outstanding claims on the assumption of immediate payment and assume that interest earned and inflation cancel each other out. To assess the validity of this assumption we ought to satisfy ourselves that the value of

$$\sum_{i=0}^{\infty}[L_0^i(1+j)-C_1^{i+1}(1+j/2)-{}^1L_1^{i+1}]$$

is sufficiently small in relation to other elements affecting profit.

Unexpired risks

12.14 The U.P.R. in the above treatment of the account has been based on the current rate of premium, i.e. the valuation basis is the premium basis. If the premium scale is not

ANALYSIS OF PROFIT

assessed to be adequate to the risks being written, then an additional reserve will be required—the 'unexpired risk' reserve of Chapter 10 which we must now bring in—or, to put it another way analogous to that of life office practice, we have to recognise that the valuation basis ought to be changed.

12.15 Suppose that the general level of premiums was increased by $100e\%$ after a proportion q of the year had elapsed. Assuming that business is spread evenly throughout the year and that the change in premium has no effect on the level of business, then the premium received will be greater by a factor of $(1+e-qe)$ and the U.P.R. by $(1+e-q^2e)$.

12.16 If it is felt that the risk on business written during the year was $100e\%$ higher than the previous year, then this is tantamount to a change in valuation basis and the U.P.R. held should be greater by a factor of $(1+e)$,

$$\text{i.e.} \frac{(1+e)V_1}{1+e-q^2e},$$

where V_1 is the U.P.R. corresponding to the actual premium situation.

12.17 This can be split into three parts:

$$\frac{V_1}{1+e-q^2e} = \text{reserve on old basis}$$

$$+\frac{e-q^2e}{1+e-q^2e}V_1 = \text{strain on change of basis}$$

$$+\frac{q^2e}{1+e-q^2e}V_1 = \text{unexpired risk reserve}$$

12.18 The unexpired risk reserve covers the extra risk arising from policies taken before the premium increase, whilst the strain on change of basis arises from policies on the new premium rates and will be offset by the extra premium collected, i.e. the non-recurrent strain on change of basis is

$$\frac{e-q^2e}{1+e-q^2e}V_1 - \frac{e-qe}{1+e-qe}P$$

together with unexpired risk reserve. On the old (valuation i.e. premium) basis we now have:

(a) Underwriting profit

$$= V_0 + \frac{(1-x)P}{1+e-qe} - C_1^0 - L_1^0 - D_1^0 - \frac{V_1}{1+e-q^2e}$$

(b) Expense profit

$$= \frac{x}{1+e-qe} P - E^1$$

12.19 Because of the way V_0 has been assumed to be calculated the expression (a) will only be valid if there has been no change in the level of premiums in year (-1). If there has been such a change V_0 should be adjusted by an amount equal to the unexpired risk reserve as defined above but calculated as at the beginning of the year.

12.20 An unexpired risk reserve may be required if the risk changes even if the change in premium levels is not proportionate to the increase in risks; for example, where the increase in premiums is smaller than desired due to government price controls.

Solvency margin

12.21 In the above treatment of the account any required increase in the solvency margin (see Chapter 11) has been assumed to be contained in the item $R_1 - R_0$. A minimum level of this margin is required by statute but the company may set a higher level. Results for the year would be better illustrated if R_0 is divided into R_0^s (= required level of solvency margin by company standard $\geq$ minimum statutory level) and R_0^F (= capital and 'free' reserves), the former only being included in F_0, the latter being shown separately. Similarly F_1 would only include R_1^s and there would be an item in the analysis of profit on account of this required increase in solvency margin of $(R_1^s - R_0^s)/(1-t)$, where t is the rate of tax.

New business strain

12.22 If the office is expanding its business the unexpired premium reserve will be increasing faster than it is being released. In the expression for underwriting profit in paragraph 12.7, V_1 will be greater than V_0 and if the claims experience is in accord with premium basis expectations, the underwriting profit will be negative on the account. This effect of the strain of building up reserves to a higher operating level is shown in Appendix 10.2 (i) of Chapter 10.

The effects of margins

12.23 The introduction of margins into the provision of reserves is prudent actuarial practice having regard to the essentially random behaviour of claims experience in general insurance. These margins may be explicit or implicit in the calculation of:
(a) U.P.R.
(b) Outstanding claims reserves and I.B.N.R.
(c) Any other reserves, especially unexpired risk reserve
(d) Solvency margin to the extent that the office standard is higher than the statutory minimum.

12.24 These margins represent a necessary slowing in the rate of release of profit as part of good financial management. There is a complete analogy between the calculation of profit in paragraphs 12.7 to 12.19 and the profit on a published valuation basis for a life fund. If an indication is required of the retardation in the release of profit, then the calculation of profit can be reproduced with all the margins eliminated.

12.25 It is implicit in the actuarial forward-looking approach that the absence of margins in the valuation basis may be regarded as allowing too rapid a release of profit.

Analysis by type of risk

12.26 We must remind ourselves of the assumption (b) of paragraph 12.7 that the data are homogeneous. To secure homogeneity we ought clearly to carry out the analysis not only by class of business but also by type of risk. In this way too an office management can see which kinds of risk are being underwritten profitably and which are not. This would be a necessary precaution before yielding to market pressures for the modification of premium scales (para. 9.3).

INDEX

Accounting regulations, 32
Accounts and forms regulations, 33, 40, 41, 44–6
Additional perils cover (fire), 25
Adequacy of claims reserves, 81, 242
Adequacy of premium rates, 70, 276, 295, 306
Adjustment of rate levels, 167
Aggregate value certificate, 45
Asset valuations, 38, 39, 46, 50, 57, 58, 280, 281, 291
Authorised insurers, 37, 38, 50
Average, in fire insurance, 27
  in marine insurance, 12, 14
  general, 12, 14
  particular, 12
Average cost per claim method, 251–4
Aviation insurance, 14–17
Aviation Insurance Offices Association, 15

Bonus/malus, 194, 201
Burning cost rating method, 218

Cancellations, 90–8, 153–5
Cargo insurances, aviation, 16, 17
  marine, 12–14
Catastrophes, 207, 208, 214, 232, 237, 259, 260, 274, 282
Census method, 118–121
Certificate of motor insurance, 18
Chain ladder method, 244–8
Claim amount distributions and analysis, 2, 84, 103, 106–9, 114, 130–4, 164, 219, 229, 230, 279
Claim frequency analysis, 45, 46, 88, 103, 104, 106, 110–12, 114, 115, 163–6, 178, 235, 279
Claim ratio, 102–6, 114, 241
Claim settlement analysis, 45, 46, 88, 110, 111, 113, 134–6, 243–54

Claim settling agreements (motor), 20, 21, 79, 82, 182, 183, 188
Claims, causes of, 86, 87
  equalisation reserve, 237, 260, 283
  estimates, 79–81, 102, 103, 242–59
  expenses, 147, 153, 238, 241, 304
  experience, 66, 67, 71, 72, 79–89, 102, 111
  payments, 79–81, 83–5, 107–9
Classifications of general insurance, 4, 5, 36
Co-insurance (fire), 30, 31
Collision clause, 13
Commercial vehicle insurance, 20
Commission, 146, 153, 158, 160, 212, 217, 227, 231
Comprehensive motor insurance, 18, 189, 194–6
Compulsory insurances, 47
Consequential loss insurance, 28
Constructive total loss, 12, 13
Contingency reserve, 272
Contribution, 27
Counter Inflation Act 1973, 47, 48, 295
Cover note (motor), 18
Credibility, 162–6, 171, 179–81
Currency restrictions, 58, 208, 210

Deferred acquisition costs, 278
Delays, in claim reporting, 122–4, 235, 254–9
  in claim settlement, 134–6, 235, 241, 244–59
  in processing records, 77–9, 89, 90, 118
Deposit premium, 118
Domestic policy rating, 169

E.E.C., Establishment Directive, 49–51, 277, 281, 284, 285, 291

E.E.C., harmonisation of legislation, 33, 34, 37, 51, 52, 61
Eighth's method, 119–21
Employers' Liability Act 1969, 6, 47
Employers' liability insurance, 6, 172, 173
Equalisation clause, 215, 222, 223
Estimated claims, 79–81, 103, 242–59
Estimated maximum loss, 212, 213, 217, 218, 222, 229
Excess of loss insurance, aviation, 16
motor, 19, 104–6, 204
Excess of loss reinsurance, 32, 84, 212–26, 229, 231
Expense ratio, 148
Expenses, 139–55, 160, 194, 236–8, 241, 263, 279, 303–5
Expenses, by class of business, 141–4
claims, 147, 150, 151, 238, 241, 303, 304
fixed, 149, 150, 153–5
initial, 150, 238
new business, 153–5
type of, 139, 140
variable, 145, 146
Experience rating, 162, 163, 172, 173, 178–82, 187, 199–203
Exposure to risk, 3, 4, 63–5, 69, 98–103, 111, 115–21, 240, 241

Facultative reinsurance, 31, 210, 211, 215
Fidelity guarantee insurance, 22
Fire and theft cover (motor), 18
Fire business, perils insured, 25
Fire insurance market, 26
Fire Offices Committee, 30
Fire Protection Association, 30
Fire reinsurance, 212, 213, 222, 229
Fixed costs, 149, 150, 153–5
Fleet rating (motor), 20, 168, 199
Floating policies, 13
Fluctuation of claims, 56, 57, 149, 162, 163, 206, 207, 229–31, 237, 260
Free reserves, 282–7, 303, 308
Freight insurance, 12, 13

Gearing, 58

General average, 12, 14
General insurance, classifications, 4, 5
definition, 1, 4, 5
General liability, 8
Generally Accepted Accounting Principles (G.A.A.P.), 297, 298
Green card, 19
Guarantee fund, 51

Heterogeneity of risks, 4, 125–30, 177, 187, 191, 235, 236, 309
Hospital expenses cover, 25
Household insurance, 29, 30

Income profit, 305, 306
Incurred But Not Reported (I.B.N.R.) Claims, 46, 60, 66, 122–4, 218, 235, 237, 249, 252, 254–9, 276, 303–5
Indemnity, principle of, 3, 202
Inflation, 56, 103, 107–9, 172, 215, 218, 222, 238–40, 242–4, 246, 247, 250, 252, 286, 306
Insoovency, 37, 46, 57, 58, 271–3, 280, 281, 291, 296
Institute of London Underwriters, 11
Insurance Companies Act 1974, 4, 32, 34–46, 61
Insurance Companies (Accounts & Forms) Regulations, 40, 44–6, 59, 60
Insurance Companies (Valuation of Assets) Regulations 1976, 38, 39
Intervention by the Department of Trade, 41, 42
Investment expenses, 143
Investment policy, 55–9, 236, 280, 281, 283
Investment return, 54–7, 174–6, 259, 287

Knock-for-knock agreements, 20, 21, 79, 82, 84, 182, 183, 188

Lapses, 90–8, 153–5
Large claims, 133–5, 147, 208, 215, 219, 220, 227, 237, 260
Liabilities of an insurance company, 276

INDEX

Liability insurance, 6, 7, 172, 173, 214, 229, 235, 242, 243
Liability insurance, Employers', 6, 172, 173, 243
  general, 6
  product, 7
  professional, 7
  property owner's, 7
  public, 173
  sportsmen's 7
Lloyd's, 5, 8–10, 26, 47, 209, 285, 286, 297
Log Normal distribution, 131, 132, 219
Loss of profits insurance, 28

Marine insurance, 7–15, 214
Marine Insurance Act of 1906, 7, 12
Marketing, 64, 69, 89, 90, 156, 157, 168, 201, 204
Medical expense business rating, 169–72
Minimum premiums, 153–6
Motor business, comprehensive cover, 18, 189, 194, 195
  multiple claims, 128, 129, 191, 196
  points rating premium system, 152, 185, 186, 188, 189
  statistical systems, 73–111
  typical premium calculation, 160, 161
  underwriting factors, 18, 19, 76, 77, 85, 86, 184
Motor cycle insurance, 20, 199
Motor fleet rating, 20, 168, 199
Motor Insurers' Bureau, 21, 83
Motor Risk Statistics Bureau, 111
Motor vehicle insurance, 17–22
Motor Vehicle (Passenger Insurance) Act 1971, 18

N.A.I.C. 'Early Warning System', 298–300
Negative binomial distribution, 191
New business, 91, 92, 95–8, 294, 308
New business, expenses, 153–5
No-claim discount (N.C.D.), 19–21, 73, 84, 148, 178, 181–204
No-fault insurance, 204

Non-proportional reinsurance, 31, 211, 213, 214
Non-tariff fire insurers, 30

Operating ratio, 299
Outstanding claim reserve, 60, 79–81, 237, 242, 278, 279, 303, 304
Overseas travel (motor), 19
Overtrading, 281

Pareto distribution, 132, 219–22
Partial credibility, 165
Particular average, 12
Pecuniary loss insurance, 22
Personal accident (aviation) insurance, 17
Personal accident and sickness insurance, 22–5
Poisson distribution, 163, 196, 220, 226
Policyholders' Protection Act 1975, 37, 48, 49, 297
Portfolio premium, 227, 278
Price control legislation, 47, 48
Pricing policy, 144–57, 168, 201
Private car insurance, 18, 19
Private dwellings insurance, 29, 30
Profit, analysis of, 302–9
  emergence of, 235, 261, 262, 279, 297, 298, 302, 309
Profit margin, 174, 175, 238, 288–91
Profits insurance, 28
Property insurance, 25
Proportional reinsurance, 31, 211–14, 224–6, 279
Proposal (motor), 76, 77
Protection and Indemnity Associations or Clubs, 13
Public liability, 173

Quota share reinsurance, 212, 214, 216–18, 227, 230, 231

Rates, adjustment of level, 167
Rating, basic routine, 157–60
  of domestic business, 168, 169
  of excess loss business, 218–22
  of fire business, 27

of medical expenses business, 169–72
of motor business, 98–100, 160–2, 168
Reciprocity, 209, 228
Records, delays affecting, 77–9, 89, 90
of cancellations, 90, 91
of claims, 66, 71–5, 79–85, 88, 89
of lapses, 90, 91
of premiums, 65, 74, 75
of underwriting factors, 67–9, 85, 86
for motor business, 73–113
Recovery of claim monies, 7, 83, 84
Reinsurance, 30–2, 44, 61, 84, 206–32, 243, 265, 266, 277, 279, 282
Reinsurance, excess of less, 32, 84, 212–22, 224–6, 230, 231
facultative, 31, 210, 211, 215
non-proportional, 31, 211, 213, 214
proportional, 31, 211, 212, 214, 224–6, 279
purposes of, 207, 214, 229–31
quota share, 212, 214, 216, 217, 227, 230, 231
stability clause, 215, 216, 222, 223
stop loss, 32, 84, 214, 216, 225, 229
surplus, 212, 214, 217, 222
taxation treatment, 61
treaty, 31, 84, 211, 216–18, 266
Reinsurance Offices Association, 210, 212
Reopened claims, 107
Retentions, 206, 207, 215–17, 222–7, 266
Revenue account, 303, 304
Risk distribution, 177, 178, 226, 227
Risk factor models, 125–9, 152, 177, 178, 187
Risk Theory, 223. 224. 274, 275, 283
Road Traffic Act 1972, 18, 20, 47
Ruin probability, 223, 224, 232, 274, 275, 283, 287, 288, 300
Running down clause, 13

Salvage Association, 10

Salvage corps, 30
Self rating point, 180
Separation method, 248–52
Simulation of claim amount distribution, 133, 232
Solvency (definition), 271–4, 291
Solvency guarantee fund, 297
Solvency margin, 36, 37, 45, 46, 50, 51, 54, 57, 58, 226, 272–4, 280, 282–91, 294–6, 298–300, 308
Stability clause, 215, 222, 223
Standard deviation, of claim numbers, 163
of total claim amount, 164
Statutory returns, 33, 40, 41, 44–6, 109, 110, 280, 295–7, 304
Stop loss reinsurance, 32, 84, 214, 216, 225, 229
Surplus reinsurance, 212, 214, 217, 222

Tariff fire market, 30
Taxation, 56, 57, 59–61, 259, 257, 289
Technical reserves, 50, 59–61, 234–70, 276–80, 285, 288, 303, 304
Third party cover (motor), 18, 21
Three year accounting, 264, 265, 279
Treaty reinsurance, 31, 84, 211, 216–18, 266, 279
Twenty-fourth's method, 119, 121, 238

Uberrima fides, 1, 26
Underwriting factors, 67–70
Underwriting factors, for fire business, 27
for motor business, 18, 19, 73, 76, 77, 85, 86
for personal accident business, 23, 24
Underwriting profit, 305, 307
Unearned premium reserve, 59–61, 227, 277–9
Unexpired premium reserve, 236–40, 303, 306–8
Unexpired risk reserve, 59–61, 236, 240–2, 277, 306–8

U.S.A. ratemaking practice, 173, 174, 181, 200
U.S.A. solvency requirements, 284, 285, 298–300
Utility theory, 229

Valuation of assets, 38, 39, 46, 50, 57, 272, 280, 281, 291
Valued policies, 13
Variance, of claim numbers, 163, 164
  of excess claims, 219–22
  of total claim amount, 164, 206, 207, 221, 223, 225, 226, 229–31, 280, 287, 288
Voidability, conditions for, 27
Voyage policies, 12

Warsaw Convention of 1929, 15
Winding-up, 43, 44, 48, 49